# A Preface To **Politics**

# A Preface To **Politics**

## sixth edition

### David Schuman
*University of Massachusetts,*
*Amherst, Mass.*


### Rex S. Wirth
*Central Washington University,*
*Ellensburg, Wash.*

Chandler and Sharp Publishers, Inc.
NOVATO, CALIFORNIA

We are grateful to the following publishers and individuals for permission to reprint from their works: page 262 excerpt from *Zen Buddhism: An Introduction to Zen with Stories, Parables and Koan Riddles of the Zen Masters* (Mount Vernon, N.Y.: Peter Pauper Press, 1959), pp. 24–25; page 267, from "Friendship" by Cole Porter, reproduced by permission; page 273 from ONE FISH, TWO FISH, RED FISH, BLUE FISH, by Dr. Seuss, ® & copyright © by Dr. Seuss Enterprises, L.P. 1960, renewed 1988. Used by permission of Random House Children's Books, a division of Random House, Inc.

Chandler & Sharp Publishers
11A Commercial Boulevard
Novato, CA 94949

ISBN 0-88316-572-4

Library of Congress Cataloging-in-Publication Data
Schuman, David.
   A preface to politics / By David Schuman and Rex S. Wirth.—6th ed.
      p. cm.
Previously published: Itasca, Ill. : F.E. Peacock Publishers, c1991.
Includes bibliographical references.
 ISBN 0-88316-572-4
1. United States—Politics and government. I. Wirth, Rex Sylvester, 1944–
II. Title.
   JK274.S44 2003
   320.973—dc21
                         2003008476


Design by Studio Star, Berkeley, California
Art Direction: Eileen Starr Moderbacher / Interior Design: Jen Thomas
Cover Design: Stewart Cauley, Pollendesign

Typeset: Steven Hiatt, San Francisco, California
Printed in the United States of America

# contents

"Everyone is entitled to know everything" (But this is a false slogan of a false era; far greater in value is the forfeited right of people not to know, not to have their divine souls stuffed with gossip, nonsense, vain talk. A person whose life and work are meaningful has no need for this excessive and burdening flow of information.)

— *Aleksandr Solzhenitsyn*

# chapter 1

# Introduction:
# The Life of the *Preface*

This book was born as *A Preface to Politics* in Berkeley as the war in Vietnam was winding down. It is about something that most people already know if they have taken the time to think about it. More specifically, it is about the failure to think about it. Through good times and bad, war and peace, through five editions and six presidents to fighting terrorism in Afghanistan and airports the non-thinking continues.

What is the problem?

Perhaps it starts with our textbooks. Anyone with reasonable intelligence and enough courses in political science can outline an American government textbook. First, there is the secret language to explain. This means that at least one chapter must be devoted to defining terms. Politics is … science is … therefore, political science is … It certainly seems reasonable to expect people who use the same language to use similar words to mean similar things. So the ideal textbook strains toward purity of definition. It strains toward standardization.

After definitions—after laying the parameters—a text must do at least four things. First, it should give examples of the system, proving that it is good or bad, but giving tacit support in either case. Second, it must include as many "facts" as possible. Third, it needs a couple of case studies to make the whole thing more "real" and appealing. Finally, an effort should be made to consciously integrate material from other fields to show the interrelationship of all the social sciences.

Worthy aims, all.

There are, of course, other things that ought to be done. Every text needs a discussion of how a bill becomes a law, and/or how power is spread less or more evenly around, and/or how elections count with an appropriate quote from old Abe Lincoln. Anyone who can manage to do this and come up with a CD-ROM with true-false questions of medium difficulty and an Internet package will have succeeded in writing a standard—and possibly even successful—textbook.

These elements a text doth make.

It seems difficult to fault the typical textbook, because it sounds so reasonable, so obvious, and so normal. It is what was, what is, and what always will be. There is nothing terribly wrong with such an introduction to our political system—nothing wrong, that is, unless it goes unquestioned. Certainly we should know about the political system, absorb a certain number of "facts," and carefully define the terms we use. All these things may at some point be critical.

Nevertheless, there is work that must go on before this begins. The investigation of the obvious may not be the obvious place to begin. There are questions that are logically prior to the "facts" of the empirical world. (This failing in our textbooks may be related to our failure to think.) Let me try to explain.

Built into the typical college text are assumptions about politics, about the political system, and about knowledge itself. Each of us gets one edition of one book. Any text is correct if readers (students looking for a grade) agree to accept its "truths," its accounts of the empirical facts of the "real world." Once we agree not to question such "truths"—not to question what they mean or whom they benefit—most of our problems are solved. That's the magic of textbooks—we accept what they say and can stop thinking for ourselves.

There is, of course, no good reason to accept the truth of our political science texts. Politics, in a real sense, affects everything we do. To begin to understand politics, we must begin by understanding the range of politics and the power of ideology. To look at politics in this manner is to open up a whole series of problems—problems that do not seem to be political, but that really are. Politics—in spite of what we have been taught to believe—may have something to do with how we think about happiness or with why we seem to be lonely. It may have a great influence on how we view each other, or on how we react to rules, or on what we think is important. For certain, politics is more than voting, and to understand it requires much more than trying to integrate the social sciences. )

What I want to argue is that what you do means something, that your actions are connected with what you believe—or were taught to believe—and that these actions are important for at least two reasons. First, most of our learned behavior supports the status quo, supports what is. Our political system—in fact, every political system—is geared to self-survival. This is achieved, in no small measure, by teaching the people who live under that system to support it. No great news in that. Second, our behavior is important because it defines who we are. If you act like an ass but think like a saint, you are still an ass.

( For thirty years the *Preface* has helped teachers and students explore how we think and act, why such behavior is political, and what all that might mean. )

There is little reason to assume that all that we write is true. Of course, it is not( Politics is often unsure and sloppy, a lot like life.)To write a book using only those things we can all agree upon would be as boring as it would be useless(To begin to understand politics is to begin to understand how we got to where we are—as individuals and as groups of individuals and as a society. The quest is incredibly complex, and is made up of many different truths. )

## Reintroduction

> ... *you think this is too horrible to have really happened, this is too awful to be the truth! But, please. It's still hard for me to have a clear mind thinking on it. But it's the truth even if it didn't happen.*
> —*Ken Kesey*

(The world, of course, changes. I'm not, and you're not, and the world is not 1976, or 1986, or even 1996. But the world is still a whole lot the same. You and I and the world are basically much like we were at any point during the last quarter-century and the same will be true in the coming century.)

If I understand correctly, both of the things you just read are true. Part of the tension of being a student or a teacher or a citizen is learning how to sort out what is really different and what is really the same. I'm still wearing glasses. I've had several pairs (they do wear out), but the prescriptions change faster than the frames. To rewrite this book (for the sixth time) is an exercise in trying to come to terms with what has changed, how I/we have changed and how a changed me/us looks at a changed world out there.

The attack on the World Trade Center was instantly and seemingly automatically equated with the Japanese attack on Pearl Harbor in 1941. Our response to a new crisis seemed to be as predictable as our normal responses to new issues, personalities, or fashions. The lesson, which is hidden in normal times, was the news{ Each generation generally responds to the same underlying tensions and themes. To know the themes—here we're talking "remember" as in "Remember the Alamo" or "Remember the *Maine*"—is to help your chances of knowing about American politics.}

In a shorthand sort of way, let me offer four generations' responses to American life. It is easiest to do this with examples from the movies. The first movie, the old one, is *Easy Rider.* The heroes are two drug dealers, big stuff in the sixties. They are apparently without families and without homes. They ride big motorcycles, have long hair, and wear dirty clothes.

All *statements.*

The heroes are, it seems, "anti" almost everything established, and they practice a kind of small-time capitalism in a corporate society. The film is, in part, a travel picture. We see the characters travel through beautiful country, stop and see beautiful communal life, party, and the like. We see them stop in small towns and big cities. We see them travel a little on acid.

Near the end of the movie, in a quiet scene, one of the easy riders has a sense that something is missing. They have, in his words, blown it. The other one is happy.

In the last scene they are both killed.

Come the eighties and we have yet another bike movie. Of course, this is a new generation, so this bike movie has to do with a bicycle. The title *Breaking Away* is an interesting name for a movie in which travel is not a theme. Actually, we do see our hero bike 50 miles in one scene; he goes from one city in Indiana to another city in Indiana. The other long trip—this one is 200 miles—takes place on an oval track.

Literally going in circles.

The hero has a family and friends. At first he is happy pretending to be an Italian. (Breaking away?) He is happy with his friends. (Breaking away?) His parents are unhappy with all of this. Our hero does not use bad language, stay dirty long, or seem to hold grudges. During the whole movie, he kisses one young woman one time, maybe twice. He shaves his legs once, there is one big fight, and many people eat pizza often.

All *statements*.

Do not be fooled. He is a hero. With limited help from his friends, he wins the big bike race. He goes to college. His father (a used car salesman) begins to ride a bicycle and to take pride in himself. His mother gets pregnant. In the last scene, our hero—now a college freshman—meets a French exchange student and likes her. He begins to speak French.

Each movie, in its way, is good. Each movie, for our purposes, tells us about what to expect.

*Breaking Away* is a 1980s Indiana version of the Waltons/Huxtables. The point seems clear enough. This generation is ready to get back to the American Basics: clean living, close families, optimism, a college education, modesty, pride, and so forth. This generation will live out—or act out—the dreams of its parents. And, if this is the best of all possible worlds, its parents will be reformed by their own offspring.

The title of the film is accurate in a strange way. People do not want to break away from the traditional liberal/capitalist values, they want to break away from the last generation. No more protests (big ones anyway). No more rebelling (not big rebellions anyway). No more mess. No more wandering. No more insecurity.

Given the, at best, very mixed results of the preceding generation that response seems reasonable.

The next movie—like the others a "modest" one—is *Say Anything*. It is a love story: A boy (the ads say Lloyd) meets girl movie. Lots of people liked it. The movie is not heavy; it does not take itself too seriously, but it certainly gets most of what it is doing just right. So why include this little film? The story is about this really smart, successful, pretty young woman who is graduating from high school and going to England on a prestigious, one-of-a-kind scholarship. She lives with her dad and sometimes sees her mom. Dad loves her, buys her a car, and gives her an expensive ring for graduation. So she's all set.

The young man—Lloyd—lives with his sister and has a lot of fun playing games with his really cute nephew. His sister keeps telling Lloyd he has to grow up. His parents (Dad is a military man) are in Germany. No career is obvious for Lloyd, but he loves (and is good at) kickboxing, the sport of the nineties. Lloyd seems stuck.

Cut to the chase. Lloyd asks the girl for a date. She goes. The chase is on. Dad gets jealous. Lloyd's two best friends (both girls) give him lots of advice. It gets heavy. Dad is accused of embezzling money from the nursing home he runs. That's no fun. Lloyd's parents are never heard from.

Will she go to England, study important things, develop her intelligence, and be successful? (She hates to fly, so the trip itself is a drawback. Anyway, she likes Lloyd.) Will Lloyd give up his true love? Does he really want her pregnant and living on a kickboxer's salary? Will the Feds catch up with Dad? What a summer in Seattle!

Dad cops a plea (he had been stealing old people's money for years). Lloyd talks to Dad in prison and says that the thing he does best in the world is make the daughter happy. In the last scene, a nice one, we see Lloyd and his love off to England on a plane. The bell signals that it's all right to take off seatbelts, and they kiss. What a movie.

One of the most fun things about the movie, and the reason it seems to get us into the nineties, is not because it is about young love. That isn't news. The reason is in who is doing what, who is there and who isn't, and how people are portrayed.

We entered the nineties reinventing a lot of social roles. The smart scholarship winner—the person going places and doing things—is the woman. The person who is going to make her happy, who will make the bed and cook the meals, is the man. That wasn't the *Easy Rider* way, and its time hadn't arrived with *Breaking Away*. *Say Anything* was wonderful because these new arrangements had become so matter-of-fact.

Even the vices are different. The pot of the sixties and toot of the seventies and early eighties have been replaced by demon rum. Yes, alcohol is back. The most abused and deadliest drug in the United States is once again the drug of choice. We see people having fun by getting blasted out of their minds. What fun.

And parents? In *Say Anything,* one pair is never seen: Out of sight, out of mind. The divorced mother is seen once, with a cheesy boyfriend. Ah, the modern world. So it comes down to one parent out of four who has a major role. Good old Dad—the crook. The picture came out when George Bush Sr. was president, but it was written and made when Ronald Reagan was in office, a dad of the times. Had her dad been bigger time, he could have had a job in Reagan's administration.

*Say Anything* is a good movie. I suggest you see it. It takes a nice story and shows us a lot about ourselves.

It takes two movies to get us through the nineties to the new century, the new millennium: *Pulp Fiction* and *The Truman Show.* Both are symbolically on target. *Pulp Fiction* begins near the end of the story and explains how we got there. It flashes forward and backward. Good editing. It has to do with drugs and friendship and betrayal and women. Uma Thurman OD's on heroin. Quentin Tarantino becomes a star writer/director. Samuel Jackson wears a retro Afro and looks perfect.

But the key is John Travolta. Travolta was a has-been at the time, once a star, now nobody: Travolta the aging Scientologist who flew his own airplanes. No good roles; not even many bad ones. (Remind you of someone? Which president from Hope, Arkansas, kept describing himself as "the comeback kid"?) So Tarantino resurrects Travolta's career. Great movie. Great role. There is even a scene when Travolta dances with Uma, subtle, quiet, totally right. All of a sudden there are flashbacks to *Staying Alive.*

The world, retro with Travolta, the Afro, and the dance ... but somehow the nineties with heroin and clubs ... seems understandable in its garbled way. *Pulp Fiction* captured the disconnectedness that so many people felt in the nineties—Travolta/Clinton coming back to help us through a very strange decade.

But that movie doesn't quite tell us all we need to know.

It took *The Truman Show* to give us a sense of what we were becoming in the nineties. The plot was simple enough: Jim Carrey was a complete creature of television. An artificial world was built so that his every move, every word, every wave and smile would be recorded and broadcast, twenty-four hours a day: His life was an ongoing series. Happy-go-lucky Jim: the tool of technology, technology's fool.

His entire life was totally manipulated and televised. What a guy.

And what makes it so much a part of who we are is that he was the last to know. Everyone in the world knew before he did. Technology can be that good ... and we can be at its mercy that much. We hooked into email and to computers that remembered everything we wrote and looked at. And the people behind the computers ... e-business and e-stocks ... became billionaires, at least for a while in those same memory banks. The nineties were an odd time. We were caught between weirdos and technology we didn't know how to control. Uma OD'd and danced while Jim smiled and finally escaped.

The point is that while things change, most of the important things stay the same. For every clean and quiet generation, there seems to be a dirty and rowdy one. If you are uneasy with what you are expected to do and to be, know that your turn will come. Put differently, if you really believe you have found the answer to traditional American questions, the next generation will tell you that you are wrong, but the underlying issues—like individualism, friendship, and bureaucracy—remain virtually unchanged. Each generation simply puts on a new mask to face them.

No matter what goes on, there are certain things that seem to be true. For example, James Madison quit changing and revising *Federalist* No.10 some years ago.[1] Bureaucracies have just gotten bigger, organizations more complex, science more powerful; but even though, since the end of the Cold War, the military no longer wants to kill us more times over, they still need the smaller, more expensive, arsenals designed for a "new kind of war." And, with regularity, people keep trying to be elected to some office or another, and other people keep encouraging them by voting.

The basic undercurrents of our culture are still powerful, and what was

---

1   Good old Madison. My friend Ken Mayers was more than amused when he pointed out that the heart of the real-world-of-selling-America is called ... Madison Avenue.

true when the *Preface* was born is true today. The critique then is the critique now.

Knowing that, we know about half of what is necessary to get at what is going on. Like it or not, each generation acts out American themes in ways different from the one before it. The Cold War was over and while the Republicans were contracting with us and impeaching a president the deficit that had seemed so threatening disappeared. Then suddenly one morning this generation was plunged into a "new kind of war." The dot-com bubble had burst and Enron was broke and under congressional scrutiny. George (the second) was cutting taxes and spending to defeat the new enemy. It looked like a remake of Reagan and Cold War II. Of course, the deficit returned, but such things never matter when the nation is at risk.

A generation ready to ride the dot-com/Enron bubble to early retirement and undreamed-of leisure and luxury may be thrown all the way back to the sixties—protests, marches ... who knows? At any rate, the military was in Afghanistan and a new generation had to come to terms with America. "Generation gaps" apply almost as well to successive generations as to the space between parents and children. The eighteen-year-old cannot follow the twenty-eight-year-old. The CIA and the FBI jumped to the top of the most popular jobs list. Once again some things seemed more important than money.

But, of course, we all get tugged by a lot of the same forces, and because of all the big and obvious things—like language and schools and TV—we have much more in common than we often admit. We're a whole lot alike. That is the truth of it. Our environment, physical and cultural and mythical, seeps in and affects us all. In real ways we are where and when we live.

If we want to do it right (it makes more sense than wanting to do it wrong), if we want to be smarter and better than we are, part of what we have to do is understand how others have dealt with their times. Clear, but bad, advice may be helpful, even if it is offered as good advice. Part of what older generations should do is to put their knowledge into forms from which younger generations might learn. The other part is that younger generations should try to listen.

The other day I read a fact that seemed true enough: No eighteen-year-old has ever been forty years old, but every forty-year-old has been eighteen years old. There is a big problem here, one that is difficult to come to grips with. This fact assumes that the forty-year-old, because of having more experience, knows better than the eighteen-year-old. In certain things, this may well be true. This also may be true: The forty-year-old may have twenty-two years' more wrongheaded thinking than the eighteen-year-old.

It's hard to know.

But there are some things that seem right. For example, given all we know, with an amazing amount of hard work, good intentions, clean hands, and a pure heart—given all those things—sometimes we get lucky and get a little smarter and better.

> *Besides, there are some things that can't be the truth even if they did happen.*
>
> —*Ken Kesey*

## Thank You, Thank You, Thank You

For thirty years students have been reading thank-yous from David. Now it's time to thank him for the *Preface*. The *Preface* is about us and how we become who we are because of where we live—our houses, towns, schools, churches, and the people with whom we share them. So it is part of the life of the *Preface* to acknowledge the place where life is done—without it there is no home and there can be no politics. As David wrote,

> Why acknowledge this not very large, nor very famous place? The fact is this: Northampton is the home of a lot of people. In its small ways, in the texture of its neighborhoods and friendships, in its shared winter storms and its concern about asparagus blight (no kidding), a lot of life gets defined.

I have been using *A Preface to Politics* to help me teach students about politics for over twenty years. It is always fresh. It's tricky. It makes me see new things every read, as it reminds students of the simple truths that daily living obscures. It's back to the basics, not the silliness of politicians talking about schooling, but the fact that we do live somewhere and that somewhere matters.   )

Life with the *Preface* has been an adventure, a journey not unlike Hesse's *Journey to the East*, with David and Barbara, their children and their friends: Ken Dolbeare, the *Preface*'s Godfather; Larry and Maya Spence; Bob and Olivia Waterman; Ken Mayers, and Sid Olufs, all of whom live in the pages of the book—watch for quotes.

This is good company. I am pleased to join them.

Thousands (this is true—I've counted!) of students have joined me for a time on the journey. They have shaped my thinking and must be recognized for what they bring to the *Preface*. Six of them require a special acknowledgment: Shannan Kain, Tabitha Williams, Laurie Lutzenberg, Mark Raaka, Callie Ingraham, and Brianne Bowker. They were in my introductory course when we decided to revise the *Preface*. We spent the following quarter together in a seminar on writing in political science, updating and streamlining the book. I asked them to make it accessible to kids who were in high school while Bill and G.W. were in the White House. They cut the outmoded material that was no longer useful and replaced it with materials that worked from past editions and personal experience. They are now fellow travelers and live as representatives of all the students who came before and those that will follow in the pages of the new *Preface*. Most of them were over eighteen, but we are well over forty. Some of them weren't born when we were forty, others were eighteen or so—and because of them much of my own wrongheaded thinking didn't make it into the book.

Thank you, David. Thank you, Stefanie and Micah. Thank you, Manastash Canyon and Creek. Thank you, Nikki. Thank you, Carol. Thank you, Ryan. Thank you … Thank you …

*Almost Thanksgiving,*
*Rex Wirth*
*Ellensburg, Washington*

# When?

*Perhaps in time the Dark Ages will be thought of as including our own.*

Sometimes you just want to sit down, sigh, and wish you knew how you got where you are. After another sigh, another question occurs: Just where am I?

Don't look at me, I don't know. It is possible to pinpoint the century we're in—and we may learn more than we want just by knowing that much.

The last part of the twentieth century was interesting. It lived up to the Chinese curse "May you live in interesting times." The fullness of Ken Kesey's life was during those times, and he was part of them. Through Kesey, we can get a sense of the last half of the twentieth century. Kesey, born in Oregon, was a wrestler and a writer. While he was a student in a writers' program at Stanford in 1959, he agreed to be part of some medical experiments in order to make a little extra money. It turned out that Kesey not only made a little extra money, he came to appreciate and enjoy the experimental chemical. Kesey was given LSD ... he dropped acid ... for science. He liked it so much that he kept doing it long after the experiments were over.

Tom Wolfe wrote about Kesey and his Merry Pranksters in *The Electric Kool-Aid Acid Test*. The book is one of the defining works about these times. It describes Kesey and friends traveling from the West Coast to the East in a bus painted in psychedelic colors. The plan was simple: "You're either on the bus or off the bus. That was that.

More than a party animal, Kesey was an author. He wrote *One Flew Over the Cuckoo's Nest*. It was a good book that was made into an interesting movie—a movie Kesey did not like. The story is about people in a mental institution who are, interestingly enough, drugged into submission. There is a very mean nurse who represents the bad parts of all institutions, and a variety of patients. The hero of the book was a big, silent American Indian, but the hero of the movie was Jack Nicholson. Nicholson is a remarkable actor, but he is not a big, silent American Indian.

An even better Kesey book is *Sometimes a Great Notion*. It takes place in Oregon and includes all of the great American themes. There is the settling of the West ... the struggle between the individual and huge organizations ... education ... family dynamics ... and on and on. The book is quintessential Kesey—a book about a high school jock, a good guy, who is trying to live his life in a changing world. It's Kesey's song.

It was a joy to hear Kesey lecture. There he was, on the stage, sitting on a stool, burly but in shape and clearly strong. It was not hard to see that he was a former wrestler who worked on his own farm. He would just sit there and do what he did best: Kesey was a wonderful storyteller.

Here's the trick. He would tell a story, but not quite finish it. Just before the end of the story, he would start a second story. That story was related to the first but was just a little different. He would get close to the end of the second story but wouldn't end it. Instead, he would tell a third story. So there you were, knowing all but the end of two stories and listening to a third one. The man could tell a story, and you would be wrapped up in what he was saying. The first two stories might be dancing in the periphery of your brain, but mostly you were concentrating on what he was saying.

Then he would tell you the whole third story. He would tell you the ending. And this is the magic part: That ending changed the meaning of the first two stories. Somehow, and I still don't understand how he did it, the first two stories meant something different because of the last one.

And that's a lot like the last part of the twentieth century. The stories built, and when we got the last one it somehow changed all the others—drugs and organizations and individualism and all that.

Ken Kesey barely made it to the end of the twentieth century. He died in 2001. And, after 9/11 all of the stories that came before seemed to change. Welcome to the twenty-first century.

# chapter 2

# Politics as Evil People:
# *The Federalist* No. 10 and Politics

*Although I know very little of the Steppenwolf's life, I have all the same good reason to suppose that he was brought up by devoted but severe and very pious parents and teachers in accordance with that doctrine that makes the breaking of the will the cornerstone of education and upbringing ... insofar as he let loose upon himself every barbed criticism, every anger and hate he could command he was, in spite of all, a real Christian, and a real martyr. As for others and the world around him he never ceased in his heroic and earnest endeavor to love them, to be just to them, to do them no harm, for the love of his neighbor was as deeply in him as the hatred of himself, and so his whole life was an example that love of one's neighbor is not possible without love of oneself, and that self-hate is really the same thing as sheer egoism, and in the long run breeds the same cruel isolation and despair.*

*—Hermann Hesse*

## Politics: Who, What, How

There are all kinds of traditional questions in politics. The more you know about history and political thought, the better chance you have to sort things out. While there are constant themes in American politics, every generation gets engaged in its own peculiar and particular variations.

We are, it seems to me, engaged in some serious Who, What, and How questions: Whom should I sleep with? What am I going to breathe? How am I going to earn a living?

I do not want to give the impression that this list is exhaustive. In truth, one hardly knows where to begin the list of such questions. It would seem to be endless. There are times when things appear to be just plain wacky. Example: When the Ayatollah Khomeini died, the Iranians couldn't get him to the cemetery. Millions of people bumped into each other, hit themselves, and finally spilled his body out of its casket. Make sense of that.

Now there are two pillars of light rising into the sky where the World Trade Center once stood. The Audubon Society had been concerned about the number of birds that died because they were attracted by the lights of the Twin Towers. The society thinks that the new memorial of light will be even worse, so they have been allowed to set up cameras to monitor it. If a large number of birds get trapped in the beams, they can have the lights turned off.

Or this: Our everyday computers in 1990 operated at such rapid speeds that they were measured in nanoseconds—billionths of a second. Clapping your hands took 500 million of them. Who can relate to that? Now computers are 1000 times faster—try moving your hands that fast.

Better that we begin with the who of bed, the what of breathe, and the how of work. At least we might make some sense of these essential concerns.

**Who?** It might seem unusual to think of politics beginning in bed. For most people in the world—and even most people in the United States until about thirty-five years ago—"Whom should I sleep with?" was a fairly simple question to answer. Generally speaking, a person tried to find someone of the opposite sex to fall in love with, marry, and—as things happen—sleep with.

Where is the politics in that? As Americans learned (as all those closets opened), the first question might easily be: Which sex do you want to sleep with? There are more choices: choices of number, choices of color, choices of married or unmarried. There are pregnancy choices and abortion choices. Whole political movements grew up around almost every choice. And I mean the voting, lobbying, lawyering kind of politics with which we are all familiar. Most of the battles have been won and now rights are attached to each of the choices. Rights bring benefits and we are back to marriage. Although any adult can now sleep with any other consenting adult, anytime, marriage is not a right available to homosexuals—unfinished politics. Now the rub: A heterosexual couple has the right to marry, and they must do so in order to get spousal benefits in Washington and many other states. A homosexual couple, however, is entitled to benefits while living together since they can't marry. A choice for a choice: We now seem to take a political stand whenever we lie down with someone else. What does that mean?

**What?** What am I going to breathe? The question is straightforward enough. Progress, that driving force of so much American life, has somehow gotten us to the point of killing the world in pursuit of a more comfortable material existence. The fear of aerosol spray depleting the ozone layer has been replaced by concern about the greenhouse effect. We know that much of our manufacturing—from automobile assembly plants to nuclear reactors—puts things into the air that are bad for us. Cars we live with, but inhaling a single "puff" of air containing radioactive stuff can produce serious health problems. We cut back on spraying deodorant from aerosol cans, but no one, or to be more precise, no one I know is against using electricity for all kinds of things. But that is only part of the matter. The other part is that one of the great, unintended consequences of all times is that our own production is making our world unsafe to live in.

A political problem? How can that be?

It is reasonable to expect that, as a country, we should be able to regulate any number of things in the "national interest."

"Aha," the shrill, harsh voice of Political Science says, "define 'national interest.' There it is, in print and in quotation marks as if it means something. Well, what *does* it mean?"

The truth is that, except in the wake of national disaster, there seems to be no agreement on what, specifically, defines our national interest. When it comes to the "what" question, books are written about it, governmental commissions are formed to define it, politicians always believe they understand it, and newspaper editorials often proclaim it. What all these efforts have in common is their lack of success.

There are some things we can say in general. For example, we have rules about killing other people, but what about people-made things killing everybody? Aren't we, after all, guaranteed liberty as well as life, not to mention the pursuit of happiness?

If that is so, what kind of politics—what kind of national interest—allows this slow death to go on?

What you breathe turns out to be an unlikely but wholly valid political problem.

**How?** The third question—How am I going to earn a living?—is a nagging one, but one not always of immediate concern to most college students. While you may think of school as job training, the fact is that school is a career for only a few of us.

In important ways, working does not belong in the category of politics. After all, politics is, well, politics. It has to do with armies and Congress and electing mayors and presidents. Politics involves voting, not getting a job.

That, of course, is the myth.

Working—according to the myth—has to do with personal ambition and talent and whom you know and what you are paid. Working is all wrapped up in the American dream of being the next Bill Gates: making it, rugged individualism, retiring at forty, status seeking and status getting, and the like.

Jobs are private and prestigious; politics is public and dirty.

Somewhere in our consciousness we know that is not quite right. After all, government is politics and government is in the job business. More people are employed by the government than by any other employer: One out of every six working people work for the government.

While regulation of the economy is anything but a science, certainly the level of prosperity in general and many jobs in particular are affected by government decisions. If the decision is made to raise interest rates, less money is loaned, fewer things are bought, fewer things are manufactured, and, as this keeps going, the one thing to rise will be—ta-da—unemployment. What happened to the public/private myth?

Think about it: You could be bright and able and energetic and selling apples on a street corner during the Great Depression of the 1930s. You could be fighting in Vietnam in the 1960s and early 1970s. You could be collecting unemployment in the 1970s because of shortsighted energy policies, inflation, and economic stagnation. You could be underemployed in 2001 wishing you had diversified your 401K better, before WTC/Enron.

It is, to be blunt, nonsense to misjudge the effects of government and politics, and to think that working is a sign of personal triumph or failure.

What's going on here?

## Madison ... as in the Avenue

> *... survival of a democratic system does not depend upon a consensus that penetrates to every level of society. It is apparently not necessary that most people commit themselves to a democracy; all that is necessary is that they fail to commit themselves actively to an anti-democratic system ... It is important to keep in mind that although the masses may have anti-democratic attitudes, they are also inclined to avoid political activity ... although the masses can usually be counted on to leave politics to the elites, we should not necessarily assume that our freedoms are safe in the hands of the elites ...*
>
> *One is tempted to attribute the stability of American democracy to the actions of the elites ... This conclusion would be inaccurate ... for in times of crises, the leadership of the elites has failed to provide a protective bulwark against anti-democratic forces. Ironically, it is to the poorly educated masses ... that the stability of American democracy is to be attributed. Although the poorly educated tend toward authoritarianism, violence, and prejudice, they are also apathetic; they fail to take action on their beliefs.*
>
> *—Thomas Dye and Harmon Zeigler*

Among those who attended the Constitutional Convention in 1788 James Madison stands out. It is Madison who is the source for what went on during the convention, since he kept an informed and intelligent diary of the convention debates. More important, along with Alexander Hamilton and John Jay, he wrote a series of papers defending the Constitution for the citizens of New York State. The papers—collected as *The Federalist Papers*—are brilliant propaganda that do much to explain the Constitution. The following is *Federalist* No.10, in which Madison writes about our citizens' relationships with each other, what they should be, and how they should be handled.

Two suggestions: Read it at least twice—one for what it says and again for what it does *not* say. Omission is important (especially if one knows just what to look for).

> Among the numerous advantages promised by a well-constructed Union none deserves to be more accurately developed than its tendency to break and control the violence of faction. The friend of popular governments never finds himself so much alarmed for their character and fate as when he contemplates their propensity to this dangerous vice. He will not fail, therefore, to set a due value on any plan, which, without violating the principles to which he is attached, provides a proper cure for it. The instability, injustice, and confusion introduced into the public councils have, in truth, been the mortal diseases under which popular governments have everywhere perished, as they continue to be the favorite and fruitful topics from which the adversaries to liberty derive their most specious declamations. The valuable improvements made by the American constitutions on the popular models, both ancient and modern, cannot certainly be too much admired, but it would be an unwarrantable partiality to contend that they have as effectively obviated the danger on this side as was wished and expected. Complaints are everywhere heard from our most considerate and virtuous citizens, equally the friends of public and private faith, and of public and personal liberty, that our governments are too unstable, that the public good is disregarded in the conflicts of rival parties, and that measures are too often decided, not according to the rules of justice and

the rights of the minor party, but by the superior force of an interested and overbearing majority. However anxiously we may wish
that these complaints had no foundation, the evidence of known
facts will not permit us to deny that they are in some degree true. It
will be found, indeed, on a candid review of our situation that some
of the distresses under 'which we labor have been erroneously
charged on the operation of our governments; but it will be found, at
the same time, that other causes will not alone account for many of
our heaviest misfortunes, and particularly for that prevailing and increasing distrust of public engagements and alarm for private rights,
which are echoed from one end of the continent to the other. These
must be chiefly, if not wholly, effects of the unsteadiness and injustice with which a factious spirit has tainted our public administra-
tions.

By a faction, I understand a number of citizens, whether amount-
ing to a majority or a minority of the whole, who are united and actuated by some common impulse of passion, or of interest, adverse to
the rights of other citizens or to the permanent and aggregate interests of the community.

There are two methods of curing the mischiefs of faction: the one,
by removing its causes; the other, by controlling its effects.

There are again two methods of removing the causes of faction:
the one, by destroying the liberty, which is essential to its existence;
the other, by giving to every citizen the same opinions, the same passions, and the same interests.

It could never be more truly said than of the first remedy, that it
was worse than the disease. Liberty is to faction what air is to fire, an
ailment without which it instantly expires. But it could not be less
folly to abolish liberty, which is essential to political life, because it
nourishes faction than it would be to wish the annihilation of air,
which is essential to animal life, because it imparts to fire its destructive agency.

The second expedient is as impracticable as the first would be un-
wise. As long as the reason of man continues fallible, and he is at liberty to exercise it, different opinions will be formed. As long as the
connection subsists between his reason and his self-love, his opinions

and his passions will have a reciprocal influence on each other, and the former will be objects to which the latter will attach themselves. The diversity in the faculties of men, from which the rights of property originate, is not less an insuperable obstacle to a uniformity of interests. The protection of these faculties is the first object of government. From the protection of different and unequal faculties of acquiring property, the possession of different degrees and kinds of property immediately results; and from the influence of these on the sentiments and views of the respective proprietors ensues a division of the society into different interests and parties.

The latent causes of faction are thus sown in the nature of man, and we see them everywhere brought into different degrees of activity, according to the different circumstances of civil society. A zeal for different opinions concerning religion, concerning government, and many other points, as well of speculation as of practice; an attachment to different leaders ambitiously contending for pre-eminence and power, or to persons of other descriptions whose fortunes have been interesting to the human passions, have, in turn, divided mankind into parties, inflamed them with mutual animosity, and rendered them much more disposed to vex and oppress each other than to co-operate for their common good. So strong is this propensity of mankind to fall into mutual animosities that, where no substantial occasion presents itself, the most frivolous and fanciful distinctions have been sufficient to kindle their unfriendly passions and excite their most violent conflicts. But the most common and durable source of factions has been the various and unequal distribution of property. Those who hold and those who are without property have ever formed distinct interests in society. Those who are creditors and those who are debtors fall under a like discrimination. A landed interest, a manufacturing interest, a mercantile interest, a money interest, with many lesser interests, grow up of necessity in civilized nations and divide them into different classes actuated by different sentiments and views. The regulation of these various and interfering interests forms the principal task of modern legislation and involves the spirit of party and faction in the necessary and ordinary operations of the government.

No man is allowed to be a judge in his own cause because his interest would certainly bias his judgment and, not improbably, corrupt his integrity. With equal, nay with greater reason, a body of men are unfit to be both judges and parties at the same time; yet what are many of the most important acts of legislation but so many judicial determinations, not indeed concerning the rights of single persons, but concerning the rights of large bodies of citizens? And what are the different classes of legislators but advocates and parties to the causes, which they determine? Is a law proposed concerning private debts? It is a question to which the creditors are parties on one side and the debtors on the other. Justice ought to hold the balance between them. Yet the parties are, and must be, themselves the judges, and the most numerous party or in other words, the most powerful faction must be expected to prevail. Shall domestic manufactures be encouraged, and in what degree, by restrictions on foreign manufactures? are questions, which would be differently decided by the landed and the manufacturing classes, and probably by neither with a sole regard to justice and the public good. The apportionment of taxes on the various descriptions of property is an act which seems to require the most exact impartiality, yet there is, perhaps, no legislative act in which greater opportunity and temptation are given to a predominant party to trample on the rules of justice. Every shilling with which they over-burden the inferior number is a shilling saved to their own pockets.

It is in vain to say that enlightened statesmen will be able to adjust these clashing interests and render them all subservient to the public good. Enlightened statesmen will not always be at the helm. Nor, in many cases, can such an adjustment be made at all without taking into view indirect and remote considerations, which will rarely prevail over the immediate interest which one party may find in disregarding the rights of another or the good of the whole.

The inference to which we are brought is that the causes of faction cannot be removed, and that relief is only to be sought in the means of controlling its effects.

If a faction consists of less than a majority, relief is supplied by the republican principle, which enables the majority to defeat its sinister views by regular vote. It may clog the administration, it may convulse the society, but it will be unable to execute and mask its violence under the forms of the Constitution. When a majority is included in a faction, the form of popular government, on the other hand, enables it to sacrifice to its ruling passion or interest both the public good and the rights of other citizens. To secure the public good and private rights against the danger of such a faction, and at the same time to preserve the spirit and the form of popular government is then the great object to which our inquiries are directed. Let me add that it is the great desideratum by which this form of government can be rescued from the opprobrium under which it has so long labored and be recommended to the esteem and adoption of mankind.

By what means is this object attainable? Evidently by one of two only. Either the existence of the same passion or interest in a majority at the same time must be prevented or the majority, having such coexistent passion or interest, must be rendered, by their number and local situation, unable to concert and carry into effect schemes of oppression. If the impulse and the opportunity be suffered to coincide, we well know that neither normal nor religious motives can be relied on as an adequate control. They are not found to be such on the injustice and violence of individuals, and lose their efficiency in proportion to the number combined together, that is, in proportion as their efficacy becomes needful.

From this view of the subject it may be concluded that a pure democracy, by which I mean a society consisting of a small number of citizens who assemble and administer the government in person, can admit of no cure for the mischiefs of faction. A common passion or interest will, in almost every case, be felt by a majority of the whole; a communication and concert result from the form of government itself, and there is nothing to check the inducements to sacrifice the weaker party or an obnoxious individual. Hence it is that such democracies have ever been spectacles of turbulence and contention, have ever been found incompatible with personal security or the rights of property, and have in general been as short in their lives as they have been violent in their deaths. Theoretic politicians who have patronized this species of government have erroneously supposed that by reducing mankind to a perfect equality in their political rights, they would, at the same time, be perfectly equalized and assimilated in their possessions, their opinions, and their passions.

A republic, by which I mean a government in which the scheme of representation takes place, opens a different prospect and promises the cure for which we are seeking. Let us examine the points in which it varies from pure democracy, and we shall comprehend both the nature of the cure and the efficacy that it must derive from the Union.

The two great points of difference between a democracy and a republic are: first, the delegation of the government, in the latter, to a small number of citizens elected by the rest; secondly, the greater number of citizens and greater sphere of country over which the latter may be extended.

The effect of the first difference is, on the one hand, to refine and enlarge the public views by passing them through the medium of a chosen body of citizens whose wisdom may best discern the true interest of their country, and whose patriotism and love of justice will be least likely to sacrifice it to temporary or partial considerations. Under such a regulation it may well happen that the public voice, pronounced by the representatives of the people, will be more consonant to the public good than if pronounced by the people themselves, convened for the purpose. On the other hand, the effect may be inverted. Men of factious tempers, of local prejudices, or of sinister designs may, by intrigue, by corruption, or by other means, first obtain the suffrages and then betray the interests of the people. The question resulting is whether small or extensive republics are more favorable to the election of proper guardians of the public weal; and it is clearly decided in favor of the latter by two obvious considerations:

In the first place, it is to be remarked that, however small the republic may be, the representatives must be raised to a certain number in order to guard against the cabals of a few, and that, however large it may be, they must be limited to a certain number in order to guard against the confusion of a multitude. Hence the number of representatives in the two cases not being in proportion to that of the two constituents, and being proportionally greater in the small republic, it follows that, if the proportion of fit characters be not less in the large than in the small republic, the former will present a greater option and consequently a greater probability of a fit choice.

In the next place, as each representative will be chosen by a greater number of citizens in the large than in the small republic, it will be more difficult for unworthy candidates to practice with success the vicious arts by which elections are too often carried; and the suffrages of the people being more free will be more likely to center in men who possess the most attractive merit and the most diffusive and established characters.

It must be confessed that in this, as in most other cases, there is a mean, on both sides of which inconveniences will be found to lie. By enlarging too much the number of electors you render the representative too little acquainted with all their local circumstances and lesser interests; as by reducing it too much, you render him unduly attached to these and too little fit to comprehend and pursue great and national objects. The federal Constitution forms a happy combination in this respect: the great and aggregate interests being referred to the national, the local and particular to the State legislatures.

The other point of difference is the greater number of citizens and extent of territory which may be brought within the compass of republican than of democratic government, and it is this circumstance principally which renders factious combinations less to be dreaded in the former than in the latter. The smaller the society, the fewer probably will be the distinct parties and interests, the more frequently will a majority be found of the same party; and the smaller the number of individuals composing a majority, and the smaller the compass within which they are placed, the more easily will they concert and execute their plans of oppression. Extend the sphere, and you take in a greater variety of parties and interests; you make it less probable that a majority of the whole will have a common motive to invade the rights of other citizens; or if such a common motive exists, it will be more difficult for all who feel it to discover their own strength and to act in unison with each other. Besides other impediments, it may be remarked that, where there is a consciousness of unjust or dishonorable purposes, communication is always checked by distrust in proportion to the number whose concurrence is necessary.

Hence it clearly appears that the same advantage which a republic has over a democracy in controlling the effects of faction is enjoyed by a large over a small republic—is enjoyed by the Union over the States composing it. Does the advantage consist in the substitution of representatives whose enlightened views and virtuous sentiments render them superior to local prejudices and schemes of injustice? It will not be denied that the representation of the Union will be most likely to possess these requisite endowments. Does it consist in the greater security afforded by a greater variety of parties, against the event of any one party being able to outnumber and oppress the rest? In an equal degree does the increased variety of parties comprised within the Union increase this security? Does it, in fine, consist in the greater obstacles opposed to the concert and accomplishment of the secret wishes of an unjust and interested majority? Here, again, the extent of the Union gives it the most palpable advantage.

The influence of factious leaders may kindle a flame within their particular States, but will be unable to spread a general conflagration through the other States. A religious sect may degenerate into a political faction in a part of the Confederacy, but the variety of sects dispersed over the entire face of it must secure the national councils against any danger from that source. A rage for paper money, for an abolition of debts, for an equal division of property, or for any other improper or wicked project will be less apt to pervade the whole body of the Union than a particular member of it, in the same proportion as such a malady is more likely to taint a particular county or district than an entire State.

In the extent and proper structure of the Union, therefore, we behold a republican remedy for the diseases most incident to republican government. And according to the degree of pleasure and pride we feel in being republicans ought to be our zeal in cherishing the spirit and supporting the character of Federalists.[1]

In many important ways, *Federalist* No. 10 gives away most of the plot, a plot we have accepted with almost no reservations, accepted almost unknowingly. As it seems to have worked out, we, bright and brave college students, we bright and brave future businessmen and women, we Americans, really do not like or trust each other very much. At least we are not supposed to. We do not relate to each other well enough to make mutual decisions. *Federalist* No. 10 is the story of mistrust. Madison speaks of the rabbleness, of the potential evil doings of public meetings and democratic practices. He poses the essential question: How can we trust government to the people when we have no faith in them?

People, self-serving, self-centered, selfish people, are the raw material for our state. We are encouraged to be a private, materialistic people. We are essentially an uncommunitarian, antipolitical people who may act differently in spite of—certainly not at the urging—of the state. Harsh words, these. Let me try to explain.

Madison knew something that we must learn. He knew that there was a close connection between how people relate to one another and the structure within which that relationship takes place. It is important to understand Madison's argument in different terms.

If the problem is how to create a political system that will continue regardless of the basic inability of citizens to rule themselves the answer is deceptively simple. Structure the system so that its citizens will become mired in a self-grabbing, self-gratifying way of life. Make it so that petty people, materialistic people, will be allowed, whether acting singly or in small groups, to go about the task of robbing the poor, robbing the rich, robbing the consumer, or even building a better mousetrap. Madison, in all his political wisdom, worked it out so that we could pursue our own private, material interests. The plan was not a stupid one; for certain, it has had lasting effects.

Have you ever seen a fairly large group of children "playing" on a play-

---

1   *Federalist* No. 10 can be found in various places. Clinton Rossiter edited a complete version of the *Federalist Papers,* and Bobbs-Merrill has reprinted some of the papers individually.

ground? There are balls and bats and fields and courts and sandboxes and toys. Here these young citizens of the future grab and kick and cry and fight over the toys or games they are to play. Sometimes groups form and play their own game, but mostly they just make nasty remarks to other groups. The critical element in the playground is that the whole hassle seems pretty harmless. The children are being looked after, taken care of, and ultimately directed by adults. Theirs is a choice of what to do in the sandbox. If Madison is correct, that is good training for the system, good practice for the future.

The point is obvious: Do we make decisions of any more importance than the toys we are going to play with? Houses, SUVs, powerful computers, cell phones—what difference does it make? Face it; we are playing by their rules on their playground. The strategy of *Federalist* No. 10 is to divide the citizens and make them politically impotent; it does and we are.

## Is So? (As in: Say It Isn't So)

Metaphors are helpful, no doubt about it, but the sandbox metaphor will get us only so far. We need to see if there are some real-life examples of our claimed political impotence.

What about all of those Middle Eastern countries? What about all the former Soviet states? We missed a lot that was going on in the world during the long prosperity and titillating scandal of the Clinton years. If the politics of the world was a piece of music, then the United States ended up several beats behind. Consider the following.

The government of the United States has priorities. So far, so good. The Cold War priorities were to fight communism and to support democracy. Then it was to fight a global war on drugs while letting other countries conduct their own internal business. What we ended up doing was bumping into ourselves in the most embarrassing ways—causing wars, supporting dictators, invading other countries and arresting their leaders, punishing populations because we disliked their leaders. It is possible to look back over the past half-century and see such things as the impetus for the "Axis of Evil" that the Bush administration has discovered.

Let's look back. It wasn't long after World War II ended that the wartime alliance between the USA and the USSR unraveled. The beginning of the Cold War was a line-drawing exercise. The American secretary of state drew a line between Japan and Korea and told the communists not to cross it. When they stepped up to the line, as should have been expected, we went to the UN and precipitated the Korean War. It is still going on—it's been a long truce—so the first member of the Axis of Evil is a very old enemy.

Then came the terrorists because we will not deal with them (how can you disagree with that?); for example, we would not deal with Iran. But because Iran held American hostages, we had to make a deal: exchange military equipment for hostages. We sold them the means of violence and terror in return for the fruits of terror—and Iran is now the second Axis of Evil power.

Finally, there is the saga of Saddam. A dictator who we have loved, and hated, and who we now love to hate. It seems that in the late 1980s when Kuwait began to do things that were detrimental to the Iraqi economy the US ambassador assured Saddam that we had no defense agreement with Kuwait. We basically gave him the go-ahead to invade, but when he did we called out the UN again. This time the job could have been finished, but we decided it would be better to embargo and bomb the country for a decade—so there was nothing new with the third party to the new axis.

There you have it, the three partners in the Axis of Evil, America's enemy in the war against terrorism. Unfortunately, no matter how it's cut, action against the axis will be more of the same. By the time this gets into print, we may have already declared war, fought it, and "won" … whatever that means in our most unsettled of times.

In a lackluster, nearly meaningless election campaign, the loser (by popular vote) was elected president of the United States. Another four years of silly controversy, investigative journalism, and news flashes was in the offing, but the era of good feeling came to an end. The nation was brought back to the world beat when our own airliners were converted into bombs that struck symbolic targets in the heart of our country.

So now we are fighting a "new kind of war." One the "experts" say could last twenty years or more, and civil rights advocates argue will cost us not only money and lives, but also some of the very freedoms we say we cherish. Big Brother (via the PATRIOT Act) is watching—and it's for our own good! And all the while we citizens can't do much more than watch it all on TV. We can cheer the people we think are right and boo those we think are wrong, but only those in the same room can hear us.

It takes no great insight to see that the government makes decisions in which we have no say. As the Cold War wound down and ended leaving us with no one to blame (the Russians made it easy for a long time), this tension became apparent in two important respects.

The first point has to do with the faith each of us has in each other and in the country. The fact is that the United States is just not all that bad. Neither are we. We have some freedoms and a lot of material things that make life easier. Even many of our public officials seem to have good intentions.

The second point, and the one that is not easy to live with, is that the faith we have gets systematically abused. Our power is power to react, not to act. So what if we had nothing personally against the people of Central America? So what if we are against opening more of Alaska to oil exploration? So what?

Given the fact that we control neither information, nor debate, nor decision-making, we are essentially powerless. Without power. Power-less.

No power.

Of course that is the way it was set up to be. Built right into our political structure and our ideology is the dynamic that we should be grateful for what little we have; built right into it is the pressure to forget that there is much more than we have the right to do. Our myths support our powerlessness. Each of us discovers it in his or her own way, but the important fact is that each of us discovers it.

The idea of a political state built on the evilness—and, hopefully, the powerlessness—of its people sounds pretty silly. It should. Regrettably, to consider what students are taught about our system is to consider just such thoughts. The following questions are quoted from a reputable textbook:

1. "How is it possible to maintain a real equality of influence and power over government?" (In other words, won't a minority of people gain power?)

2. "If everyone is to have an equal say, how can the decisions of government be made with sufficient knowledge and expertness?" (How can we expect "ordinary citizens" to understand?)

3. "How can a popular government act vigorously, speedily, and decisively, particularly in crises?" (Citizens are just too slow.)

4. "How can a system of popular government ever cope with ... larger groups ... tyrannizing smaller groups?" (We count on the worst in people coming out.)

5. "Can a system really operate with the consent of all?"

These are not abstract questions but live issues... In one way or another every popular government must surmount these problems...[2]

These are no doubt hard questions. While not exactly in the same class as "Have you stopped beating your wife?" they are close. At the root of these questions lies an unarticulated, seemingly reasonable bias: How do we form a popular government in spite of the weaknesses of people? Look at those five basic questions and at what they assume about you. That, among other things, you are probably not able to understand the complexities of government; that you will probably get more power than others if you are able; and, finally, that if you have the power to do so you will tyrannize over others. The beauty of it all is that we have been taught that *we* are not like that—but that other people are. The self-protective mechanism is simple: "If others were only as good as I am, then I could begin to act as kindly and generously as I really am." Score another one for Madison.

## Crossing Ourselves

In *Federalist* No.10, Madison wrote about what he called factions. The notion of factions has had a noble history in our political thinking. These groups of active citizens have formed the basis of many theories of politics in the United States. The most powerful of these theories is called pluralism, which we will come back to later. In another chapter, there will also be a more complete discussion of social science and group theory, but I want to introduce the topic here in order to give you a sense of some of the underlying meanings of our interest groups, or factions.

A standard textbook on American government by James Q. Wilson includes a chart showing the percentage of people belonging to "interest

2  Robert Dahl, *Pluralist Democracy in the United States* (Chicago: Rand McNally, 1967), pp. 10–11.

groups" in five Western nations:[3] the United States, Great Britain, Germany, Italy, and Mexico. The chart shows conclusively that more Americans belong to interest groups than do people in those other countries. The reason that is wonderfully good news, according to the theory, is this: It is because of "the greater sense of political efficiency and the stronger sense of civic duty among Americans."

There is a logic behind this statement. We all join interest groups, and as each group grows in number it also grows in strength. The groups then pressure the proper governmental agency or official to make decisions in their favor. In this way, the theory assures us that our interests are taken care of.

While the shortcomings of the theory (and they seem to outweigh the advantages) will be dealt with later, there is an emotional reality that is important to understand now. There is a name for this theory of interest groups, one that sounds fairly nasty: cross-cutting cleavages. The name has merit as one of the most descriptive in political science, and it is, in truth, on the cutting edge of theory.

The theory, to repeat it in a little different way, is that society is broken up into competing groups. It is clear that groups vie for power. It is equally clear that there are power struggles within any particular group. All of this cleavaging leads to at least two things. First, the struggle of many groups against each other leads to a kind of hyperactivity that may result in the groups canceling out each other's activity. Second, and more important, it leads to political stability. We each have a small amount of power that gets dissipated in many different groups. To put it in the language of Madison, factions fight factions, and the whole is undisturbed.

At the level of the political system, if the political system is the most important thing, then a theory that aims for stability seems sensible. While it is normal to think that those cross-pressures work out best with groups, it is important to remember that those cross-pressures are aimed at each of us. We are the target, you and me. It is here we can see the cleavage part of the theory.

Each of us gets caught up in our own cross-pressures. We are taught to believe in our own self-interest, in our own ineptness, in our own evilness.

3  James Q. Wilson, *American Government* (Lexington, Mass.: D.C. Heath, 1983).

The theory is a powerful one because we get trapped in ourselves and are not given much of a sense that there is something beyond the selfish pursuits of our very own interests.

And we are cut up by it.

How can we support more homeland security and the family values agenda, and protect our constitutional rights and individual freedoms? Cross-purposes. How can we be members of a group that is for lower taxes and another that is for better public education? Crosscutting. How can we be for a "strong" country and spend what it takes to win the war on terrorism and be for tax cuts and a balanced budget? Hmmm.

We have a political arrangement that turns each of us back on himself or herself. Much is missing from the theory of groups that represent people, not the least of which is a citizenry active in politics. We are urged to be unpolitical and private, alone to tend to our wounds. When we read Madison we read a truly amazing version of who we are. He was able to visualize a mechanical way of creating a nation-state in which the distrusted citizen could appear active yet remain virtually powerless. In many ways that is the un-kindest cut of all.

As it turns out, we are much like our parents. Maybe there are style differences—choice of drugs, styles of dress, and the like—but the basics are similar. We know we must train ourselves to be private, to get ahead on our own, if we are to fit into this land of the free. So we go to college to learn a trade, to become a professional, to prepare to be rich. Education for increased earnings. Education in how to live a life geared to privacy. We must learn to listen to and follow directions well. We must produce when told.

The structure of college is the structure of society, and the ends are the same. We go from class to class, learning truths contradicted by truths. We write our own exams and our own papers. Those who can best compartmentalize truth, who can learn most of what they are told, and who can do so alone get prizes. To excel is to be super-average. To excel is to be rewarded materially.

That is like the state and our parents. We all agree on ends and on how we are to be judged and rewarded. We understand at a subtle, sophisticated gut level why the state protects its property. Our institutions and our ideology are geared to similar principles. In important ways, we agree with what is. We agree to mistrust ourselves with our own ruling, we agree to judge ourselves, in large part, in terms of what we buy, and we agree on the basic rules of materialism, capitalism, corporate wealth, and the like. James Madison would be proud.

Some problems are obvious. Because we mistrust others, we have lost control of all those things we might have in common. Every issue, every topic, every decision that might include all of us, is denied most of us because we have so little faith in the ability of people to make political decisions. Let us review what the Federalists, as exemplified by Madison, believed:

1. People could not be trusted to rule themselves. Indeed, the only thing worse than a few people trying to rule themselves was many people trying to rule themselves.

2. The morality of the system was in almost no sense public. Morality was a private thing, a commodity of the individual based on self-interest.

3. Citizenship was based upon an individual's remaining private. The system depended upon materialism, self-seeking-ness, self-interested-ness, and the struggle for personal advantage, and the citizen became trapped in this self-view.

4. The system was created by people of the Enlightenment who believed that if only the right (read rational) set of institutions was discovered, then the system could run indefinitely, in spite of people.

## A Wholly Hostile World

*This, I think, has been our most devastating and enduring impact on this continent and its indigenes: Europeans furnished it all in fear. After the wreck of the* Santa Maria *off the coast of Hispaniola and the remarkable rescue of the crew and cargo by local natives, Columbus decided to leave behind a small outpost of men and supplies till his return. La Navidad, as he called it, was a fort erected where none was needed: these people were unbelievably generous and "timorous." But the admiral was by now a firm believer in his own lurid fantasy of the man-eating Caribs, who, he imagined, preyed upon these gentle, unarmed people. Thus, shortly before leaving, he shot off the cannon at the hull of the* Santa Maria, *dere-*

*lict out there on the reef, to brief the natives on "how far it possibly carried, and how it pierced the side of a ship, and how the charge went far out to sea." Next, he "had the people of the ships arm themselves and engage in a sham fight, telling the cacique that he was not to fear the Caribs even if they should come. All this the admiral says that he did, that the king (chief) might regard the Christians whom he left as friends and might be frightened and have fear of them.*[4]

—*Calvin Luther Martin*

Built into what the America of Madison means is that each of us acts in certain kinds of ways. We are, in truth, often-threatened folks. It is, after all, a way to relate to the world we've come to know and—I mean this—to love.

The national debt was the specter that haunted and threatened the future of post–Cold War students, but one day it disappeared and there seemed to be nothing to fear. High schoolers brought fear back when they started shooting their teachers and classmates—or such things, at least, became big nationwide news. Then came the World Trade Center: Nothing, it seems, is safe anymore. We live in a world that appears to be wholly hostile. The "big" problem—terrorism—has eclipsed drugs and school violence. Our nuclear weapons are headed for the warehouse and it seems that a focus on AIDS and deadly wastes of all kinds will have to wait until we achieve victory in this "new kind of war." But those are easy things. We are nervous about big government, and about not enough government. That is to say, in the 1990s we worried about big government—after all, shouldn't we "the people" spend the surplus? Now it seems there can't be enough government to protect us from those who would destroy our way of life. The fact seems to be that, after an all too brief respite while the debt was lifted from our shoulders, the world is, once again, becoming increasingly uncomfortable for a large number of people. It is a threatening place. To see how fear dominates our lives, think about its role in a day in college: grades, money, popularity, professionalism, sex, roommates.

4  Calvin Luther Martin, *The Way of the Human Being* (New Haven, Conn.: Yale University Press, 1999), p. 168. Quotes from *The Journal of Christopher Columbus*, trans. Cecil Jane and L.A. Vigneras (New York: Clarkson N. Potter, Bramhall House, 1960), pp. 132–33.

School is spring training for life.

Why are you in school? Just what are your motives? In an amazingly optimistic way, let's start our list with something nice. It is possible that people go to college to gain wisdom. Or (less grand and noble) we fear ignorance; or (more accurately) we don't want to appear stupid. That, of course, is at the top of our list—the most impressive of our motives.

Why the hell are you in school? To make more money in the future? Maybe. To find a wife or a husband with a college degree? Maybe. Because your friends or parents silently (or not so silently) demanded it? Could be. Just a terrific set of reasons. But they are, in the end, not the most important or interesting topics. What counts—at least two things that count—is what you see and what you do.

We know, as one of those "facts," that college or university can put you through changes, personal changes, value changes, social changes, which you will probably like, and which are for the good. It has been known to happen. There is even a kind of secret history of people who have gotten wiser and better and who started doing it in school. In spite of a whole lot of mindless effort and activity, learning can and does go on. It is learning that has to do with serious and important questions.

But two things seem to get in the way: students and teachers.

We are painfully aware that there is a very good chance that any class you walk into will be fairly shallow, uninteresting, and destructive to your good mood and desire to learn. After all, those who have, in a strange way, done the very best in the most ordinary way people the university. More precisely, if we learn from example it is important to remember that people in the university are often malignant forms of what is normal and ordinary. That a person made good grades and got high scores on standardized tests means nothing more than this: A person made good grades and got high scores on standardized tests. There are an amazing number of other reasons why teachers aren't good at teaching, but what I wanted to say was they are mostly just normal—malignantly normal.

Students often aren't much better. What has always been most curious to me are those who know what's wrong: those who know their compulsions, and who are so "sophisticated" that they laugh at themselves. We announce our anxieties about grades or money or whatever—we then explain why the anxieties are silly and talk about how we are "stuck" with them. After this formal announcement we then go about being anxious, unhappy, unpleasant, or the like.

That kind of self-analysis doesn't really do much good. In fact, it is often little more than self-delusion, which we "smart" people do. It works in a wonderful way: As we make fun of ourselves in sophisticated ways (but still act out those myths we are supposed to act out) we just make fools of ourselves. We're simply much less witty and insightful than we think we are.

So we all walk around threatened by one thing or another. We are forced to miss many things—like an education in college—because we fear either looking for the truth or looking at ourselves. Every time we step back, or turn our head, or close our eyes to those things, we have only ourselves to blame. Being threatened is another way of saying we are afraid, and that is another way of acknowledging the force of the system in which we live. If we can go to school and be scared enough to avoid being educated, what chance do we have when we leave college and try to do good? If you're scared now, you're on your way to becoming a dynamite citizen.

## Politics

But we must understand more than what the Founding Fathers wrote. We must go beyond their words and even our own actions. We must begin to get at what was not said. We must try to figure out what the world of James Madison lacked.

What Madison excluded, what he feared and so eloquently attacked, was politics. Those things shared, the things we have in common, were to him not best served institutionally. He does not mention the idea of community—only "interests." If politics were a science, then there could be a fairly accurate definition of those things political. Regrettably for accuracy, politics seems to be beyond the precision of science and the impurities of language. The best that can be done at this stage is to discuss a few of the concepts involved in politics.[5]

5  For various but obviously related discussions of politics, one might see Max Weber, "Politics as a Vocation," in Hans Gerth and C. Wright Mills, eds., *From Max Weber* (New York: Oxford University Press, 1958); Hannah Arendt, *The Human Condition* (Chicago: University of Chicago Press, 1970).

Politics, to overgeneralize, is the activity by which people live together. It is working to adjust aims and activities between you and others: the one and the many. Aristotle believed that it was society's highest form of activity. It was, he thought (and I believe rightly), through citizenship—through people deciding how to act and then acting that way—that an individual could develop his or her capabilities to the fullest. Through participation in politics people helped define themselves.

This definition implies much. It is meant to link politics to morality. What is implied is that politics means taking a stand, being passionate about something, defining what you believe to be right or wrong, good or bad, and then acting on that belief. It is not an easy thing to do, especially when one is taught to reject just such propositions. But it seems to me that politics involves the inner tension of trying to figure out—and then doing—good in a world where we do not know what good is and where no choices seem clear-cut.

Politics, then, is something profoundly human, something with its roots in morality and its sources of action in a deeply felt inner tension.

Through political action, the individual becomes responsible. To either destroy or check the power to act is to destroy an individual's capacity to do good. By destroying the personal responsibility for power, one destroys its moral roots. It is precisely this kind of equation that Madison failed to acknowledge. We are denied the possible joys of making joint decisions—yet we seem to be responsible for the actions of others. Politics includes the possibility of sharing happiness or unhappiness—but not so in the state laid out in the *Federalist Papers*.

Finally, there must be some place for politics to take place. Politics needs an arena, a public space. There must be arenas, in terms of issues and ideas and even physical space, where citizens can come together and work out courses of action. Space is both psychological and physical. Thus far, our only public space is the ballot box, which is neither public nor really space. There is always the idea of going into the streets, or of sitting in a building, or of bombing monuments. Those are only the choices of how to create space, a problem that is ahead of where we are now. To deny the citizen a public space is to suffocate political activity. That is very close to the precise state of our political life.[6]

6  Hannah Arendt, *On Revolution* (New York: Viking Press, 1965), discusses the idea of political space and why it does not exist in the United States.

But we have a tradition, a view of ourselves that denies us the opportunity to share. Certainly we give something to charity, or buy Girl Scout cookies, or avoid littering. But we do not involve ourselves in those decisions that control our lives. Madison talks about dividing power, pitting it one against the other; he talks about the selfishness of people, pitting them one group against the other.

We are structured not for cooperative acts but for private ones; we are given a form of government that calls not for the best in people but only for the minimum from them. What we must realize is that we are living a self-fulfilling prophecy: That by founding a government geared to selfishness, we can maintain it only by being selfish. By participating within the structure, we are acting out Madison's belief that we are unworthy.

To repeat, Madison outlines a life alone; a life of technical skills, of savings bonds, and of SUVs that carry our hopes for happiness; a common life without community, a public life without politics, and popular decisions without people.

What I am arguing is that our basic view of humanity condemns us to an autistic public life. We are powerless over ourselves. We are mute. We consider ourselves an evil people condemned to a life without trust, without power, without politics.

> *I know a place where you can sometimes sing along with yourself ... "Row, row, row your boat, gently down the stream ..."—and just when you get to your merrily-merrilies, the echo comes in "Row, row, row ..." right on cue. But you must be careful in choosing your key or your tempo ... because an echo is an inflexible and pitiless taskmaster: you sing the echoes away. And even after you have left ... you cannot help feeling, for a long time after, that any jig you whistle, hymn you hum, or song you sing is somewhere immutably turned to an echo yet unheard, or relentlessly echoing a tune long forgotten ...*
>
> *—Ken Kesey*

# chapter 3

# Politics and Knowledge: Epistemology

*But even worse was the way he talked about science—in which he did not believe ... it was a belief, like any other, only worse, stupider than any; the word science was the expression of the silliest realism, which did not blush to take at their face value the more dubious re-flections of objects in the human intellect; to pass them current, and to shape out of them the sorriest, most spiritless dogma ever imposed upon humanity. Was not the idea of a material world existing by and for itself the most laughable of all self-contradictions?*

*—Thomas Mann*

*Truth is always in poetic form; not literal but symbolic; hiding or veiled; light in darkness. Yes, mysterious. Literalism is idolatry of words; the alternative to idolatry is mystery. And literalism reifies, makes everything into things, these tables and chairs, commodities. The alternative to reification is mystification.*

*—Norman O. Brown*

*Knowing and being are opposite, antagonistic states. The more you know, exactly the less you are. The more you are, in being, the less you know.*

—*D. H. Lawrence*

## Knowing Things

All of us act as if we know things. Moreover, we act as if we know how we know things. Every society is built, in great measure, on a method of knowledge gathering, on a way of knowing things. This is normal enough, but what does it mean? How much do we really understand about how we know things, about why a fact is a fact, and why knowledge is knowledge? What if our approach to knowledge is more closing than opening, more confining than freeing—in essence, more mechanical than human?

What if our "facts" are unclear, misleading, or false? In an important way, this chapter is simply an extension of the preceding one. We now know something about Madisonian people, about ourselves. In this chapter, we will consider how we look at the world, what we know, and how we know what we know. To know about knowing is to begin to fill out our knowledge of politics.

The Madisonian person is, in a sophisticated sense, scientific. Put most simply, the link between the two is materialism; the link is an extraordinary reliance on the reality of objective things. We have a notion of what is real, of how to analyze reality, and of what that analysis means. It is that method—science—and its accompanying myths that form the basis of this chapter. It is "evil" people in a scientific, material, objective world who will be our main concern. In essence, our society's knowledge gathering rests on what has been called (and I believe correctly) the myth of objective consciousness. It is the kind of myth that needs to be looked at in pieces, as well as whole, to be fully understood. For a start we might say that the myth of objective consciousness assumes that the only "facts" in the world—the only things that are real—are those things that are apart from us. According to this myth, things have a reality if we can perceive them objectively.

A fact is a fact, in and of itself. Without help. A rose is a rose.

All that, simple as it is, sounds reasonable. Certainly it is what we have been taught. Indeed it sounds so right that we rarely examine the assumptions upon which it rests. We think that all facts are objective things, but we fail to realize that we tie facts with moral codes. We seldom see that the result of our myth of objective consciousness may be trauma-filled. Yet the myth fills our lives in many ways, in many ways we are often unaware of.

The myth makes scientists of us all—we become counters; the more sophisticated of us, statisticians. We add and subtract reality. We use our fingers and toes, calculators and computers, to find facts, facts which become truths. This is our style: precise, calculating, objective.

Certainly, there are those who will object to this whole attack. It would be foolish to deny that this style has led to a great many things. After all, somehow those numbers are able to make airplanes fly and bridges span, and offensive and defensive missiles project. Science does produce a kind of magic; but the problem is more complex than that. To quote Theodore Roszak, "If we believe there is some place to get and if we believe it is important to get there very, very fast—despite the dangers, despite the discomforts, despite expense, despite the smog—then the automobile is an impressive piece of magic."[1]

The tension is obvious enough: Objectiveness is the stuff of science; but is it the stuff of politics?

## Science: Real and True and Its Application

Science, in its approach to knowledge, in its gathering of it, and finally in its view of what is real, is little more than a value system of impressive proportions. To find these values, we must look at the elements that make up science. We must study what it studies, approach its own approach in a critical way, and try to make a judgment about the reality it produces. We might begin by clarifying what we mean by objective reality and then go on to examine the method of science.

It is important to realize that what is being discussed is not an isolated

1   Theodore Roszak, *The Making of the Counter Culture: Reflections on a Technocratic Society and Its Youthful Opposition* (Garden City, N.Y.: Doubleday, 1969), p. 259. For an interesting work on the nature of scientific discovery, see Thomas Kuhn, *The Structure of Scientific Revolutions* (Chicago: University of Chicago Press, 1962).

phenomenon that may or may not be personally interesting to me.[2] Again to quote Theodore Roszak: "Objectivity as a state of being fills the very air we breathe in a scientific culture; it grips us subliminally in all we say, feel and do. The mentality of the ideal scientist becomes the very soul of society." He continues to say that the stuff of this soul is objectivity and that the belief in objectivity becomes myth:

> The myth of objective consciousness is to cultivate a state of consciousness cleansed of all physical distortion, all personal involvement. What flows from this state of consciousness qualifies as knowledge, and nothing else does ... (Scientific knowledge) is a verifiable description of reality that exists independent of any purely personal considerations. It is true ... real ... dependable ... It works.[3]

It is real. Better yet, it is concrete. Yes, science is just what we can believe in because it deals with the real world, and if there is one thing we have learned to agree on, it is the real world. Of course, that is part of the myth—that we think we know what the real world is. Let us not accept that we know what the real world is; let us not accept the definitions that underlie science. It seems reasonable to begin to understand the myth of objective consciousness by trying to understand the term "real."[4]

What I would like to argue is that it is no easy thing to know what is "real." To say that what one sits on is a real chair does not tell us quite enough. Are other kinds of chairs "real," or are they false? If we worked at the silly example of the chairs long enough, we might get to the point of knowing exactly what was included in, and excluded from, the phrase "real chair."

2   For example, see Floyd Matson, *The Broken Image,* (Garden City, N.Y.: Doubleday, 1966), or Abraham Maslow, *The Psychology of Science* (New York: Harper & Row, 1966).

3   Roszak, *The Making of the Counter Culture*, pp. 208, 216. In the third edition of *The Preface* this quote evoked the image of the consciousness of the corporate liberalism of the Pentagon.

4   This is taken in large part from J. Peter Euban, "Political Science and Political Science," in Philip Green and Sanford Levinson, eds. *Power and Community: Dissenting Essays in Political Science* (New York: Vintage, 1970), pp. 3–59

When we go from chairs to the "real world," everything gets more complicated. Maybe the "real world" consists of only those things that one can see, touch, or count. If that is so, and scientists including most social scientists would have us believe that, then we should know something about that reality.

To believe solely in the scientism of our time is to believe in a fairly static and, to me, fairly boring, state of affairs. To begin with, the bias is clear: If the scientist studies the "real world," then presumably the rest of us study the "false world." They have hard "facts," we soft; indeed, they have facts, we have only values. The scientific method, as we all know, insists that all of its experiments be repeatable and that all of its hypotheses be verifiable.

Think about a world in which everything that is true (could there be a "true fact"?) must be able to happen again and again and again. If that is what "true" is, and if it comes from things that are real, then "real" is nothing more than what we already have. To put it differently, to accept the scientist's vision of reality is to accept a world in which change is neither probable nor perhaps even possible, and is certainly not desirable.[5]

Part of what I would like to argue is that politics is an art, a practice, and a part of life that is beyond the validations of the scientific method. Maybe an example will help make my case more clear. Scientists build reality carefully, finding those "facts" in the "real world" that are "true" and making them into hypotheses that are potentially verifiable. Simple enough—just find enough truths, find enough facts, and one can build a real world.

Several years ago, someone studied how people voted in Congress.[6] What he wanted to do was to build a model that would predict how each legislator would vote. The work was impressive, sophisticated science. There were numerous tables and charts and models of the most advanced type. Correlations were made and statistically his results were at an important level of significance. With all this work, the author was correctly

5 Thomas Kuhn discusses in *Structures of Scientific Revolutions* what changes in views have occurred and how they happen.

6 The following figures suggest a very complex model found in Michael J. Shapiro, "The House and the Federal Role: A Computer Simulation of Roll-Call Voting," in the *American Political Science Review,* vol. 62 (1968): pp. 494–518.

able to predict how each member would vote 87 percent of the time. Pretty impressive—87 percent.

Of course, an 87 percent correct prediction rate is not all that impressive. As an unsophisticated (methodologically, that is) student, you could predict outcomes almost that well. Just by knowing whether a legislator was a Democrat or a Republican, you could accurately predict his or her vote 84 percent of the time. The point is simple enough: The politics of Congress takes place in that 13 percent of the vote that cannot be predicted. Most of the really interesting votes concern precisely those issues that are in doubt, those issues on which Republicans and Democrats do not vote a straight party line.

In part, I am suggesting that to be successful in science, one must necessarily be limited to very ordinary, repeatable events. To have a social science is to think in rather limited, sometimes unimaginative ways. To use the words science would imply for us, maybe we should consider more carefully the "unreal world."

## A Warning and a Suggestion

Before the attack on science continues, a couple of things should be made clear. First, just because a person is a scientist, or a social scientist, there is no obvious reason to believe that he or she is a conservative son-of-a-bitch who is hopelessly involved in wasted effort and useless endeavors. That would be foolish. All I am trying to argue is that the world in general, and politics in particular, is much more complicated and involved than science is able to comprehend. Second, I am not suggesting that we, personally, are the source of everything; or, more precisely, that what each of us thinks is right, or that what we say is accurate, nor even that what we do is not good simply because we think, say, or do it. To ignore science entirely would be about as bright as to accept it entirely.

Finally, I am using the popularized notion of science. What it is, really, is a technique and not science at all. A good deal of our troubles come from misunderstanding just what real scientists do. Still, I will be talking about images initially. Just be warned that things are not always what we believe them to be.

What I would like to suggest now, and to explore later, is the idea that the distinction between objective and subjective reality may not make sense.[7] Indeed, one does not make sense without the other. A more reasonable formulation of the world might be this: The interaction between our conscious selves and the world—the relationship between the objective and the subjective—creates what we know as reality. This view implies that science and objectification are simply less significant, less accurate ways of dealing with the world than is the more unconventional, and yet well-explored, phenomenological view.

## Science: Compartmentalization, Objectification, and "Political" Style

We are problem-solvers, we Americans. We think about something, analyze it, and then do it. We think of all the different ways we can do it, but we rarely consider the reasons for what we do. Values? Ethics? We God-fearing citizens get these every Sunday. But we practical people are mostly "manual" oriented: how to program our own computer, how to make a killing in the stock market, how to have sex. What I want to suggest is that this emphasis on technique is a natural by-product of the emphasis that science places on method; moreover, that somehow we get divided—method from feeling, parts from the whole. To describe the techniques of science may help clarify the point.[8]

To begin with, we are taught that everything is a problem (therefore, solvable) and that each problem is to be analyzed. So we do. We analyze. We take our lives or our problems or our relationships and break them down into manageable parts. We seek units of analysis. We make components; we compartmentalize. We ignore the whole. We dissect; we cut up; we make small.

What happens is clear. We have the impulse to reduce complex things to simple ones. Science urges us to devalue the rich—which we find difficult to understand—so that we can get to the common—which we might

---

7   This approach is called phenomenology, and was first explored by Edmund Husserl around the turn of the last century. It was furthered by his student Martin Heidegger. Phenomenology is very difficult to read, but there are explanations that make sense—for example, the introduction to William Barrett and Henry Aiken, eds. *Philosophy in the Twentieth Century*, vol. 3 (New York: Random House, 1962).

8   Kenneth Keniston, *The Uncommitted: Alienated Youth in American Society* (New York: Dell, 1965), p. 254.

easily understand. We sacrifice the unique. To quote Kenneth Keniston: "Theories of learning frequently proclaim that human learning is essentially no different from animal learning—that Michelangelo in his studio is to the cheese-seeking rat merely as the large computer is to the small."[9] We are intellectual disintegrators. For the most part, we perceive only pieces of problems.

The obvious way to go about problem solving is by counting and comparing. We measure, we total, we add up the sum. Then we can compare reality and see which is the most, which is the best. Quality is too difficult to measure, or to compare; but horsepower, income, and grade averages are not.

And all the adding depends upon what one thinks reality is. To count depends upon those things that are external, that are objective. It is firmly rooted in the metaphysic that individuals must always turn outward, never inward. Insight is worth nothing if it cannot be made tangible. Science shuns the invisible: magic, art, religion, love. By doing so, we split our knowing from our being, our knowledge from ourselves. To do that enough is to be crazy. People who are able to divide themselves well are often considered successful; people who do not do it well are diagnosed clinically as schizophrenics.

"Crazy" is a later topic. For now, I would like to argue that our gathering, quantifying myth gives us an odd perception of anything public, of anything that should be political. We have a public style of numbers, a politics of volume.

For example, each week we were given the number of people killed in Vietnam. Body counts, they are called. It is instructive to think about what they mean. To look back on that war is not very happy. While the obvious lessons of what war does have been repeated and repeated, it seems important to look at how we learned about what was going on. Where one starts helps explain just where one can expect to go.

With each fact, there is an implied value. Because Americans were reported to have killed more Vietnamese than Vietnamese killed Americans, we were led to believe at least three things: 1) God was on our side; 2) we were better fighters than they; and 3) we were winning the war. How-

9   Ibid., p. 256.

ever, this turned out not to be the case. All we know for certain is that these figures—these objective "facts" of the war—cannot be trusted, they do not tell the whole story, and that they are absolutely incapable of conveying what was really happening. By objectifying reality, an effort is made to reduce war and killing to numbers and to measure success in columns—surely insane. But we kept getting facts—real facts from the real world—and were led to believe that there were related values.

Then we were hit by another fact: In less than a month 10,000 young men from everywhere in the USA died during the Tet offensive—too many families, too many sons. It made no difference how many enemy were killed, the war was over.

Counting bodies would never be the same.

But as the Cold War ground to an end NUTs (nuclear utilization theorists) brought body counting back. We could fight and win a limited nuclear war because the numbers were in our favor. We, of course, would lose tens of millions of people (gigadeaths), but the Russians would lose more. How could you disagree? The numbers just don't lie.

Now small is beautiful—the war against terrorism in Afghanistan became a success in a matter of months with only two real American battle deaths—even better than Desert Storm. The secretary of state home from his first visit observed that rebuilding Afghanistan would be harder than ending terrorist domination of the country. He had just pledged $296 million toward that effort. In response to allegations that the contribution was miserly given the estimated $1.7 billion price tag, we returned to the numbers game by counting the $4.5 billion spent driving the Taliban regime from power as part of the rebuilding. Money talks.

Now these numbers are given to us with different kinds of emotion. Some are sad numbers, others are happy ones, and still others seem to be amazing. But, and here is the trick, the belief is that the numbers—in themselves—mean something, that they are important. That we should take careful notice and really learn something.

There is something very natural about the affection we all have for quantity. Of course, as we think more carefully about it, the affection is not at all natural but is like many other things ... it is learned. Let me give you an obvious and gross—but very real— example. It is about a friend of mine, and his son.

One day the son came home from elementary school very upset. He was good in math but had gotten a bad grade. His parents sat down with him and tried to figure out what was wrong. The problem revolved around a series of questions like this: There are two piles of pennies. In one pile there are 1,000 pennies, in the other pile there are 100 pennies. Which would you rather have?

In every case, the boy chose the pile with the *smaller* number. When asked why, he explained that he really did not like pennies very much. They were, after all, dirty and not worth very much. So given the choice, he would take less rather than more, a clear value choice. His parents understood the argument, so they went to talk with the math teacher.

The math teacher was having none of that thinking. Math, the parents were informed, was an exact science. There was one right answer to any single question, and everyone knew that more had a higher value—that more was, by definition, better.

The mind boggles at the overwhelming wrongness of the teacher, but that is not quite the point. The point is that we are *taught* to believe in this way. We not only learn certain skills, like math, but we learn a whole ideological way of dealing with the world. In the end we may forget our fractions or geometry or whatever, but the informing ideological bias stays and stays.

It has staying power, in part, because it is not so much taught as simply assumed. It is difficult to examine because it is rarely articulated. It remains at the root of things and as such remains very difficult to uncover.

The values of facts are in the eyes of the beholder. Is marijuana much worse than alcohol? Is it as bad? Is marijuana all right when a doctor gives it to you, but bad if you merely want to get high? Are prescription diet pills good, and speed bad? Is it good to put recreational drug users in jail (at huge costs to taxpayers), and then not have room in jail for those who commit violent crimes?

And money. How smart is it to know that billions of dollars in sales go untaxed while we don't have money to spend on our public schools? Why are we cheering when punk dealers are rounded up, and why don't we listen to serious proposals to legalize and clean up drugs? Many of the numbers that sound so good, looked at in a different way, may not be so good after all.

All this, of course, sounds foolish. We know that the examples are a bit overdrawn, and are probably wrong—somehow. It is offensive to think that we can be given a list of numbers and then be expected to find meaning and social value in them. Upon reflection, it is an outrage to believe that those numbers represent anything meaningful, except perhaps to an individual who is insecure personally and must relate impersonally; who is less interested in understanding the "why" of values than in being almost wholly dependent upon material worth.

The point is not that facts should not be used as ingredients in any moral argument. Facts and values are dependent upon one another. Each helps to inform and define the other. The point is which "facts" we look at, study, and are given, and what we infer from them. The point is that for us Madisonian people—in a scientific, objective world—more is better than less and that we regularly make qualitative judgments from quantitative facts.[10]

The sad truth seems to be that the example offers a fairly clear vision of the world we inhabit and provides insight into the way we view reality. The scientist is closer to truth than the magician—at least, that is what we are taught to believe. But we must question our knowledge.

Is it possible that there is a kind of knowledge that is not objective, but that is nevertheless real? Must we measure everything—ourselves and our environment—in material terms? Can there be a better kind of politics that is related to a different kind of knowledge? Can there be an "us" that responds to a less gross ethic? What are the kinds of questions we can ask that will lead us to a different, and maybe better, set of answers?

## Something Else

> *I suppose it is tempting, if the only tool you have is a hammer, to treat everything as if it were a nail.*
> — *Abraham Maslow*

In a simplified way, I have argued that objects are facts, that lots of facts seem to imply value, and that these values appear to indicate moral worth.

10 For a full description of the psychological processes involved, see Murray Edelman, *Symbolic Uses of Politics* (Champaign-Urbana, Ill.: University of Illinois Press, 1964).

The conclusion, stated just as simply, is that there is a kind of insanity in that view. It seems to me that we must begin to understand ourselves as makers of both fact and knowledge, as makers of both value and morality. To make the world more understandable, indeed to recapture some personal power and meaning, we must think in terms that supersede the coldness of rationality and the sterility of science. It is necessary to go back and seek an explanation.

At the base of every social system—and ours is no exception—there is a series of rules that most people follow. Many of the rules are not obvious, but they are nonetheless remarkably binding. For example, most of us either do not know why we are in college or are here just because it seemed the thing to do. Either our parents wanted us to go or all our friends were doing it. More self-consciously, we are here to find a wife or a husband or so that we can land a better job.

In all these cases, we are getting ready to fit into the system. We are following its laws, obeying its rules. But what if our arguments have been correct, what if these laws are based on a reality that really is not human? It is unpleasant to think that the system is based on a kind of magic that can produce cars more easily than it can handle human cares; that spends more on bombs than on babies; and that is tuned more to the values of science than to the good of humanity. The argument, so far, has led us to the point of generalizing that to have a basic view of the world as being only objective can produce the kinds of rules and laws that function not to help a person grow, but only to produce more material reality.

Our politics are as sterile as our reasons for being in college or our experiences in high school or—in all too many cases—our own lives.

There are thinkers who believe that knowledge is the result of more than objective reality, more than those things we can touch. They argue that knowledge is the result of the interaction between the object and the individual: a kind of mingling of the "what is" with the "what might be"; the personal and the impersonal; the I and the thou. Let us begin with two individuals who meet and talk. They are strangers who view each other with what we know as typical insecurity and fear, two Madisonian people in our modern world. Each views himself or herself as "I" and the other person as an "it." There is no real exchange of anything between them. Each has his /her own little social act, own little game to put on the other.

Both become dehumanized, both objects. People become things; politics becomes impersonal and impossible.

What seems necessary is to begin again. Objective reality is not the only place to begin and science—when you get right down to it—is science; just as there is knowing and knowing, so there is science and science.

What our sciences have to teach is truly amazing. Part of what is truly amazing is that they don't teach us what we generally expect them to.

Just see.

## Science and Science

> *Now it's time to further an understanding of nature's order by re-assimilating those passions, which were originally fled from. The passions, the emotions, the affective domain of man's consciousness, are a part of nature's order too. The central part.*
>
> — *Robert Pirsig*

One of the critical political tasks ahead of us is to understand that life is at least as strange as science fiction; and if we do it (life) the right way, maybe even stranger. Before you argue that I have misunderstood, that "strangeness" not only does not seem a critical task but also certainly not a critical political task, let me try to explain myself.

Science fiction and similar kinds of fantasy can be interesting and instructive and even good escape. There are lessons to be learned from *Star Trek,* and *Star Wars,* and what passes for the future on TV and in the movies. But an amazing amount of science "fiction" is pretty lightweight stuff. Fun for sure, and certainly a way to play, but it is generally just a logical extension of what we have and know.

Science fiction is instructive for showing ourselves as we are. It often looks strange because, if you happen to be in the mood to see it, much of what we do is strange. We worship gods and machines and things; we kill others and our earth and ourselves; we do marvelous and wondrous things for no reason beyond the fact that we can. In the end, it all makes only a limited amount of sense—at best—and our science fiction really doesn't do much to help us. It's a lot like angel food cake: I never pass it up—it's good and light and fluffy, but all I get is a good taste in my mouth and a pimple or two.

What I want to argue is that it makes sense to understand the world in a way and do life in a manner that puts the particular "fantasy" of science fiction in the limited box where it belongs.

It seems necessary to take seriously the multiplicity of meanings of any event or of "facts." We are faced with a curious situation at the beginning of the twenty-first century. It is our legacy, in part, to be emotional heirs of a kind of despair and ultimate meaninglessness that has been powerfully argued for the last hundred years or so. Until that time, there were the twin assurednesses of religion and science. Philosophers took on religion and, in many important ways, seemed to have won. We know that by the beginning of the twentieth century scientists had begun to make the theoretical breakthroughs that forever removed science from the realm of Truth with a capital T, removed it from certainty.

With Einstein's theory of relativity, you literally had to triangulate your position in the universe just to know where to hang your hat.

It is a misleading and cheap shot to say that because there is no certainty, everything is relative. In a technical sense, that may be a fact—but that does not necessarily make it true for us. There are categories, concepts, and human convictions that do not easily fit into the casual name-calling style of being "relative."

Multiple meanings mean multiple meanings. The trick is that each of us—in some preconscious, inarticulable place—has a sense of the rightfittingness of the world. To know about knowing is to begin to know why we see what we do, why we ask the questions we do, why we may be "right," and why those who disagree with us may also be "right." We must look and act as well as look at looking. Things must mean and mean.

Let me try to sort that out.

## False Stuff, if Wholly Believed

*Between cockroach and codfish there were only structured differences—their substance was the same and this substance itself was a lie.*

*He saw the entire Universe wheeling, made of a fine shimmering pattern, a lie of such grand and incredible artistry his own vain dream of political empire collapsed—the White House was a doll house played in by childish fibbers. He left the University that morning, disappearing without forwarding address, becoming a nameless wanderer.*

— *William Kotzwinkle*

The effort of this section is not to say that all science is wrong. (In "correct" writing, I'm told, no one should begin with a defensive paragraph. The truth is, I simply don't want people to misunderstand that point.) What I want to argue is that there is an amazing amount of stuff that science either cannot deal with, or that science mishandles, or that science ignores, or that science tries to destroy. If possible, I would like to begin to work us out of the binding myths of science. That work will include some stuff that will make something between limited and no sense to you.

That's all right. Work at it, think hard about it, but relax. None of us, after all, really understands.

This is the order to what follows. We will consider science, our heads, what things might just possibly be, and some of the implications of change. Put differently, fiction is stranger than life, but not very often.

It makes sense to go about knowing in several different ways. Since I'm convinced and will argue that there are intensely individual aspects to how we see the world, it would be foolish to believe that one argument would satisfy everyone. One could say, quite rightly, that if there is a "system" in our country, at its base it is a system of thought. The genius for politics—or the villainy of it—is located, first, in our heads. It is how we see and structure our world. Our system of thought may well be our first unnatural act.

That is one way to begin our argument. Better, we could begin with a man described by his biographer as possessing "authentic magic," we could start with Albert Einstein. Read this: "Einstein's physical intuition, though not infallible, had certainly stood him in good stead. All science is based on faith. The many strange developments that we have already seen … should have convinced us by now that great science is not built on cold logic." [11]

---

11 Banesh Hoffmann, *Albert Einstein: Creator and Rebel* (New York: Viking, 1972), p. 193.

As we have seen, our science wants us to believe in a predictable universe. Not only is that bad life, it is even wrong science. The logic of the argument about how to get from predictability to chaos is fun; it is also useful to know.

The classic function of science is to "discover" those few elementary laws from which the universe may be built up by pure deduction.[2] This, as we know, comes from careful following of the scientific method. The method, in shortened form, is 1) stating a problem, 2) stating a hypothesis to explain the problem, 3) designing tests for the hypothesis, 4) predicting the results of each test, 5) conducting the tests and observing the results, and, finally, 6) making conclusions from the results.

Fair enough. We are taught to believe that if the same results occur each time a particular test is given, it may be a "law."

In repeatability we trust.

But this is simply what we have been told science is about. The facts seem to indicate that this is not what scientists do at all. It is science for popular consumption; it certainly does not produce the kind of social knowledge we need to help improve our social conditions, our social lives, or our own selves.

What we are not taught are all of the problems with this method, or with the method's relationship to the truth. Einstein: "Evolution has shown that at any given moment out of all conceivable constructions a single one has always proved itself absolutely superior to the rest."[12] Let's accept that, and then look at what we have just accepted. In essence, we are accepting the idea that truth, in part, is a function of time.

No pretense about it. Something is true, in measure, because we are who we are, and live where we live, and exist when we exist. Those are odd kinds of criteria for truth.

But there's more. The scientific method works well, for those physical things to which it can be applied, only after the problem has been stated and the hypotheses have been formulated. The part we never seem to remember is that there are an infinite number of hypotheses for any given phenomenon. The whole basis of the scientific method rests on our own

12  Robert Persig, *Zen and the Art of Motorcycle Maintenance: An Inquiry into Values* (New York: Morrow, 1974), p. 115.

imaginations. We make up problems and tests and truths; we base our science on our myths.

Listen to Einstein: "The concepts and fundamental principles that underlie [theoretical physics] are free inventions of the human intellect, [and they] form the essential part of a theory, which reason cannot touch."[13] When we get to the nub of the most central of our sciences—theoretical physics—we see a group of people who believe in something more basic than logic, who often think in terms of beautiful pictures and of how they believe the physical world may be.[14]

The heart of science is not reality, but one or another myth.[15]

We may do the argument another way. Even if you don't know or understand the details, you probably know that there are Euclidian and non-Euclidian geometries. For that matter, there are several non-Euclidian kinds. What is interesting (are you listening, you hard-core-science types, you left-over believers in the absoluteness of science?) is that these geometries contradict each other.

All of them, as it turns out, are "right," but some just happen to be more convenient than others. To quote: "Geometry is not true, it is advantageous."[16] That, at one level, is just outrageous. With little trouble, we can get to the same outrageous point with math as we did with the concepts of physics that math is used to "prove." Mathematical solutions have a harmony, a beauty, an elegance to them, and are often chosen for those reasons. It seems that our most hard-core, hard-science, high-powered magicians are not seekers of truth, but of beauty.

13  Hoffmann, *Albert Einstein*, p. 170.

14  In 1916, a distinguished astronomer reported on Einstein's general theory of relativity. In part, he wrote, "Whether the theory ultimately proves to be correct or not, it claims attention as being one of the most beautiful examples of the power of general mathematical reasoning." Ibid., p. 129.

15  Maybe the biggest myth is being worked on by the most brilliant mind of our time. Stephen W. Hawking, in his remarkable book *A Brief History of Time,* concludes by saying that his is merely a part of a discussion "of the question of why it is that we and the universe exist." He ends the book by writing that "[i]f we find the answer to that, it would be the ultimate triumph of human reason—for then we would know the mind of God." To read the book is to understand that Hawking—even with his assumption that there is a God and that God's mind works with human reason—is well beyond the methods of social science.

16  Pirsig, *Zen and Motorcycle Maintenance*, p. 264.

What is astounding is that we keep believing in the myth of scientifically verifiable truth. The system in our heads is systematically wrongheaded.

If one pushes science, if one sees the way hypotheses multiply until there are too many to keep track of and too many to test, if one sees that scientific "truth" keeps changing at an increasing rate, and that the half-life of truth keeps getting shorter and shorter, or if one sees that underlying the basic principles of science are people's senses of beauty, one can come very close to seeing the obvious: The most impressive product of modern science is anti-science.

By understanding the work of our science, we can understand our world as chaos.

## Real Stuff

William James tells us that the world "is a turbid, muddled, gothic sort of affair, without a sweeping outline and with little pictorial nobility."

Terrific. Start with knowing about knowing and end up with the idea of chaos. You want facts and you get beauty.

Think of it this way: When you are working out how you know what you know about reality, there may be no simple answers. It's equally possible that there may be no complex answers. There are ways to get into all of that, and what seems necessary is to sketch at least one way other than science.

Let me be specific about a thing or two: I am not suggesting that theoretical physics be our model for politics. All I want to argue is that if we are really hung up on the Truth of our science, we may as well admit to ourselves that some time ago science admitted its fundamental relationship to magic. Equally important, human lives and events are much more complex than "physical" events. Trying to live a day, much less a lifetime, with some meaning and social "goodness" makes discovering elementary particles of the universe seem like a piece of cake.

To get on with the topic, we will take up just where we find ourselves, what that might mean (or not mean, in this case), and how we can begin thinking about it.

We live in a world that quite literally never stops. While myths and often social institutions stay fixed for limited times, our world just keeps changing. Reality, in part, consists of all of the "facts" of our existence, plus relationships, functions, motives, ideologies, and the like.[17] Reality, to put it a little differently, simply keeps becoming. Jean-Paul Sartre writes: "For us, truth is something which becomes, it has and will have become. It is a totalization which is forever being totalized."[18]

We are what we were and what we will be in situations that will not stay set. As we will see, we become creators and definers in the context of our times and our surroundings.

The world in which we find ourselves—and now I'm talking about the physical world, the one science "deals" with—may well be, in its essence, just stuff, basic, primal stuff. No few basic particles from which to create or recreate the world. Stuff. The stuff in our head is the same as the stuff of a desk, a car, or a flower.

Our universe, if we care to look deeply enough, is fundamentally chaos. The argument goes further. Each of us begins from that general chaos; we sort things out and make distinctions that help make sense of the world and that allow us to have some communications with those around us. We try to understand—more to the point, often we invent—the world around us. We often do well at it, but we fool ourselves if we believe we tap into anything more ultimate than our own myths—our own ghosts, as Robert Pirsig would say.

Part of what I want to warn about is that we should be careful of what we take as "given." For example, we know that there are many people in the world who really do see ghosts of one kind or another: old friends, dead relatives, and supreme spirits. We have just a terrible time seeing those ghosts. But fear not, we have our own ghosts. We can, for example, see " the law of gravity," which is a ghost many others simply cannot envision. In any lived day one ghost is no more real (or false) than the other. After all, when we finally admit it, the world is relative and we really

---

17 To quote William James, "Life in the transitions as much as in the terms connected; often, indeed, it seems to be there more emphatically, as if our spurts and sallies forward were the real firing line of the battle, were like the thin line of flame advancing across the dry autumnal field. ... Mainly ... we live on speculative investments, or on our prospects only." *Essay in Radical Empiricism and a Pluralistic Universe* (New York: Dutton, 1971), pp. 46–47.

18 Jean-Paul Sartre, *Search for a Method* (New York: Random House, 1968), p. 30.

don't even know which way is up.[19]

Here we sit, in the midst of chaos, ultimately understanding that even the "basic" split between the objective and the subjective is a distinction we make. Please don't misread that. It was written to say that, originally, everything simply is, and we continually add meaning to it. That does not mean everything is subjective or objective, but rather, it just is.

And each day, each instant, we are confronted with objects and actions and events. Confronted with much more than we can deal with or sort out or make sense of. Much passes us by—or, we pass by much—because our world is cluttered and chaotic. We memorize whole lists of things (a pen is a pen, a desk is a desk) that help us in the world a great deal. However, we are left with two critical points: What we choose to consider, and how we put it together.

In the messy world, we are constantly experiencing, and that experience immediately becomes a part of our past. From that past we choose to recall parts, and we grant meaning to those parts because we pay attention to them and we give them added meaning by thinking about them the way we choose to.

Nothing—no part of our experience—has self-evident meaning.[20] Once we are conscious of something, we add meaning to it. Not only that, we get those meanings from our surroundings. The myths of our society, the values of our parents and peers, the kind of day we're having, all contribute to how we make sense and meaning of the events around us. We make meaning within the context of meaning; we make history within history.

That is half of it, the choosing-of-the-events half. The other half has to do with how those events are arranged in our heads. There are scientists (maybe they are really pseudoscientists) who would have the inside of our heads look something like a great pyramid—things (blocks) arranged neatly, in a hierarchy, in a way that reflects the way they arrange the world on paper.

Life, and learning, for those scientists, is a matter of stacking up reality

---

19  It makes sense to try to imagine a good scientific "law." So far, I've come this close: What goes up must come down, most of the time, if we only just knew which way was up. I'm attracted to this law because of its preciseness.

20  For much of this, see William James, *Essay in Radical Empiricism.*

in a prescribed order. I suspect that when some people speak of the building blocks of knowledge they aren't speaking figuratively at all.

A way to think of the world that seems more useful—even more accurate—is to envision the arrangement of the events of our lives as a mosaic, not a pyramid. Each of those events, those happenings, and those striking elements finds a place in our mosaic; each finds a place in our understanding of the arrangement of the world.

But the events, the tiles, of our mosaic are just part of our reality. Equally important is the glue that holds the tiles together, the relationships that place events in order in our heads.[21]

In important ways the key is in those relationships—in that glue. Much of how we do our arranging has to do with what we are taught both to see and to value. The more rigid we are about our reality, the more fixed the relationships, and the less likely we are to change, to rearrange. We all know someone—a friend or relative or teacher—who just cannot "see" something very obvious to us.

In politics (more accurately, in our daily lives) we run into that non-seeing, that "blindness," all the time. Some people have bought into the myths so deeply, have set their mosaic so firmly, that change for them seems out of the question. Later, there will be a chapter on voting. It is, in a way, a tile in your mosaic. My guess is that it is a tile well set, and that whatever age you happen to be, you will resist rearranging your mosaic even if you agree with what I say.

If we arranged chaos in a pyramid based on firm scientific data, then change would really be incredibly difficult. We would probably have to replace one huge edifice with another. No wonder that damned hierarchy is so tough to get rid of; not only is it taught to us as Truth, it is taught in a way that makes it replaceable only with another Whole System. That, in short, is bunk.

In a mosaic, change is still difficult but certainly possible. With it, we can rearrange, "see," play a little with the facts of our life. I am not saying that fundamental change (whatever that means) is an easy thing, but it is possible.

21 The eloquence of Einstein: "I am grateful to destiny for having made life an exciting experience so that life has *appeared meaningful*" (emphasis added); or, "approached rationally that fear [of death] is the most

Our—or any—culture constantly provides patterns of commonly held relationships. We just know what is expected of us, whether in a classroom or drinking beer or in a serious discussion. From the pattern of our speech to the pattern of our political and economic system, we are silently (and sometimes not so silently) given directions on how to put our act together in fairly particular ways. We are presented with the "proper" relationships of events.

The world is chaos and we're forced to make meaning out of it. But it's more complicated than that. We want to be members of society, and society tells us how to order that chaos while being chaotic itself. How do we live in a way that satisfies both our society and us and still remember the chaos?

We must continually consider a world of multiple truths and realities, and on-going social-political-economic truths and realities, all of which help us form powerful and inter-related facts. To keep the tension and chaos close at all times is tough, but really necessary.

All of that, it seems to me, provides the conditions for optimism.

It is about time we do a little "politics." We can do it in laundry-list fashion. Politics can/should/might mean living together so that:

(1) Important decisions are decided in a collective way (of the people, by the people, for the people).
(2) Each of us has both responsibility and power when it comes to actions we each take.
(3) Justice and excellence are alive with meaning for the decisions made.

Since our world is not set, does not rest on any ultimates, does not rely upon scientific methods to be verifiable—since our world is in constant motion and is given shape by each of us individually as well as collectively—then our job is nothing short of this: We must re-form and re-inform ourselves, and then work to have our society reflect that re-formation.

All of that doing and re-doing is political. It is, in its essence, the basis of politics.

I am convinced that each of us has a sense of how the world fits together in a good—and beautiful—way. That sense, or picture, or whatever, should be the touchstone of our mosaic.

There is no reason to believe that each of us will share the same sense of the rightfittingness of the world. Not only that, there is reason to believe that these differences will not be simply of taste or beauty, but will extend from our moral values to how we wish to arrange ourselves organizationally, to what we understand as politics.

As the monolith of our scientifically socialized heads and then society begins to break up, we should look forward to an America of united states or cities or towns or neighborhoods or blocks. A place where we can begin with our own self-conception of the way the world looks best; a place to join like-others to create an environment in which that sense can be worked out; in which we have a duty to be our best selves because the whole community will depend on it.

If we are creatures of myth, it makes sense to take it seriously and choose to live with the myths of our choice.

One could, I suppose, imagine whole groups of people who choose to think of themselves and others as evil, who will base their reality on the science of a hundred years ago, and who will wholly believe in the myth of objective consciousness.

How weird.

## Of Human (Language) Bondage

I would like to change the focus in order to put what has been said in a little different light. In this section, the focus will be on the person doing the wrong-headed kind of science that has been described. The discussion is based on a fine book by Larry Spence titled *The Politics of Social Knowledge*. What follows is my shortened version of just one of his arguments.

The point is this: The person who uses this kind of popularized version of science is not practicing science at all. In fact, this person is not producing knowledge, but is producing myth. In order to see this more clearly, it is necessary to see the different parts of the argument.

In all communications (don't worry, we will get to the point in due time) there are at least two levels. The first level is what is actually said or done, and the second level is the context in which what is done takes place. We can take the example given by Gregory Bateson, who asks us to imagine two animals. Then he has us imagine that one animal bites the other. That is the first level, and from it we really know nothing. Finally, we imagine that these animals are playing, and immediately we know that the bite is nothing more serious than a little nip.

What is important to remember is that the context (often unstated or invisible) is critical to the meaning of what is said or done. That is the background we must know.

Back to the person doing research. What this person does is divide him- or herself from the context of what is being studied. He or she denies personal experience and knowledge in order to be "objective." The person looks upon an event from a separate, exclusive, and polarized position. Spence says that this is "heroic research." The heroic researcher stands outside of life itself, and asserts *"a* general, contextless knowledge of social order." When context is dismissed, the meaning of the findings depends absolutely upon what the investigator says the meaning is. The heroic researcher makes the context of the findings the myth that he or she has created.

If Spence is right that a worthy task of the social sciences is "the prediction of the effects of social contexts on human capacities for adaptation and the control of such contexts" (and I think he is), then heroic research will never get us there. We can, in fact, never become unbound from their talk, since we never know the context in which they put their facts.

Heroic research is the research of political and social power, not necessarily the research that leads to social knowledge. For Spence, heroic research is not science.

## Politics as I: A Tie

Classically, one is supposed to state what is about to be said, then say it, then repeat what has just been said. In a funny way, that is what I'm about to do. Let me repeat myself in different words and a little more to the point.

In order to challenge the amazing accumulation of facts lying between us and significance—the world of body counts and grade points—we must know ourselves and our actions well enough to teach and learn from others. An I-thou relationship is, in many ways, revolutionary politics.

The burden of the argument is clear: How one understands knowledge and how one does politics is interrelated. If by knowledge we mean only those things that are objective, then we may never have politics, only an elite of science, a mythology of numbers. We will be organized as a bureaucracy and each of us will be reduced to a statistic of the state. Ours will be a well-ordered, rational world where rules replace revelation.

It is important that we become seriously involved in the search for social knowledge. To do that, several things must change. For example, we must be aware and able to describe the context in which speech and action take place. We must no longer be heroic researchers, taking ourselves out of our own experiences and trying to control others by making myths. Heroic researchers produce mystification; the job of good social science is to help develop practices that will better serve the needs of all of us.

In order to do research that will improve our world, it is important not to be heroic, not to believe that there is only one right way. It seems much more honest and accurate to bow to the multiplicity of right ways and acknowledge the beauty of many aesthetics.

Given that, good social science is a real possibility.

Knowledge is neither entirely objective nor rational. We must insist that those who lead share their knowledge with us; moreover, that those who lead follow us as we share our knowledge with them. One task of political science is to make clear as many different ways of living as possible. To do this, there must be a whole new series of questions we can ask. We must understand our present as well as our potentials. Henry Kariel has written that by "postulating functions which have the effect of shifting our perspectives, we expose previously unseen institutional forms. We perceive new reality—lives not lived (or not lived decently) because of decisions not made. When the empty space in which potentialities might have been realized is bared, we become aware of our losses."

> *Weakness is true and real … faking only proves weakness is real, or you wouldn't be so weak as to fake it. No you can't fake being weak. You can only fake being strong.*
>
> — *Ken Kesey*

# Rightfittingness

*Bob Waterman*

The argument is that division of knowledge exclusively into objective and subjective dimensions without recognition of the third alternative of rightfittingness misleads us when we think about politics. Rightfittingness—an evocative concept novel to the discussion of political knowledge—was explained as a triangulation from the objective-subjective dichotomy. It synthesizes some elements of each with new elements to create an independent third perspective. In everyday language, rightfittingness could also be called judgment: A determination reached through the human capacity to make up our minds based upon our feelings in response to what we know about the objective world of things and other people. For example, a person may judge a house "right" after consideration of several feelings about its objective characteristics—such as joy about the craftsmanship which went into it, disappointment about the layout of the kitchen, and so on—based on that individual's idea of what is best for that person and the world. According to the notion of rightfittingness, the house is judged right because it will encourage that person to be his or her best self, and enable that individual to be that best self with family, friends, neighbors, and acquaintances. Out of the houses available in the world, this is the chosen one because it fits rightly or best with who that person is.

Rightfittingness is based on a person's deep moral roots as well as on transitory emotions. It is connected with a person's careful thoughts about how the world should be and how that particular person should fit into it. Because rightfittingness fits a person together with the world, it must also take prudent account of the world's existing arrangements in order to know what might be changed and what must be accepted as given. Rightfittingness, then, combines moral roots, thought about what should be, and prudent calculation about power into a compass for giving direction to human action.

Politically, a central question for rightfittingness is whether a person feels in his or her deepest being that participation in elections suffices for citizenship or whether one wants the opportunity to debate and exercise political power more directly. Nineteenth-century American townsmen knew that voting was only one and not the primary element of their public life. In the language of this chapter, they believed that living together politically meant dealing publicly and in a dignified way with the rightfittingnesses of themselves and other people as they were shaped and made apparent in public meeting. Because their town meetings gave nineteenth-century Americans the opportunity to hear, confront, and persuade others, the townsmen were willing to take on the chores of politics, including administration. The townsmen were drawn regularly to political activity because it gave an almost objective reality in laws and public agreements to their deliberated sense of collective rightfittingness; that is, as they legislated and instructed delegates, they went on formal, public record about what was right and wrong politically in their world; what should be changed and how; what they enjoyed or endured. In doing so they had to reveal things about their interior selves and their identities because they endeavored to justify their public stands with reasons connected to their political beliefs and moral convictions.

At first glance, town meetings look like a burdensome task that must have interrupted more productive activities and leisure time. No doubt the meetings were burdensome and would be so today. But on second thought, they also are the few occasions when one's considered opinions count to the community as a whole. Since one is directly helping to conduct the common business, one becomes essential to the history of the community, and perhaps becomes known for what one says and does. This possibility of public reputation, together with the joy of living out rightfittingness, has reportedly been the central attraction of political life in the past (see Hannah Arendt in *On Revolution* and Machiavelli in *The Prince*).

Since the objective-subjective dichotomy reduces political opinion to mere preference, it obscures the stabilizing and directive role rightfittingness can play in political matters, especially when diverse people are able to deliberate to a common public conviction, thus allowing people with different rightfittingnesses to act and live together effectively. The dichotomy is misleading for politics because political agreements are neither scientific truths nor mere subjective feelings, but the results of political actions. These agreements are the best that diverse human beings can do in the political realm. They can keep a diverse nation of people together in a civilized manner generation after generation despite whether they agree about the truth or have the same feelings.

This is not a partisan argument; it advocates a role in politics for rightfittingness that is general rather than any single political ideology or viewpoint. It assumes that political discussion will be immensely more fruitful when citizens in public arenas discover their own rightfittingnesses and give attentive respect to the genuine rightfittingnesses of other people. The ideal is a variety of individuals holding differing political viewpoints who in addition are able to agree on a basic constitution for their community or nation, a basic framework that will encourage them to be their best selves together with other people. That goal was certainly the aim of the nineteenth-century townsmen and their predecessors of the revolutionary and constitutional eras in the United States. In other words, while the word *rightfittingness* is a new one, the idea behind it and its political ramifications have deep roots in the American past.

chapter **4**

# Politics as Rules: Organizations and Bureaucracy

*Robots have no future. They merely have a past that has not yet occurred.*

*—Robert Boguslaw*

If how we view the nature of people means something to our politics and to our personal lives, and if how we view the world and knowledge means something, then it seems pretty obvious that the way we organize is also important. The way we organize ourselves and the accompanying ways those organizations dominate our behavior are the concerns of this chapter.

One way to begin to understand the effects of organizations, and to understand their ideology, is to look at a concern central to political science: power. One of the debates of scholars of American politics is Who has power? Who rules? Do the people rule, or an elite, or elites? The optimists say "the people" rule, the pessimists, "the elite." Personally, I think either position may well be optimistic. If someone is in charge, if someone has power, if someone has control, then that someone can be changed. To believe that one or a few or many have power is to have faith that human beings are making decisions about the future. That is optimistic. What if, ultimately, nobody is in charge?

The whole idea that no one is in charge, that we have a tyranny without a tyrant, is an unhappy one.[1] It is an idea tied directly to the nature of large organizations and how they work. To begin to understand how large organizations operate, to understand the rules by which they operate and the rules they impose on our world, is to begin to recognize that a large organization is greater than the sum of its human members.[2]

There is a very natural tendency to believe that because people work in organizations, organizations are simply the reflection of all those people. Such a tendency ignores the point of this chapter: That large organizations may easily set the rules for our society, and that those rules will be geared toward organizational—not human—ends. That may be a description of our reality. To understand what it means to be involved in this kind of reality, this kind of societal/governmental machinery, is to understand what it means to be little more than a small cog in an impersonal machine—a cog that is interchangeable with other cogs, one that wears out and is replaced with no loss to the machine.

Before describing and analyzing large organizations, it might be useful to make this point: To understand what is going on, we cannot ignore the study of large organizations; they exist, they are "real," and they seem unwilling to go away.

## Organizations as a Historical "Fact"

It is my intention to argue that many problems facing us today are related to the size and workings of complex organizations. Right now, all I want to show is that to look at the history and dynamics of organizations is to understand that these problems will increase with time.[3]

---

1  For an excellent discussion of this, see Hannah Arendt, *On Violence* (New York: Harcourt, Brace & World, 1969).

2  Probably the most clearly spelled-out statement of why organizations act as they do is to be found in James Thompson, *Organizations in Action* (New York: McGraw-Hill, 1967).

3  This discussion draws heavily on Robert Presthus, *The Organizational Society* (New York: Vintage, 1962), and Kenneth Dolbeare and Murray Edelman, *American Politics*, 3d ed. rev. (Lexington, Mass.: D.C. Heath, 1979), pp. 23–24.

It is not news that from the middle of the nineteenth century until now, organizations in America have gotten bigger and more complex. Indeed, bigger and more seem to be the dominant organization themes:

Bigger: General Motors is the biggest. Only twenty-four countries can match it, and its revenues are larger than thirty-seven of the states.[4]

More: In 1903, when Ford Motor Company produced its first car, it employed 125 people and had an authorized capital of $150,000. It took Ford six months to conceive and produce the first automobiles. In 1964, when the Mustang was introduced after three and one-half years in preparation, Ford had assets of $6 billion, employed 317,000 people, and spent $9 million on "engineering and styling" costs and $50 million on tooling costs for the new car.[5] In 2001 Ford Motor Company had sales totaling $162.4 billion.

Bigger and More: Brothers Sam Walton and James "Bud" Walton opened Wal-Mart in 1962. By 1970 the company had eighteen stores. Thirty years later it has over 4,000 stores, including 440 outlets in Mexico, 236 in the U.K., and 166 in Canada. Not more enough? They teamed up with America Online to offer Internet service to Wal-Mart customers, who can now purchase 600,000 products on the web.[6] Wal-Mart was number two in 2000 with $166.8 billion in sales.

A mainstay of the Reagan Revolution was big tax cuts for the rich that, it was hoped, would spread the wealth to everyone. This is an old story that keeps returning in new clothes. In our mythical reality it works like a series of chain letters, and just when our payoff is due some "nonvoter" always breaks the chain—better than Catch-22. It always brings more and better now, but we never make it to the bank. It should work, but the employees at the top of corporations, who take care of the windfall for their nonhuman bosses, never do what they should. Instead of investing in new plants and creating new, high-paying jobs—the mythical reality—they buy, cannibalize, and consolidate what is already there to rack

---

4   This information was complied from tables in Richard H. Robbins, *Global Problems and the Culture of Capitalism* (Boston, Mass.: Allyn & Bacon, 2002), pp. 123–24; and Herbert Jacob, Russell L. Hanson, and Virginia Gray, *Politics in the American States: A Comparative Analysis* (Washington D.C.: Congressional Quarterly Books, 1999), p. 18.

5   John Kenneth Galbraith, *The New Industrial State* (New York: Signet, 1968), pp. 23–24.

6   See http://vault.com/profiles.html.

up huge paper profits. When the Reagan round began there were "Five Sisters" of big oil, and these big fish ate all of the small fish and then turned on one another. One day Chevron ate Gulf and then there were four. Exxon is now the largest, perhaps the only fish in the American pond, the third-largest global corporate bureaucracy, beating Ford with annual sales of $164 billion in 2000.

Tax cuts returned at the dawn of the millennium. In the new world where every other motorist and shopper was making deals on a cell phone, responsible drivers used hands-free models. Microsoft and Intel want to gang up and take over the market—lots of small fish. A good feeding frenzy could put "MicroTel" in the running for a medal in the annual corporate games.

On the cable side, Congress thinks it may be necessary to restore AT&T's monopoly to protect our nation's competitive position in the global marketplace. After all, AT&T had slipped to 27th place, with only $63 billion in revenues.

The history of growth—of industrial consolidation and mergers—means that we are all becoming more involved in big organizations and bureaucratic conditions. The facts are these: Large organizations are more likely to survive than smaller ones, and people are now likely to be employees, not their own bosses. This quotation from Robert Presthus has appeared in every edition of the *Preface:* "Huge capital resources, experience, and good will enable established firms to survive. Statistics support this interpretation, showing that small firms have a very high failure rate, while big enterprises rarely fail. In time such a pattern probably increases concentration."[7] Small firms still fail, as the rise and fall of the dot-coms shows, but now big and even old firms fail.

In his farewell address, President Eisenhower warned about the military/industrial complex. Beware, he said, of the mixing of those giant corporations that were in the business of making war with big government. What we know now is that there was no reason to stop with companies that had connections to the military. Eisenhower should have said this: Big business and big government will be in bed together, and it won't be a pretty sight.

---

7  Presthus, *Organizational Society,* p. 74.

The story of Enron is interesting in many ways. Greed and power and sex are just the beginnings. One of the important things to know is that it was our nation's current faith in the free market that helped create the problems. The belief that government control just screws things up almost ensured that an Enron, or something like it, would happen. The details of Enron are so complex and convoluted that complete accounts will probably be found only in business textbooks (under "Case Studies in What Not to Do") and law books (especially those dealing with fraud). Here is a short account.

About fifteen years ago two natural gas pipeline companies merged. Their business, basically, was to buy natural gas from producers and sell it to companies that used it. But a smart economist, Kenneth Lay, saw that because the markets were being freed from government control (deregulation) there was an opportunity to do business in a different way. His was one of those good ideas that are rewarded in the free market.

The idea was to deal with what are called derivatives. If, for example, a company wanted to make sure of the price it would pay for natural gas in, say, 2005, Enron would insure that price. Enron would then go out and make a contract to buy natural gas at that price from a producer. It costs very little to do this, since the biggest chunk of money is exchanged when the gas is delivered. After the deals were made, Enron would then sell these derivatives, called futures.

It was a simple idea that helped stabilize prices for everyone, and in an unregulated market that kind of stability is a good thing.

From there, the story gets almost totally out of control. Enron thought that if derivatives were good for natural gas, they would also be good for just about everything else: fiber-optic cable capacity, newsprint, and even the weather (I really don't understand what that was about). To make things more complicated, Enron created independent partnerships to do business. Generally, these partnerships were very lucrative for those in Enron management who were a part of them. They also seemed to be a way to hide the financial goings-on at Enron.

A timeline, and numbers, might be useful.[8] The merger of the two gas

---

8  See Jeff Madrick, "Report of Investigation by the Special Investigative Committee of the Board of Directors of Enron Corp.," in *New York Review of Books,* vol. 60, no. 4 (March 14, 2002), pp. 21–25.

pipeline companies happened in mid-1980. The price of a share of Enron stock was about $10. By the early 1990s Enron was trading in futures. Management asked that the trading be exempt from governmental oversight, and the government said OK. Enron grew, went into businesses in other countries, and became one of the most admired corporations in the United States.

By the year 2000 a share of Enron stock was trading at a little over $90. Congress passed a law further exempting energy-derivatives trading from regulation, and Enron became the sixth-largest energy company in the world. They were the business of the future. Enron even had a deal with Blockbuster to sell you movies on demand in your home. What a company; what a country.

In June 2001, federal regulators imposed strict price controls in some electricity markets and Enron's profits fell. In August, CEO Jeffrey Skilling resigned so he could "spend more time with my family." In mid-October Enron announced a third-quarter loss of over $600 million. Later that month, the Securities and Exchange Commission began a formal investigation. In November Enron admitted that it had overstated its earnings by $587 million since 1997. By January 2002 Enron was belly-up.

What does this have to do with politics and government? Enron and Kenneth Lay made large contributions to George Bush when he ran for governor of Texas. In 2000, they gave presidential candidate Bush $500,000. Bush campaigned, in part, in an Enron jet. Bush called his friend Lay "Kenny Boy." When Enron first asked the government to not regulate its trading, Wendy Gramm was the head of the commission that agreed that no regulation was necessary. Ms. Gramm was the wife of the then senator from Texas, Phil Gramm, who in turn was chair of the Senate Banking Committee. Enron was a huge donor to his campaigns. Wendy Gramm left the commodity commission and became a member of the Enron Board of Directors.

Here is a short list of people in the Bush White House who had dealings with "Kenny Boy": Thomas White, secretary of the army, was an Enron executive for more than a decade; John Ashcroft, the attorney general, took money from Enron when he ran for office; Spencer Abraham, head of the Department of Energy, took money from Enron when he ran for the Senate; Lawrence Lindsey, top economic adviser to the president, was a consultant to Enron; Pat Wood III is said to be Lay's choice for federal energy regulator. Lay gave money to Poppa Bush's campaigns and had many meetings with Vice President Dick Cheney and his energy task force in order to craft an energy policy for the new Bush administration.

When the walls came tumbling down, the number of calls from Enron to the White House was amazing. While all those contributions helped get the phones answered, they were not enough to buy any more help from the government. Kenny Boy was all of a sudden Mr. Lay. The president, it seems, suffered from sudden and politically helpful loss of memory.

But this is a story of our world—it's not the old, simple world where big business just bought into government. Enron was at the top of the list of those businesses that understood the future. Part of this understanding was that power lay not only in formal governmental structures, but also in the media. Enron bought into the media by paying well-known journalists and political commentators "unusually high sums" to be "advisers." A short list: Paul Krugman, *Fortune* magazine; Irwin Stelzer, *The Weekly Standard;* Lawrence Kudlow, CNBC; and $100,000 a year to William Kristol, also of the *The Weekly Standard* and a frequent commentator on television. For what are big bucks to commentators but peanuts to a multibillion-dollar corporation, Enron helped ensure that it got good press. Put differently, Enron was a successful complex organization that understood how other complex organizations worked, and had the money to make its will felt.

Two things are now in place to help us understand the Enron story. First, there was a good idea that would help Enron stabilize recently deregulated markets. Second were very close ties to those in government who had the power to let these "free" markets work without any oversight. For good measure, Enron tried to ensure that it would have a sympathetic press.

Greed and fraud followed.

For our economy to work, people who buy stocks need to have confidence in the information they receive. There are companies who do nothing but research businesses and give advice. More importantly, huge accounting firms check the books and make certain that companies give out accurate information. If an investor can't believe what an accounting firm certifies as correct, if an investor can't believe the best advice of Wall Street analysts, the stock market simply cannot work.

The accounting firm hired by Enron was Arthur Andersen. It had been, for years, one of the most highly respected firms in the business.

Enron also hired Anderson to consult. In 2000 Enron paid Anderson $52 million for auditing and consulting. For that $52 million, Anderson gave its stamp of approval to the "aggressive" accounting done by Enron. As it turned out, that accounting was actually criminal. Enron overreported profits, underreported debts, and used private contracts to hide much of what was going on. Had Anderson done its job, it would have forced Enron to change its accountants and be more responsible in what it reported. For example, in the late 1990s Enron lost about $2 billion on telecom capacity, $2 billion on water investments, $2 billion on a Brazilian utility, and $1 billion on an electrical plant in India—and failed to make any of that information public. Indeed, between July 2000 and October 2001 Enron reported $1 billion in profits that it did not actually earn.

Enron was playing fast and loose; Arthur Anderson was playing fast and loose; and, just before Enron restated its earnings in the fall of its fall, sixteen of seventeen securities analysts placed a "strong buy" or "buy" rating on the stock. The entire system was completely out of whack.

It seems reasonable to assume that some people knew what was going on. Of course they did. A vice president of Enron, a woman named Sherron Watkins, even sent a memo to Kenny Boy that outlined all of the problems. He had the charges made in her letter investigated by Enron's own lawyers, who then reported that they were false. They were not false at all.

Even as the facts of Enron's financial problems were being kept from the public, those in the know began to sell their stocks.

Kenny Boy sold more than $200 million of his stock, all the while telling the public as well as his own employees to buy. Other examples of those who seemed to know the right time to sell: Between May 2000 and August 2001, Jeff Skilling (Enron's CEO) sold almost $14.5 million of his Enron stock and Lou Pai (a unit CEO) sold almost $63 million. In all, Pai sold about $250 million in Enron shares. As the ship went down, the captains made certain that their life rafts were waiting.

As luck would have it, as I was writing this section there was a story in the Sunday paper.[9] It began by talking about an Enron employee who was now out of work. The story, in part, was about how he could now spend more time watching his son play baseball. There was a nice picture of a good-looking man, probably in his forties, and his son. They had baseball equipment. As an aside for this human-interest story, it mentioned that the man had made $50,000,000 in the last five years while working for Enron.

It turns out that there are a surprising number of people who live in Houston, Texas, with a huge amount of money and nothing much to do. But the stories we hear most about are the pension funds and individual investors who lost huge amounts of money. Those who got the most press were Enron employees who lost what would be their retirement money when their stocks became worthless. We heard over and over again stories about people who went from being millionaires in the summer to being broke by mid-winter. It is interesting to look a little deeper into those stories.

First, everyone who bought Enron stock was by the end lied to. The information was just plain false. Arthur Anderson was crooked. They even shredded evidence to avoid looking as guilty as they were. Because their business is built on trust, what they did with Enron has destroyed them. Greed got the better of good sense.

The other liars were, of course, Enron executives. Kenny Boy testified before Congress. What he said, essentially, was this: I am innocent and I refuse to answer questions on the grounds that it might incriminate me. He then said that he was unhappy that he could not tell the real story. Hmmm. One executive felt so badly he committed suicide; greed again at work. As I watched some of the congressional hearings, one of the networks added this nice touch: As each member of Congress asked a question, they showed how much money that person had received from Enron—holier-than-thou members of Congress ignoring the fact that they were part of the problem. It was one of those wonderful television moments. Greed had helped Enron make sure that there would be no governmental oversight of its futures trading.

9  Barbara Barboza, "From Enron's Rubble, Life on a Luxury Tightrope," *New York Times,* May 19, 2002, Section 3, p. 1.

Back to the Enron employees who had gone broke. Every stockbroker will tell you this simple lesson: diversify. Make certain that you have stocks from many different companies and in many different areas. It is the best and only way to ensure, over a long period of time, that your investments will be relatively safe.

But many Enron employees were as greedy as everyone else. They took the same ride up everyone else did, and when the $90 stock was suddenly worth $0.26, they were as angry as they were broke. They had been lied to. They had been taken advantage of. And, what they rarely would say is this: I didn't listen to my stockbroker. I refused to diversify. I thought I could be even richer if I kept all my money in Enron stock.

In terms of the Enron story, all of the fun was getting there. While it ended badly, there were some very good times along the way. Enron was the land of milk and honey. There was a big electronic board in its building that flashed the price of Enron stock, a visual sign of how rich they all were. There were the three-hour lunches at men's clubs and the parties in the private rooms with expensive champagne and more expensive women, the affairs with secretaries, the multi-million-dollar mansions, a wedding where Asleep at the Wheel played for an hour for $80,000.

Jeffery Skilling made the secretary he was having an affair with secretary of the Board of Directors. Her salary increased to hundreds of thousands of dollars a year. He then got a divorce so he could marry her.

Let me try to be biblical again. Enron walked that thin line between milk and honey and Sodom and Gomorrah. It was excess in just about every imaginable way. Fun, yes, but it had everything to do with fraud and greed and the great hope that it would last forever. Free markets have never worked and greed has never been good.

The Bush administration, rightfully scared about the harm Enron could do politically, ran away from the problem as fast as it could. They let Enron die. Indeed, Bush's main political adviser said that the failure of Enron was proof of "the genius of capitalism." How scary is that? What Enron showed was the absolute failure of capitalism. It showed how, with enough money and no government regulation, a huge, complex organization could corrupt both the private and public sectors.

What has become of the organizational structure that we are all a part of? What's going on in our organizational environment?

The point remains the same: Organizations are all around us. If we were fish, they would be the water we swim in. Not just organizations, but huge organizations dominate our environment. Eighty-five percent of us are directly involved in the organizational apparatus and are susceptible to an organizational ideology. It is an ideology of impersonality, rules, interchangeability, and productivity. The history of organizational growth seems to indicate the following: What we have Now is an extension of What Was; and what Will Be will be a bigger and more Now. Now that we've seen Enron, let's go back to the beginning and try to understand what bureaucracies and large organizations are and what they do.

## Bureaucracy

> *There was only one catch and that was Catch-22, which specifies that a concern for one's own safety in the face of dangers that were real and immediate was the process of a rational mind. Orr was crazy and could be grounded. All that he had to do was ask; and as soon as he did, he would no longer be crazy and would have to fly more missions. Orr would be crazy to fly more missions and sane if he didn't, but if he was sane he had to fly them. If he flew them he was crazy and didn't have to; but if he didn't want to he was sane and had to. Yossarian was moved very deeply by the absolute simplicity of this clause of Catch-22 and let out a respectful whistle.*
> *"That's some catch, that Catch-22," he observed.*
> *"It's the best there is," Doc Daneeka agreed.*
> > *— Joseph Heller*

Most automobile manufacturers, certainly the Department of Defense, and any Big State University qualify as bureaucratic organizations. In each, there are few at the top and many at the bottom, the leaders and the led, those with positions of power and those without. The point of a bureaucracy is that those at the bottom feed information to those at the top, and those at the top give orders to everyone. Information up, orders down, that is the simple story of bureaucracy. It makes sense in a perverted kind of way. But that is getting ahead of where we are.

When dealing with a bureaucracy, there is at least one vital lesson to learn. The lesson is simply that information is the stuff of power, the stuff necessary to control an organization. People who study organizations seem to be fascinated by charts and graphs. They are, in fact, picture-drawers. So, to illustrate the "information is power" point, picture the following. As a student at Big State U, something bad has happened. The administration has somehow messed up your record. You expected to graduate in June, but now the computer printout card from the registrar says that you lack enough credits. That rude news could mess up your plans to go to Europe, to hitch across the country, or to retire to a villa; so you decide to see someone about it. Where would you go?[10]

Begin at the top of the organization chart. At many universities, there is a Board of Regents, or a Board of Trustees, which has a great deal of power. One could try to go to them, but common sense suggests that that would be a wasted trip. Below the regents, there might be a president, a chancellor, some vice presidents, and some vice chancellors. But again, they seem a bit too high up. Theirs are problems of millions of dollars or whole faculties or new buildings or doing politics with state legislatures or huge private corporations. None of these are of direct relevance to a person who simply wants to graduate.

Next down on the chart is an administration of deans and assistant deans and various divisions and an incredible number of secretaries. Lower yet, but a little more accessible, are department chairpersons, vice chairpersons, administrative assistants, undergraduate faculty advisers, undergraduate secretaries, faculty, junior faculty, graduate students, and, finally, undergraduates. Where does one go? Whom does one see?

Reasonably, one should see a secretary. The business of the secretary is to know, to have information about how things work, to know whom to call to find out important facts. In an important sense, secretaries are everyone's best friends in beating the bureaucracy. While deans and presidents, faculty members, and graduate students pursue a variety of goals, the secretaries help human beings with the workings of the organization. Characteristic of bureaucracies, those at the bottom of organizational

10 The story of school as bureaucracy is an oft-told one. In my opinion, one of the best and most complete analyses of the problems confronting the student and the university in contemporary society is found in Sheldon Wolin and John Schaar, *The Berkeley Rebellion and Beyond* (New York: Vintage, 1970).

charts—the very individuals who are in direct contact with the public—are those members of the organization with the least formal power.

To repeat the point of the story: Information is power.

## Government as Bureaucracy

> *"No, you can't go home," ex-P.F.C. Wintergreen corrected him. "Are you crazy or something?"*
>
> *"Why not?"*
>
> *"Catch-22."*
>
> *"Catch-22?" Yossarian was stunned. "What the hell has Catch-22 got to do with it?"*
>
> *"Catch-22," Doc Daneeka answered patiently... "says you've always got to do what your commanding officer tells you to do."*
>
> — *Joseph Heller*

This section of the book is the one that comes closest to dealing with what is traditionally considered the governmental process. While it does not exactly deal with "How a Bill Becomes a Law," it does have to do with what we think of as politics in government.

There are several lessons in this section. Some of them are these: The government can be understood in part as a large-scale bureaucratic operation. The bureaucracies that make up the government fight among themselves. Finally, policies often seem less the result of reason and good sense than the result of bickering and fighting among people who want power. Remember this: Power is gotten when Congress funds projects. If you are in government and want power, it follows that it is critical to get funding for your project. We will see that this is important to those in the different bureaucracies, as well as to those in Congress.

Congress is set up so that it is possible for an individual to get more, rather than less, power. It helps for an individual to work hard and to follow the rules and to be intelligent. But it helps most to be re-elected over and over and over again. The longer a congressman or congresswoman lives and continues to be re-elected, the more power he/she will accumulate.

It's almost as foolproof as that.

Congress, like any complex organization these days, is set up to produce specialists. This means that committees are formed, and then each committee is broken down into subcommittees. If you want power in Congress, it is very helpful to be in charge of a subcommittee that controls a lot of money. In the old days, a senator from Oklahoma named Robert Kerr headed the Subcommittee on Rivers and Harbors. Rivers and harbors in Oklahoma?

Ah, but here is the beauty of the position. Kerr had a say about every river dredged or harbor built or dam constructed in the United States. All of those projects had to go through his subcommittee. Would a senator trade a project for a vote on something else? Sure. It turns out that because of Kerr there is now more mileage of artificial lakeshore in Oklahoma than in any other state. Robert Kerr corrected God's oversight.

Glenn English, who was also a representative, chaired one of the key subcommittees that funded the War on Drugs. He was friendly with U.S. Customs Commissioner William von Raab. (No surprise so far.) Customs claimed it needed a new center to coordinate its air surveillance efforts along international borders. English's subcommittee agreed. (So far so good.) We know that most drugs that come into the U.S. come through Florida. The big question is this: Where should the new Customs Coordination Center be located? If you said Oklahoma City, Oklahoma—the home district of Glenn English—then you would have been right.

This is not, to make a little different point, Republican and Democratic stuff. This chapter is about how organizations work, and how to get power in a bureaucratic setting. Nor is it a story of graft and corruption. We will see that later. No, this is simply one kind of bureaucratic business-as-usual.

What goes on between bureaucracies or between Congress and bureaucracies inside our government extends into relations among bureaucracies internationally. As we engage in the "War on Terrorism" it might be useful to look back on the Cold War—just so we'll know what to look for: Bureaucracies need bureaucracies. The Central Intelligence Agency is an amazing example.

In a Cold War–era Senate hearing about the CIA, it was learned (read *revealed*) that the Soviets, by using antennae on their missions in the United States and by using orbiting satellites, could spy. (Something—if not somebody—really was up there looking at you.) The Soviets monitored and recorded thousands of telephone conversations carried by microwave.

It turns out that we were doing the same thing in the USSR.

What's interesting is that we could have jammed the Soviet interception of our microwave communications. Of course we didn't because then *they* would have jammed ours in Moscow. These bureaucracies needed each other. The CIA needed the KGB—they saw the world in the same way. What organization is/will be the replacement for the KGB?

Information is power in a bureaucratic world, and bureaucrats from different organizations share knowledge when they share a common aim. What we must understand now is just what kind of style bureaucratic politics has, what the bases of its decisions are, and what are the built-in limits of its organizational structure. What underlies and what motivates the actions of a bureaucracy?

## Bureaucracy: The Ideology

Ideally, a bureaucracy is a hierarchy, with few at the top, many at the bottom. Those at the top—ideally—have the authority to make decisions; the others have the responsibility for carrying out those decisions. As we know, information from the outside world comes in through the bottom and is sent up the organizational ladder if it seems important. Decisions stem from this information.

A bureaucracy is supposed to be a human machine. Each position in it is defined, described as to function, and limited in its freedom of action. The position becomes standardized; as a piston does only the work of a piston, so a clerk does only the work of a clerk. When either malfunctions, it is replaced.

The human machine is geared toward productivity. It must produce something, and that something must be measurable. Whether it is measured in terms of profit, sheer quantity of goods produced, or number of diplomas granted, the output of a bureaucracy must be measurable. So the basis of information for a bureaucracy is both measurability and precision.

All of us know that in school forms have to be signed by advisers; everything has to be "just so." Back in 1990 I had to have an operation. Nothing horrible (tennis-related stuff), but I was going to miss some school. I tried to remember to do everything, including putting in my courses for the spring schedule. When I got back, I looked in the spring schedule to see where my classes were. Imagine my surprise when I found out I wasn't listed. I went to see the person in charge.

Why aren't my classes in the schedule? You never turned them in! I know I was nervous, but I'm pretty sure I did it. No, you didn't; here, I'll show you. Out comes a big black book. Teachers listed in alphabetical order. Turn, turn, turn the pages. Then, there I was, and there was my little piece of paper with the courses on it.

See, she says.

I'm looking, but it looks to me like I had turned in my request.

See, she says, you put it on the wrong form. With more than a little satisfaction, she closed the book.

The point is that bureaucracies try for precision, and a lot of that comes from things that are objective. It is very important to understand that bureaucracies are too gross, too inexact, and too unsubtle to comprehend quality. Huge organizations like our bureaucracies function "efficiently" and are capable of understanding functioning only in terms of how many in how short a time and at what material cost.

Like any machine, a bureaucracy works best when it is well insulated from the outside, well protected from different elements. In a real sense, bureaucracies are afraid of the outside, afraid of the public sector. Paranoid, if you will. So they grow. They keep trying to occupy more space and to control more sectors so that their internal workings will be protected. The larger a bureaucracy grows, the more the world will look like a bureaucracy. The more the world is like that, the greater the likelihood that more decisions that should be made publicly will be made privately and that the criteria used will suit organizational demands rather than societal ones. The style is production-oriented, paranoid, and private.

## The Future

> *When man invented the machine, for which there is no external model in nature, he invented it in his own image. The machine does not come from nowhere—it mirrors man's mechanical head.*
> — *Philip Slater*

There is logic to large, complex organizations that we must understand. In question form, it is this: If a bureaucracy were a human machine (and, therefore, vulnerable to human mistakes), wouldn't it be better to develop machines that would eliminate many of those mistakes? This kind of thinking has led to a technology and an organizational style with implications far beyond organizational efficiency.

Large organizations are coming to rely more and more on the centralization and standardization of information gathering. This is particularly true in the case of the military. Computerization has become central to organizations, causing the organizations to change their operations. In the early 1970s, when the *Preface* was in its first edition, Judy Merkle had already observed that

> Because the computer does not process general information in the same subconscious manner as human commanders, and because errors are incredibly costly, computer technology forces an immense clarification of thought and a precision of action in preparing computer inputs. The rules governing the operation of organizations and the decision process must be determined, the routine business must be separated from functions requiring human judgment, and the procedures for computerized functions must be laid out before actual computer calculations. In creating a man–machine network to process information, more and more effort must go into the precise definition of organizational requirements ... Technology has not merely merged with organization theory, it has become organization theory.[11]

Thirty years later computer technology continues to change the nature of society. It not only requires a particular kind of behavior, it facilitates it. User-friendly programs that help us adjust have replaced the confrontation between users and pages of error messages on green-bar printouts.

The intensive application of computer technology and the creation of databases allow authorities to monitor most anything. Now only two

11 Judith Merkle, *Command and Control: The Social Implication of Nuclear Defense* (Morristown, N.J.: General Learning Press, 1971).

types of political potential are free from predetection by computers and databases: genuinely spontaneous mass action and well-run, well-funded, organized groups. But funding is relative; in a technology race, as in the arms race, the richest will win. If government radically increases spending on the technology of surveillance, even tightly organized, technically competent, politically uncompromising opposition groups will be unable to keep up.

Look what happened after terrorists with suspected ties to al Qaeda attacked the World Trade Center on September 11, 2001. Within three weeks of the attack the United States had analyzed 241 credible threats, conducted 540 interviews, conducted 383 searches, issued 4,407 subpoenas, and arrested or detained 439 persons. Al Qaeda had assets in the multi-million-dollar range and was still unable to avoid detection with the use of technology.[12]

On the flip side of this argument the average American can access most of this information. We are in an age where high-school–age hackers (or even old dogs who can learn new tricks) can gain admittance (illegally, of course) to government databases using affordable software and a phone line—anyone can be a threat.

Other changes: Civil disobedience returned to the hands of the common man. The World Trade Organization was met in Seattle by protesters. Using the Internet to plan their campaign, an assortment of unrelated organizations and individuals, from militia groups to environmentalists, were able to synchronize their efforts, resulting in the convergence of thousands of activists in Seattle all at once. In this case the protesters were prepared and the police were surprised.

Where are we headed? Who knows?

Just a bit of bureaucratic craziness: The news media—definitely large-scale organizations—seem to have decided for us that the FBI and the CIA should have been able to detect the attack on the World Trade Center "because it was so well planned." Obviously, that would be the reason that they could not detect it in advance. If it had been poorly planned, this logic would work, but that's why they plan. Who's planning what, now?

---

12 See http://usinfo.state.gov/topical/pol/terror/01100118.htm.

## Bureaucracy in a More Personal Sense

> *"Did he tell you how I could ground you?"*
>
> *"Just by filling out a little slip of paper saying I'm on the verge of a nervous collapse and sending it to Group. Dr. Stubbs grounds men in his squadron all the time, so why can't you?"*
>
> *"And what happens to the men after Stubbs does ground them?" Doc Daneeka retorted with a sneer. "They go right back to combat status, don't they? And he finds himself right up the creek. Sure, I can ground you by filling out a slip saying you're unfit to fly. But there's a catch."*
>
> *"Catch-22?"*
>
> *"Sure. If I take you off combat duty, Group has to approve my action, and Group isn't going to. They'll put you back on combat status, and then where will I be? On my way to the Pacific Ocean, probably ... all they've got in the Pacific is jungles and monsoons. I'd rot there."*
>
> *"You're rotting here."*
>
> — *Joseph Heller*

Although it's not an extraordinarily precise way to present an argument, I would like to introduce one with a physical law: For every action, there is an equal and opposite reaction. That is the sense of what I would like to argue. While the following contains a good deal of speculation, there seems to be enough truth in it to take it seriously. If possible, accept what is right and reject the rest; my feelings will not be hurt.

Basically, bureaucracy develops only half of an individual. It so concentrates on some personality factors that it wholly ignores others. What I shall argue is that as we become more highly skilled bureaucrats, we develop urges equal and opposite to those skills. For example, as we become more developed "rationally," we may also become more anxious to be "irrational." Simply stated, bureaucracies may be driving us crazy. We may be going mad—in part—as a result of the organizational imperatives that have such a disproportionate effect on our lives.

It may be easiest to understand what I mean by visualizing how one learns to diagram a compound sentence in ninth-grade English. As I recall, it looked something like a straight line that was split into two lines. What I want to argue is that in the beginning an individual has some kind of wholeness, some kind of merging of qualities. At some point—indeed, we seem to have reached that point—bureaucracies overdevelop certain of these qualities, while leaving others underdeveloped. The individual with integrated skills slowly becomes an individual divided. Like our diagrammed sentence, the person is split in two. There are three areas that help illustrate the point: rationality, time, and relationships.

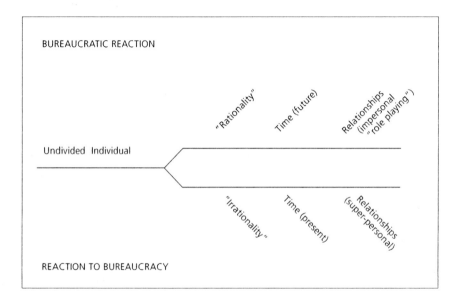

A basic assumption of this line of thought is that a healthy individual is able somehow to integrate the various factors of his or her personality. To a greater or lesser degree, the rational and the emotional would mix. One would not always be employed, nor would either be used alone. Our undivided individual would not be concerned for the future at the expense of either the past or the present. Indeed, each would have its own importance. Finally, he or she would not participate in relationships exclusively on the basis of roles, according to the positions held by each person. Nor would all relationships be of the encounter-group type: extra-tense, personal, and in a sense, tyrannizing. Somehow, a middle ground should be sought.

But bureaucracies develop extremes. By that I mean that the human cogs in the organizational machine are forced to divide their feelings, emotions, and actions into extremes. Let us begin with rationality.

## Rationality

There is a certain rationality that a bureaucracy fosters. Most of its parts we understand, for in a sense the logic of bureaucracy is the logic of science. It assumes an objective reality, one that is "real" and quantifiable. The aim of the bureaucracy is to produce a countable product at the lowest possible cost. The most for the least, just so long as it is objective. All questions must be technical, all problems soluble in terms of costs and benefits. To build a house or an atomic bomb cannot be judged as "good" or "bad" per se; it can be judged only in terms of organizational credits and debits.

So the bureaucracy constructs its own world and makes its own rules about what is real. For a person to get ahead in that world, that person must act according to its rules and its rationality: keep within the framework, produce and behave, stay in step to get ahead. If one believes in the outputs of bureaucracies, one is forced to admit that it functions effectively. But the point is that it seems to be very difficult for a human being to be so confined for very long, difficult to leave one's emotions at the front door in exchange for wholly rational thought.

The use of the words *rational* and *emotional* is, I am afraid, a bit sloppy. While I am using them as most people do, it is important to remember that relating to the world "rationally" is simply one kind of emotional stance. To put it differently, rationality is, at its root, only another emotion. The idea of a human machine in which human beings are confined to the rationality of cogs means inevitably that in some part of life "irrationality" must come out. If an individual is rational eight hours a day, we certainly should expect signs of something different when he or she is not at work.

We can begin to understand our irrationality by exploring the ideas of religion and violence in America.[13] Religion first.

---

13 For an example of how dysfunctional bureaucratic organizations are in France, see Michael Crozier, *The Bureaucratic Phenomenon* (Chicago: University of Chicago Press, 1967).

There are, of course, all kinds of religions and all kinds of worshipers and "faithful." From polite Episcopalians to Jesus freaks (read *Children of God*), people take their religion with differing degrees of intensity. It seems that we Americans have a rather singular expression of conviction: We are the land of the revivalists. Always have been—from one fire-breathing, hell-talking preacher to the next, and almost gladly we vent our emotions at a good revival. A good Sunday revival seems as good for the pent-up, rational person as a good Saturday night drunk. Maybe the best of each world would be to have both.

A minister named Albert Barnes once said, "The religion of forms is the stereotyped wisdom or folly of the past, and does not adapt itself to the free movements, the enlarged views, the varying plans of this age."[14] The age in which he spoke was 1844, and his idea was to return to the pure conditions of primitive Christianity, to get back to the basics. In a land where social movement is in unique combination with the confinement of work, people naturally looked for a release. They turned to God with a vengeance—or, if not with a vengeance, at least with an emotional intensity that would help ease the rest of the week—redneck religion for the confined, a perfectly rational response to a "rational" life.

Moreover, it is good business. Billy Graham, Oral Roberts, and T. L. Osborn are in the noble tradition of evangelists in America. From the days of tent revivals to contemporary TV, revivalists are not only saving souls but making a little money, too. For example, by the 1880s, Dwight L. Moody was into the God business the way Andrew Carnegie was into steel and P. T. Barnum into circuses.[15] It was big business and the hard sell. Moody had "expenses" for his meetings: $32,000 for Boston, $30,000 for New York, $140,000 for London. Once there, he would give his pitch: "Who'll take Christ now? That's all you need. With Christ you have eternal life and everything else you need. Without Him, you must perish. He offers Himself to you. Who'll take Him?"[16] Jim and Tammy Faye Bakker knew that religion was good business. They made a bundle of money helping people find salvation. Behind their driveway full of luxury cars—

14  Richard Hofstadter, *Anti-Intellectualism in American Life* (New York: Vintage, 1963), p. 137.

15  Ibid., p. 110.

16  Ibid., p. 111.

behind their upscale home—was an air-conditioned doghouse. As with junk bonds and old people's money, business got too good and Jim went to jail.

The point I am trying to make is not that all religion is insane, or that every evangelist should be institutionalized. All I am suggesting is that we are attuned to a particular kind of religious experience. We have a kind of therapy, a societally approved place in which to be emotional, to be "irrational." The bureaucrat and the evangelist may be the two sides of our selves.

The other and obvious reaction to rationality, at least obvious in our experience, is violence. It takes no keen insight or imagination to argue that violence in America is not a new phenomenon. There is no need to list examples from the Old West, or from television's version of the Old West. The ongoing violence in the South, where it was always open season on blacks, included burnings, beatings, rapes, and hangings. White men in white robes, being irrational, relieving their frustrations in an American tradition.

There is also the violence of the lonely: The seemingly senseless killings in almost every community, done by a person alone, are now so commonplace as not to make the national news.

We have the ongoing violence of war. It does not matter too much where the war is, or who is fighting; we Americans get a dose of violence if we decide either to watch the news or read the paper. Both foreign and domestic terrorists have attacked us. We have, over the years, watched everything from Vietnam to the British invading the Falklands. (Remember that?) We watched O.J. Simpson, at one time our hero, crouch in a semi-speeding vehicle, and waited to see if he would shoot himself. Even our sports are violent. We witnessed a boxer bite the ear off his opponent and opposing major league baseball teams engage in fistfights. The news repeatedly reports stories where sports heroes are being brought up on charges of rape or assault. There is a beside-the-point that should be added here. There is a kind of violence that we do not see but is just as real. There are poor people who freeze to death because of bad energy policies; there are hungry people who do not eat because of rules that protect the government from "cheaters." There are children who need special education but cannot get it because they live in a school district that does not provide it. There is real violence done that never gets on the news. But that is beside the bureaucratic point that is being suggested.

War may well be too obvious an example. As we know, not all violence is acceptable. "Innocent" violence is all right. Acts that are obvious reactions to the confinement of normal existence, the return of panty raids or eating goldfish, are permissible. What is not acceptable is violence against the "rational" system. It is all right to relieve oneself of the tedium of the day, even irrationally—just so long as one is willing to return to that tedium. But when violence begins to mean something, when it becomes a weapon instead of a release, an important political act instead of just a childish prank, then it becomes dangerous.

So we are allowed to engage in meaningless (save to those we harm) violence so that we may be good bureaucrats during the day. It is one way in which we can be emotional, have a little fun, and feel unconfined. Our violence is as normal a reaction as it is "irrational." While it would be foolish to claim that bureaucratic rationality was responsible for all violence, it would be equally foolish never to make that connection.

## Time

It was Ezra Stiles who in the 1700s came to believe that the "multitudes were seriously, soberly, and solemnly out of their wits."

Bureaucracy creates a fairly definitive view of time. As a large, ongoing organization, it points to the future, it plans on contingencies; it is problem solving. It lives not in the Now but in the Will Be. There is no real end in sight for a bureaucracy. The compulsion to produce, the ideology of production, means that the organization will continue to look ahead until there are no more raw materials to consume. In other words, bureaucracies live in the future until there is no more life to destroy.

This fits well with our Christian heritage. It goes well with the idea that if we work hard now, if we continue to deny ourselves in the present, then we will go to heaven. Heaven is the ultimate bonus, the best fringe benefit. So we live in the future. Let me try to explain it in a different way.

My example is really a comparison between the French view of time and the American view. Imagine a truck traveling along a road. The person from France will sit on the back of the truck, facing the road just traveled. His or her ability to see clearly from there is like a perception of time.

The past is most clear, the present is whizzing by so fast that it is a blur, while the future, the road before him, is simply unknown.

Now the American sits in the cab, facing front. The future, for that American, is most clear. The present is a blur, while the past is behind him/her, completely unknown. Our vision is best when we anticipate. We live there, not here. For example, we go to high school in order to get into college; to go college in order to get a job; get a job in order to have a family; and have a family so that our children can have those things we never had. We have an endless future, as does a bureaucracy. That is what we are taught; yet we know the reaction to that vision of time has been almost "irrational."

One way to do time was tried several years ago: There was an effort to reject both the past and the future. The emphasis became the Now, and the Here and Now. Everyone wanted to be current, or hip, or with it. Time became the present and just those things the senses were currently sensing. Plans were middle-class hang-ups, the past was dead, and the future had not happened, so why not light up, lighten up, and live in the here and now. Even nostalgia became the "current rage," with no connection to history or the past. Old might have been funky, but it surely wasn't meaningful.

Bureaucracy condemns us to the future, while we react by claiming the present. Neither the richness of the past nor the lessons of tradition are in much evidence in such an arrangement. To reclaim a never-to-be-reached future, or ourselves from the demands of a hectic, meaningless Now we might consider understanding the past: learning about the culture that produced us and a variety of styles that are so different from our own.

## Relationships

> *"Well say, buddy, is this the way these little meetings usually go?"*
>
> *"Usually go?"*
>
> *"Is this the* usual *pro-cedure for these Group Therapy shindigs? Bunch of chickens at a peckin' party? ... [A peckin' party is when] the flock gets sight of a spot of blood on some chicken and they all go*

*to* peckin' *at it, see, till they rip the chicken to shreds, blood and bones and feathers. But usually a couple of the* flock *gets spotted in the fracas, then it's their turn. And a few more gets spots and gets pecked to death, and more and more. Oh, a peckin' party can wipe out the whole flock in a matter of a few hours, buddy, I seen it. A mighty awesome sight. The only way to prevent it—with chickens—is to clip blinders on them. So's they can't see."*

— *Ken Kesey*

There are many who argue that a bureaucracy is, basically, little more than the sum of its roles, which are "linked psychologically."[17] In other words, one can understand an organization simply by studying the roles of those in that organization. What is important for us is to try to get to the real meaning of such a view—the costs of role-playing to those within the organization. In a sense, the heart of the question revolves around the problem of defining the individual.

Let me state the problem in a personal way. It is possible that a person could relate to me in terms of the roles he or she ascribes to me. I could be seen as playing the role of family member, tennis player, teacher, and television watcher. Those would be my roles. The sum of them would be me. If I were to die suddenly, couldn't there be another person who would fill my roles: a tennis player, a part of the family, a teacher of classes, and a watcher of television? In bestowing roles, society can both give identity and take it away. By relating to roles instead of to people, we are continually in danger of being no one, knowing nobody.

The sociologist Ralf Dahrendorf describes the tension in the following way: "[An individual's] roles are conferred on him, and he is shaped by them; but when he dies, the impersonal force of society takes his roles away from him and confers them on somebody else in new combinations ... man has turned ... from the individual into the member, from a free and autonomous creature into the sum of his alien characters."[18]

Roles depersonalize. They provide an easy means whereby people can

---

17 For example, see Daniel Katz and Robert Kahn, *The Social Psychology of Organizations* (New York: Wiley, 1966).

18 Ralf Dahrendorf, *Essays in the Theory of Society* (Stanford, Calif.: Stanford University Press, 1968), p. 75.

ignore other people; roles are an excellent device through which an individual can hide from the facts of his or her job. In consciously playing a role, one is doing exactly what the bureaucracy demands. One no longer acts as a human being, but instead as a functioning, rule-following, member in good standing of an impersonal organization.

In part, role-playing means that we are replaceable, interchangeable. To be a good vice president is to be a good vice president. It matters little why, or where, or for whom one might be vice president. A secretary here and a secretary there are simply the same parts in different machines. It is critical for an individual to play a prescribed role correctly so that the bureaucracy can guarantee its own survival, no matter what happens to any particular person.

Robert McNamara, Elliot Richardson, George Schultz, and Colin Powell represent generations of good (interchangeable) top executives. They run this corporation or that department. They are CEOs or secretaries (generals or diplomats or spies or educators or social workers or cops) floating from one bureaucracy to another (governmental, corporate, academic), replacing and being replaced. We grew up with McNamara and lived with Schultz, so let's take a look at him (Chicago Ph.D. and professor of economics, secretary of labor and secretary of the treasury; director of the Office of Management and Budget; CEO, Bechtel International; secretary of state; and professor, Stanford University). After oil, the UN, and the CIA, George H. Bush included the presidency on his resume. Today it's Donald Rumsfeld (director of the Office of Economic Opportunity, director of the Cost of Living Council, White House chief of staff, secretary of defense, CEO of GD Searle and Company, and back to the Defense Department).

In the realm of example, of course, they are all the same person. From here they all look alike. Or, to put it a little differently: In a large class, all you students look the same.

There seems to be a real desire among many to play more than a role, a longing to relate in more personal ways, a reaction to the system. So we go to extremes, to the superpersonal, to encounter groups. Lonely role-playing people pay their money to be tyrannized by a group of lonely role-playing people. One wonders if in an artificial environment, instant intimacy will solve any long-range problems. There is little doubt but that encounters are beneficial, but very possibly they provide only temporary relief.

Some organizations set up encounter sessions once a week for a whole office. Can you imagine the incredible emotional relief in one hour, after emotions have been stored up for thirty-nine hours? But organizations are wise to do it. People are able to react to the inhumanity of their roles in an equally foolish way by overcompensating and being inhumanly personal. The beauty of it is that it all takes place in an institutional setting. It is harmless to the organization. People yell and scream and cry and kiss and then go back to work, emotionally spent, able to endure until the next session.

Now that's depressing. We know the "truth" of how our surroundings affect us: The warning is that we can always be right but miss certain truths.

To act on the basis of the intellectual framework we know is accurate may be both wrong and destructive.

Not all that long ago I was called an intruder by another person. My first reaction was "of course." It was like being a stranger or an outsider, which is a fairly normal American condition. That impression was a little off the mark. I was felt to be an intruder, which was exactly right. When you know or want to know another person you should and do intrude into that person's life.

It is not at all a corporate/capitalist/liberal/legalistic idea of separation.

In the real world of family and friends, loves and hates, we should suspend some of our correct knowledge and figure out what may really be happening, what may be possible.

What I want to argue is that much of your identity, the who-you-are-in-the-world is contained and cemented in close relationships. In a tangible way, other people carry around a great deal of who you are. I believe it's true that a person's death diminishes absolutely all those people who have surrounded that person.

How we treat the people around us, and how they treat us, forms an arena of unlimited opportunities for acts of integrity. It is the primary location of good and evil. From it, we should be able to generalize and enter into the broader world of actions and politics.

What we get is at the same time something fragile and dramatic. It certainly won't guarantee wealth or fame or even happiness. Those all seem to be the wrong words and belong to different scales of measurement.

What intrusions may do is turn the world upside down, and allow each of us—in interesting combinations—to become creators.

Beats being a bureaucrat.

## An After Word

To take this chapter seriously is to begin to understand the world in a different, depressing way. To take large organizations as lifestyles that convey a very definite ideology is to limit the use of certain kinds of analyses.

For example, much of the economic interpretation of society—an analysis that depends heavily upon the class conflicts inherent in capitalist, but not Communist, societies—makes little sense. There is no doubt that wealth is concentrated in our society, that there are the rich and the poor, and that there are "managers" and "workers." But the whole dynamic of organized society—the impersonality and role-playing and ever increasing institutional growth—affects everyone.

What I am arguing is that the ideology of organizations will not change, whether they are public or private, national or global, in Communist or capitalist countries, in America or England, China or Japan, Russia or Brazil.[19] The bureaucrat recognizes the bureaucrat, inter-office or inter-nation-state. Regrettably, class analyses are too optimistic. To eliminate the "ruling class," the upper class, would be in effect to trade one set of highly placed bureaucrats for another. A class analysis in a bureaucratic world leaves too many essential problems well hidden.

Essentially, it seems obvious that in an organizational society potentially everyone might get hurt. People at the bottom—the poor, the minorities—are forced to deal with powerless organizational employees who represent an impersonal set of rules. For those in the organization the pay may be higher, but so perhaps are the costs. Organizations do more than buy people's time; they represent an impressive way of purchasing an individual's individuality.

19 For the classic statement of bureaucracy, see Hans Gerth and C. Wright Mills, *From Max Weber* (New York: Oxford University Press, 1958). There are, of course, alternatives. For some examples you might begin with some of the selections in Terrence Cook and Patrick Morgan, eds., *Participatory Democracy* (San Francisco: Canfield, 1971).

The world is safe for bureaucracy only when everyone is a bureaucrat.

There is an eternal tug in America between the bigness of bureaucracies and the individualism of the little engine that could.

It would be a real relief if I could honestly write that all we had to do was to destroy all bureaucracies and all large complex organizations in order to solve our problems. Of course, I can't. That our organizational structure is helping to drive us mad is, I hope, now more obvious. We are surely becoming divided, and are in the process destroying ourselves. The less together we are, the more potentially successful we become. But we can split ourselves just so much.

The problem of how much organization is complex. We seem to be social as well as political animals. There are things we can do in groups—things that are beneficial both physically and psychologically that we cannot do alone. So we must create new modes of organization and different ways of perceiving each other.

As long as we are simply unimportant, replaceable parts in an impersonal social machine, the best we can hope for is that some day we will go sane and become irreplaceable.

# chapter 5

# Politics as Tacky: Economics, Money, and Everyday Life

*Most people sell their souls and live with a good conscience on the proceeds.*

*—Logan Pearsall Smith*

*Work is of two kinds: first, altering the position of matter at or near the earth's surface relative to other matter; second, telling other people to do so. The first is unpleasant and ill paid; the second is pleasant and highly paid.*

*—Bertrand Russell*

*The prean is a sea monster with the body of a crab and the head of a certified public accountant.*

*—Woody Allen*

## Money

There was a great cartoon in the *New Yorker* showing two pilgrims on the deck of the *Mayflower.* "My short-term goal," one is saying, "is freedom of worship. But in the long run I plan to make a killing in real estate."

The more things change, the more they stay the same.

Welcome to the United States of America, where people make killings in real estate and the stock market all of the time. In the great cycle of things, economics has reemerged on the top of the priority list for a majority of our citizens. The great triad of politics, society, and economics has changed. It is now mostly economics and the little two. What started in the 1980s exploded in the 1990s, then the dot-coms and Enrons came tumbling down along with the symbol of it all—the World Trade Center. There was honesty in the admiration of money during the last quarter-century: of who made it, how much was made, and how much money could buy. It will be refreshing to look back on this time if we succeed in the War Against Terror and manage to put Humpty-Dumpty back together again.

But things were never that simple. We know from reading Marx that there is more to money than merely earning it and spending it. One way to understand society is to understand who controls wealth. Our infrastructure, the argument goes, is dominated and manipulated by the wealthy among us. From tastes in clothes to who gets elected, the moneyed have more than their share of the say.

Wealth is the bedmate of power.

What makes the study of politics more interesting to me than the study of economics is that grand and unexpected things happen in politics. In economics, for the past fifty years, people have been understood to be "rational actors." Thankfully, that just is not the case.

The point is not that economics is unimportant. The point is that I do not accept the premise that economics is the center of our existence. That, I readily admit, has not been a mainstream idea of our times. Unfortunately, it seems that the catastrophes of 2001 will only make economics more central.

We now seem less able to recognize the fact that it is a real and live outrage that there are some so rich and many so poor. That there are whole groups of people who take their identities from their financial inheritance, dividend checks, or savings bonds has been eclipsed by the losses of a few newcomers and a lot of small players. While those who starve because they were not "smart" enough to be born rich or of the "right" color are still with us in increasing numbers, events and the problems they created have made them invisible.

But that is just the obvious bad; there is much worse. We hide real issues with false ones; we hide moral problems with material ones. We reduce everything to our pocketbooks, and then we shoot from the hip. We convert every potential political discussion into the vocabulary of currency, and then cannot figure out why our souls are so poor.

Just how many things do one person or one family need? Why do we keep looking out for our financial interests when more often than not they will not solve our real problems? There is no guarantee that being rich will help us be ourselves, or that by gathering money we will avoid being destroyed by that very process.

The urge to acquire, more exactly the proportion and magnitude of that urge, is a sign of something cancerous in our ideology. There can never be enough things—there will never be enough "thing-security." When we put the problem of economics at the center of the universe, we guarantee that our problems will not be solved.

It would be nice to believe that we are now involved in a "noble cause" that makes us different, to believe that things have changed (I remember when Vietnam and Desert Storm were noble causes). It's ROTC and the CIA, not money, that counts today. There are things that are more important than stuff, but what do we hope for in our struggle—what is our vision? What is their crime? What is the fast track to the top? Place your bets!

Here we are in college so that we can earn more money (gain more status) than a high school graduate. I think it appropriate for an honest institution of "higher" education to change its motto from a noble Latin phrase to an American truism: Learn to Earn. When it gets right down to it, people seem willing to do almost anything for a salary. Being bureaucrats with split work/leisure lives is the destiny of many of us. In an important sense our vision is limited to what is called the root of all evil—we cannot get past our very own economic interest.

Money is the visible sign of the elect, of the elite, and of some of the very worst behavior we can imagine.

Enron grew from virtually nothing to one of the largest corporations around inside a decade, but it didn't do anything except make money. This is Information Age stuff. Just hire lots of people to produce information about trading representations of stuff, and keep on doing it better. Enron was on the verge of completing its own Twin Towers in Houston when the game collapsed. All of the executives escaped with hundreds of millions of dollars, while the loyal employees lost $1.2 billion in retirement funds and who knows how much in other company stock. It seems that those at the top knew what they were doing, and it is the consensus among those who count that they deserve a bonus (in the millions of dollars) for doing it so well. After all, if they had not been rewarded, how would Enron have held its qualified executive team together? Will Congress/the law see it their way?

The point is that our economy operates on the quicksand of false equality. Better, possibly, than in the gray and barren boredom of what was Soviet Marxism. (The Russians seem to think so, too.)

There is a classic American definition of politics—who gets what, when, and how—that is a half-step away from economic considerations. We know that the rich get richer, but is that really what politics is/should be about? What about action and behavior and public space?

Oh, every now and then we get some kind of "new" economic plan. During the 1980s there was a push by the president for something called supply-side economics. The basic idea was to cut taxes. That would lead to more investment, and everyone would get rich from the growth. The Texas politician James Hightower, a relatively straightforward person, described it like this: "They give it a fancy name like supply-side economics, but underneath it's the same old greed. It's like putting earrings on a hog—you just can't hide the ugliness."

In the end I'm not entirely satisfied that economics is a topic but rather an amazingly useful symptom to study. That, in essence, is the way it will be dealt with here. In the following pages, we will look at the world, at industry as religion, and at work and leisure. What is important to remember is that many of our everyday, run-of-the-mill, commonsense concepts and myths are remarkably value-laden and exact much from us. Ideas of economics certainly fall into that category.

## Eating the Hand That Feeds Us

*For at least another hundred years we must pretend to ourselves and to everyone that fair is foul and foul is fair; for foul is useful and fair is not. Avarice and usury and precaution must be our gods for a little longer still. For only they can lead us out of the economic necessity into daylight.*

—*John Maynard Keynes*

*Will you teach your children what we have taught our children? That the earth is our Mother? What befalls the earth befalls all of the sons of the earth.*

—*Chief Seattle, 1852*

In a couple of chapters we will look at materialism in America. It will be tied to concepts of freedom, but with a minimum of imagination it should not be too difficult to see how the discussion would fit just as easily here. Our incredible pseudocapitalism works best when all of us are only out for ourselves, just producing and consuming as fast as we can. Later, we will see that one of the things we consume is our self. Here, we can start with the obvious: Because of the way we do economics, one of the stakes of our times seems to be the earth itself.

Our basic ideas about economics are really simple enough. A little more than three hundred years ago, an Englishman named John Locke wrote them down for us. Locke said, for example, that God gave us the earth and that we could do just about whatever we wanted to do with it. Individuals were free to consume and accumulate the bounty of the earth. While the earth may belong to people, the use of it was individual. The more rational and industrious the individual, the more property that person would accumulate.

John Locke, meet just about everybody in the United States. Meet all of our politicians, business leaders, jocks, and TV types. John Locke had an attitude about the land and about individualism: We bought into it.

Locke's vision—his attitude—is a powerful one about how to increase wealth and how to change the world. While the Native Americans understood nature as a friend, the Lockean settlers saw nature as something to be conquered. Nature became a resource, a kind of fantasy hunting ground where living things could be converted into spendable cash. The whole world became merely one big technical problem for production.

And we are able to solve technical problems. It is simply a fact that we are going about killing the world in very effective ways. Even in economic terms—the economics of numbers and the curious kinds of facts produced by numbers—we are doing a super job of being stupid.

There is simply some stuff that is irreplaceable. And (guess what?) we're using it up. As winters get cold, we remember that fossil fuels keep getting used up, and there is no reason to believe we will find an adequate replacement. The amount we burn is staggering enough, but the way it is distributed is even more amazing.[1]

The richest nations, according to the United Nations, have 31 percent of the people in the world, and those nations use 87 percent of the fuel currently consumed. If the basic question that concerns you is equality, what about this: "If the 'poor' suddenly used as much fuel as the 'rich,' world fuel consumption would treble right away."[2]

But the question, of course, is not equality. The question is how to stop consuming irreplaceable resources. There are two quick, "practical" responses. The first is the extension of the logic: Let's use it all up as fast as we can. Wonderful. It is interesting to read the fight about building a pipeline in Alaska during the 1970s. The pipeline and production and transport of all of that oil would threaten the natural ecological balance up there, the naysayers said. Some went so far as suggesting that part of Alaska might be ruined. Alaskans—and the rest of us—were pretty greedy. Now, as with Nixon, it seems that the new Bush administration hopes to finish the job in Alaska in the name of national security.

The other "practical" response is nuclear power. While it is unclear that we have yet to dominate the world, it is clear that there are limits beyond which our Mother Earth will not be pushed. When the Chernobyl nuclear power plant in the Soviet Union blew up, it contaminated soil, plants, and

1   E. M. Schumacher, *Small Is Beautiful,* p. 23.
2   Ibid., p. 24.

people from Scandinavia to central Asia. It poisoned an area larger than Massachusetts, bigger than Maryland. No one can live there anymore or grow crops on the land. The workers who spent a week (the maximum safe exposure) tearing down the newly constructed city of Pribyat listened to music over loudspeakers to keep them from going crazy in the ghost town.

The other three reactors at Chernobyl are still operating.

A former presidential adviser offered a little perspective on radioactive wastes: "One has a queasy feeling about something that has to stay underground and be pretty well sealed off for 25,000 years before it is harmless."[3] And, as we have seen, toxic waste is at least as big a problem as radioactive waste. Rivers are ruined, towns are abandoned, unusually high numbers of people get sick and die from dumped and buried poisons that seep into our lives. Not good, not good at all.

The point, one so elementary, is that our industry is now in the process of systematically both using those materials upon which it is based, and killing us with what is left over. Eating, if you will, the hand that feeds it.

If eating is the metaphor, then we know that digestion is a formidable problem. To be as "free as the air you breathe" is now only a sick joke. As part of our summer weather reports, we are told if it is safe to go outside, not because of the heat, but because of the "digestion" problems of our industry. Alaska now has so many pollution-producing cars that it has the opposite problem: When it gets too cold, the exhaust freezes and it is unsafe to go outside.

If you happen to be in Los Angeles, New York, or Houston, it is pretty much unsafe to go outside and to breathe at the same time. In L.A., for example, the air had too much ozone in it (violating the EPA standard) on 148 days in 1987. The L.A. basin tried to clean up its act by the beginning of the twenty-first century. Fewer cars, fewer barbecues, fewer power mowers, less industrial pollution—but are conditions any better?

That is just the way it has become. All these things are true, and much, much more. No single person has a cruel enough imagination to dream it all up.

---

3   Ibid., p. 18.

Why do we do it? Why do we eat the hand that feeds us? In 1989, there were three environmental conferences. The world leaders gathered and agreed that we had to clean up the environment or have economic decline in an unhealthy world. The truth is that a lot of people want to continue making their part of the mess. It costs money to conserve topsoil, to save forests, to burn less oil, and on and on. Taking all the steps necessary to clean up the environment might also cost jobs.

To begin to understand, we can start with markets, with the basic American value of "You Choose." Governments regulate markets, and markets are notorious for giving individuals lots of things, and leaving a mess behind.

Let's consider the idea that we live about like we choose to live. It comes down to the choices you make: You choose.

In this game of markets, you have to remember that other people are choosing at the same time. Remember, the things you choose are about how you want to live. The first constraint on you—the single chooser—is that millions of choices have come before you make yours. Not all things are possible. You may want fast, convenient, and less polluting alternatives to the automobile—but they are just not readily available in this country. Call this the paradox of not choosing first.

Second, you might make a choice that will make you very wealthy, but there is a little risk involved. For example, the semiconductors found in computers, microwave ovens, calculators, and just about everything else leave toxic wastes behind after they are thrown away. It is easy to argue that this small risk is well worth the advantages that semiconductors bring. Easy. You see the point. No single choice will kill us. Semiconductors are so small. But if you string a hundred choices like that together, they might add up to big trouble. Call this the paradox of separated choices.

Third, it takes some time and effort to find out how to make the best choices. Further, the people most able to make the choices—those who have the information, time, and maybe the training to make use of it, and the mobility to live somewhere else or get another job if they choose—are not the people who may face the worst risks.

Few of you college students will earn a living by dipping film into developing chemicals. Few of you will pack lettuce into boxes, handling vegetables freshly sprayed with pesticide. Few of you will work surrounded by lead dust in the factory that recycles your car batteries. You will probably be trying to figure out how to maximize profits. Your concern could well be how to live richer and how to avoid the worst of the risks generated by your choices. This is called eating someone else's fruit.

Could it be that we are getting to the point of having to choose between jobs that will kill us or ecological purity that will starve us?

## A Point to Ponder
The point to ponder is a simple one with radical overtones: The economy, as we know it, would fail if we built durable goods that lasted. One of the most basic economic premises we have is that we have to use things, throw them away, and get new things. Cars, clothes, computers, jewelry: just about everything.

Technological advances, consuming urges, buying madness move us all. There are times when the feelings are so strong we just have to go out and shop. Get a new thing. Get rid of an old thing. It is the American way: Shop till you drop.

Those economies that do not practice the modern art of disposable products are bound to be left behind in the advanced thing world. The economies that are at the cutting edge understand the dynamic of newness.

Think about economic leaders of the eighties: Japan and Germany. How did they get that way? Well, they simply sped up the process of modernization and stuck with it. The first trick, of course, is that they lost World War II. In the process of doing so, they essentially lost much of their industrial superstructure. They were in the perfect position to begin again. They started brand new, and have pretty much stayed there. We, as the winners of that war, were not so lucky. Our transition from a successful war economy to a state-of-the-art consumer and helper economy was pretty painful. But that was 1990, the world of the 500-million-nanosecond hand clap. Now in the Information Age we can be day traders—little Enrons instead of little engines shopping for our own killing in the stock market.

But the dynamic is self-evident; we don't move "ahead" unless we shop until we drop. Is that a great national economic policy, or what?

The point to ponder is clear: Permanence is destructive to our modern economic life.

## Industry as Religion

*Thus spoke the Devil to me once: "God too has his hell: That is his love of man."*
*And most recently I heard him say this: "God is dead ..."*
                                                    —*Friedrich Nietzsche*

*Mythology teaches you what's behind literature and the arts, it teaches you about your own life.*
                                                    —*Joseph Campbell*

Let's back up and repeat some of the things we know. We are myth-based creatures. Our myths form the way we see, order, and understand our facts and existence. It can be set up like this:

We respond emotionally to a wide range of things. We respond, in part, to what is comfortable. We are capable of creating myths in order to fill our feelings. There is another half of this whole. There are social myths—constructions of reality—that help shape and supply us with myths. When there is a connection between a self-sense and a social construction of reality, it is possible to get an extraordinarily powerful myth: a religion.

At the turn of the twentieth century, our industry was pretty "uneconomical" according to almost any standard—animal, vegetable, or mineral. There were amazingly bloody labor disputes, a great many of which can only be understood as human torture; and a man named Frederick Winslow Taylor set out to right wrongs.[4] In a very serious way, Taylor wanted to make a social revolution by bringing rationality and bureaucracy (that kind of science) to industry.

He was outraged by inefficiency and decided that each worker should be as machinelike as possible. He believed in—and worked out—a system

4   See his *Principles of Scientific Management*. The following was suggested, in part, by the work of Chuck Gleason.

to measure each movement with a stopwatch so no motion would be wasted. The calculation was that output would be greater, wages would be higher, people would be forced to get along better, and a peaceful revolution could be a by-product of industrial reordering.

It was (and still is) an interesting idea. We need not dwell on some obvious points: For example, his whole scheme is built on the twin notions that everyone is primarily motivated by money and that there really is one-best-way to do a job. Instead, we must understand that Taylor tapped a set of basic values in us, and put them together in a brilliant (and probably wrong and destructive) way. In a real sense, Taylor's set of assumptions led to a dynamic that might best be understood if we use the categories of religion. Think about it:

Sin = Loafing

Reward = Higher wages

Ritual = Very elaborate, involving stopwatches and a whole bureaucracy of specialists performing exotic acts of neatness and cleanliness.

Church = We need a Sunday school, and we get it in the form of the university. In school we are taught to deal well with structure. It is easy to argue that much of the meaning of the university, for most of us, is the structure of the university. As we learn to operate in this bureaucratic setting (spring training for a bureaucratic life), as we subconsciously learn the underlying sense of reality we are placed in, we are being shaped and molded to understand and operate in an after-university life. Grades, graduate/law/medical school: In the end we hum its hymn, whistle its tune.

Faith Itself = Traditionally, a real belief is what would stir the gods. To stop believing was to stop the effectiveness of those gods. Now, there is an extraordinarily critical difference: We can stop believing and this industrial god keeps on producing.

History = There is no doubt that we are worshipers. We go to school and learn. We become practitioners, and we strive to fulfill particular kinds of godlike urges from our past. We have come full circle from the Deists. We become small reflections of the Big God: rational, predictable, productive, well-ordered, right-working machines. We come close to filling the dreams; the personal becomes the impersonal; the I becomes the IT.

*I give human traits to machines and machine traits to humans.*
*And it is productive and it is therefore good.*
*And we all say:*
*Amen.*

## Thingness Is Not Enoughness

One of the overwhelming facts about people in the United States is the enormous number of things they have. While it is said and often repeated that things will not make you happy, and while we know a poverty of things is not all that fun, the fact is that things—material objects—fill the world we live in.

Jokes are made about our gross national product, and there are a number of very good criticisms of what appears to be obsessive consumption and speculation; but what seems important right now is to see the dynamic and what is beyond it.

In principle, insofar as each of us is able to own about the same stuff—the same cars, clothes, washing machines, and on and on—we are really becoming more equal. We can all, more or less, look about the same. The real difference between Levi's jeans or Tommy Hilfiger and Kirkland jeans is marginal, and it is impossible to tell if a person paid cash for his or her Toyota Camry or is making monthly payments. The point is that most of us, most of the time, fit into the same range of dress and action. It would follow that we are becoming more egalitarian.

I do not believe we are.

Once we are in the material mainstream, the mere having and keeping up is simply not enough. In terms of material things, most products can be had by anyone with enough money. If you do not have the money, you can generally get a bank loan. There is no reasonable limit on the number of

TVs Sony can manufacture or cars General Motors can produce.

There are times when reality leaks out in plain view. Show and tell in terms of where you are in society. Go to New York City and get from one place to another.

Egalitarianism isn't working.

From what I can tell, there are five main ways of getting around New York City. (Walking and riding a bike aren't part of this sidewalk class analysis.) From poor to rich, this is the picture: A person can ride the subway (getting from here to there with a profound sense of danger), can take the bus, can get what is called a gypsy cab (these are independent cabs that will take you to "less desirable" neighborhoods), take a regular company cab that seems cleaner and more available, or—and this is really a nice way to do Manhattan—have a limo always waiting for you.

As a good social scientist, I can report that I faithfully have tried each way. It is about as strange going on a subway at night as doing a limo during the day. People at both ends of the economic scale stare at you. There is something very unsettling when the realities of our economic life are put on display. We Americans just don't like it.

But our liberal/capitalistic society turns on competition. It is ingrained in our national ideological character (along with other things), and if competition for material goods leads nowhere, then we need to compete for something else.

Something else?

Enter status. Enter status goods.

A college education can be our first example. There was a time, in the not-so-distant past, when only some people went to college. It was not absolutely necessary for an individual to have an education in order to get a reasonably good job, to possibly get rich, to be respected, to live an honorable life in his or her community.

We know that has changed radically. Now a college education seems necessary for just about everyone, and even if you have one you may not be able to get a good job. So, again in principle, we have become more egalitarian.

But wait. That is just wrong. The fact is that there are colleges, and there are good colleges, and then even better colleges, and the best colleges, and finally the elite ones. There are two truths:

The first is that a person can get a good education at any college. There's no doubt about that.

The second truth is more intense—it has to do with status and a stock portfolio. To get a degree at an elite college means more money, more status, and wealth. It is not a mistake that competition to get into those schools is so great. It is the survival of the richest (or those who can take care of the tuition). Or it is survival of the highest College Board scores. It is competition for status, for social position. In some cases, it is the survival of those who have a parent who graduated, then gave money to that first-rate school. It is about being a "legacy admission." Because so much is available to so many, the competition will center on those things that are rare and will stay rare. It will be a race for the equivalent of gold when paper money seems worthless. Let me show you.

First there is the elite school. Then there is the job. Ah, but not any job; you will naturally want a job in management that will give you a shot at the top leadership (for example, as an Enron executive). There are many workers, some managers, but few leaders. Leadership is what you want (to get stock options and seven-figure bonuses). You will want the "right" neighborhood. Again limited, again exclusive. An address can set you apart, even if your fancy coat may not.

You will find that even vacations are cut into classes. A summer by the ocean is nice; a beachfront house is much better. After all, there is just so much beachfront. Clearly even IBM cannot produce a limitless amount of beachfront property. And the reality is this: You are either on the beach or you're not. Close doesn't count.

So, as you sit (or lie or stand) reading this—as you prepare yourself for the marketplace of things—remember that things are no longer enough. Know that the competition for status, and for inequality, is now fully functioning. Know that keeping up materially is actually falling behind in some ways.

Know that even in material things, more is no longer enough.

## Hardly Working

When I was in high school in the 1950s, a friend and I invented a person named Dub Hotchkiss. Dub was not too bright. When my friend and I met, one of us would say: "Hi, Dub. Working hard?" The other would always answer: "Hardly working."

My secret thought is that if I still lived in Oklahoma, I would continue to have that conversation with my friend.

The point is not that when I was growing up I thought dumb jokes were funny; the point is that in those days we could joke about jobs. Although there were periodic recessions, there were also a lot of jobs. My friend and I simply assumed that we would be employed. That assumption influenced us in ways that we were never aware of. It was as normal to expect to be employed after we graduated as it was to assume that there would always be very big, very powerful cars that would go fast and would consume huge amounts of cheap gasoline.

At the end of the Reagan era, the phrase "hardly working" had an edge to it. One might have been working as hard as one could and be doing very well. But it was altogether possible that a college graduate would be unemployed ... or something called underemployed. For a while, with the economic bubble of the nineties, it seemed that the good old days had returned. Now, in 2003, no one wants to hear "Hardly working!"

This section, if you haven't already guessed, is not going to be full of fun and games. But before we get any more involved with it, there is a fact that we should not forget. There have been periods of unemployment before. That is not news. What I want to remind you of is that there are whole groups of people who are at the bottom of our economic system who never have periods of *employment*. If you are a white, middle-class college student and you're angry that you do not have a job waiting for you, what if you were black or brown and not in college?

The plain truth is that whites periodically experience what many minorities come to think of as a fact of life. It is an ugly fact about our up-and-down economic system: Some groups are always down.

Currently, there seems to be enough "down" to go around. Our economic system is changing. The industries that we thought of as basic—like steel—are now not so basic. Basic, in the new economic reality, turns out to be a kind of computer language. We now deal in services (lawyers, dentists who practice in malls, a psychologist for our every need) and in high technology.

As college students, we feel that change as a free-floating anxiety, one ready to attack at any minute. Personally, it means that you have to cut your hair, look neat, and make good grades. It means being a business major or maybe going into engineering or computers. It means that you have to know exactly what is expected of you—and then do exactly that. In a real sense it is an undergraduate course in economic reality. The reality is this: pressure, pressure, pressure.

The arts, the humanities, liberal arts, literature ... all gone. They have no payoff. We are told that the bottom line for such studies is written in red ink. In a job market with few jobs, many people, and an unclear future, fear overcomes the desire for education and students are willing to trade the opportunity to get smarter for the chance to become a technician. For shame.

## Government

The awful reality behind all of this is that we are caught between our collective myth of individualism, the obvious strength of the national government and new forms of global governance, and the inability of anyone to really know what to do.

The first thing to go is our myth of individualism. Rugged individualism does not look very impressive on your résumé. The sworn enemy of bureaucracy is individualism—and entrepreneurial capitalism. The dream of starting your own business and becoming successful is one that remains attractive for many of us. The number of new small businesses is almost equaled by the number of small business failures. Not only that: When the economy is bad the first businesses to go are the small ones. As individuals, we have just about no power over our economic lives. We are no longer the little engines that could—none of us is much of an engine, and in today's economic world we do not own our own tracks. We style our hair and choose our clothes in an effort to get onto the bureaucratic track.

Our government, of course, has much to do with this. Since the beginning of the United States, the government has made economic policy. We have never had an economic system free from governmental regulation. Our capitalism has always been one that was tinkered with by the government.

At first, the government just tinkered. As the country grew, and as industry grew, the government grew. The tinkering became much more than that. By the end of World War II, the government and big business were interdependent. From regulatory agencies, to government contracts, to tax policies, to court decisions, to money supply, to trade policies, and so on and so forth, governments at all levels influence the economy.

Too frequently, when we want to talk about politics, we talk about economics.

In a way, it should all work out pretty easily. Politicians, who always have reelection in mind, clearly want the economy to be healthy. All they have to do is pass those bills that will provide jobs, money for the citizens, and the like. But the joke is this: Nobody really knows how the economy works.

Goodness knows that there are many sophisticated economic models that predict what will happen given a series of actions. They are all wonderful theories. They are all right, even though they are mutually exclusive. The one thing they all have in common is this fatal flaw: They assume that we—the economic citizens—are rational economic actors and actresses.

Well, we are; but we are a lot more than that. We are also not rational in a variety of wonderful ways. (Good for us.) Of course, that makes life tough for those in politics who want to do the right things to make the economy work. There is just no telling what those things might be.

It is even worse for the rest of us. Here we are with no control; there is the government with all kinds of power; there is the economy that is almost always out of control. Free-floating anxiety for sure. In a world without answers, the economy is right at home.

How depressing.

## On Hard Times

> *"What's your first reaction when the phone rings in the morning and it's a job call?"*
> *"Oh, crap."*
>
> —*Studs Terkel*

*An evening of violence and brutality on the television screen is deemed a morality play because the culprits are punished in the last*

*moments of the last act. But Satan dominates the play ... When the*
*devil is denied, he manifests himself nonetheless ...*
—Kenneth Keniston

Work and leisure, two everyday economic topics, are almost too close to us to figure out. They are givens—facts of life. They are so common and commonplace that we really don't, or maybe even can't, think very clearly about them. After all, we know that there is work-time and play-time: You do one and enjoy the other, and that is just the way it is, so why worry about it? What I want to argue is that somehow work and leisure are important—things that we should make an effort to understand.

Following the logic of the topic, the order will be work now, and leisure next.

I thought it would be interesting to see how a textbook defined work. Interesting to see what the scholars had to say. I quote: Work is a "form of activity that has social approval and satisfies a real need of the individual to be more active. To produce, to create, to gain respect, to acquire prestige, and incidentally, to earn money ... the paycheck must mean different things to different people."[5]

So that is what work is in serious language. One of the truly fantastic things about textbooks is that they often hide, deflect, or obscure meaning. Sometimes they just lie—and teach us a great deal by what they systematically miss.

We still have our problem: What does work mean to a person? In a most serious way, maybe it means this: To many people, most of the time, a job is a job is a job. Work is what you do eight hours a day to get money to buy things. If you do not work, society will shun you. You will not be able to participate; you will not be able to do or make or buy. Let's face it: Work is one way society has to keep you off the streets.

It's cheaper than jail and very effective.

The tempo is no longer ours. It is not of people, but it is made by people. Ours is an environment genuinely not human. We still serve the rhythm of mechanical movement (the joy of mousing), but at computer speed. La-

---

5  Milton Blum, *Industrial Psychology: Its Theoretical and Social Foundations* (New York: Harper & Row, 1968).

bor might have been noble when it was our own relationship with our-selves—but what we have now is a job. The brutal logic of the time clock—where we had a past and a future and could actually count time—is gone for the college student and graduate. Work now moves at the speed of a computer game that ties us to a future that has already been plotted.

In our crazy, complex, capitalist, consuming setting—in our work and leisure life—the individual comes unglued.

Think about it. There is no clear relationship between a job and a fin-ished product. That no longer exists—and often there is no product at all. One person does one small thing: We are a nation of experts, full of sound and fury, separately signifying nothing.[6] Certainly we know that raw ma-terials are transformed—dead trees or high school graduates are turned into the finished products of paper or consumers. What is magical is that no person involved in that organized work process ever seems either in-volved or responsible.

We get separated from our very own work. And we get separated from people around us. And we get separated from our own imaginations.

So here we are. Work fills time and space; it displaces our self-worth for money; it divides us from others for material reward; it speeds us up in order to satisfy the logic of machinery.

That is hard work. Enough.

Enough. It's time to relax, take a break, and get into leisure.

---

6  Early science was exciting and helpful and—sadly—restricted. Here's an example: "The Royal Institute, which existed in England to further the progress of science and its application to industry, was forced, when it became a fashionable place to visit and wished to preserve its exclusivity, to brick up its back door to keep out the mechanics who stole into the gallery." In Harry Braverman, *Labor and Monopoly Capital: The Degradation of Work in the Twentieth Century* (New York: Monthly Review Press, 1974), p. 134.

## On Easy Times

*"He did nothing in particular and did it very well."*
—W. S. Gilbert

In a real sense, the key issue is the conclusion the two bikers reached in *Easy Rider:* "We blew it." What do we do when we are free from work? One thing, of course, is that we fill our social and economic obligations. We spend money to fill time, to fulfill our ego, to try to fool our frustrations. We spend and consume, spend and are consumed.

Then we're broke—spent, if you will—and we go back to the highly structured situation of work. So we repeat ourselves.

It is more involved than that. We watch television, see a movie, get drunk, chase men or women. Essentially, we just escape. We get our minds off things, off school or work or whatever, dull ourselves, and become mindless and meaningless in our "off" hours. Leisure, to be sure.

What the hell good is leisure, if it does not somehow relate to work? We work so we can escape, but our escape is all too often uninterestingly blah. Our work and leisure should be extensions of each other. To put it differently, without meaningful labor we cannot expect meaningful leisure—to isolate the two leads directly to all kinds of alienation.

We should feel cheated. We need work and play in order to feel good about ourselves, in order to feel needed. Easy times, it seems, aren't necessarily easy in the long run, and not necessarily a blessing if you use time poorly.

To talk about economics, to get right down to it, we might want to begin with saving our lives—socially and spiritually. A reasonable economic question would be: How do we make the world safe for itself and for its people? Maybe the way to begin is by not taking anything on faith. There are enough bad examples of our corporate capitalism that it would truly be foolish to keep up the way we've been going. On the other hand, there are enough bad examples of socialist/Marxist economics to convince us that we do not want to adopt the Soviet model.

The first point, then, is that these are good times to look around. Not only would it be foolish to dismiss anything out of hand, it would be equally foolish to pretend to know what is coming next—WTO and

*Rollerball?* Who knows, maybe we will enter an era of smaller collectivism, or even one in which more durable goods are produced.

In an essay entitled "Buddhist Economics," E. F. Schumacher writes that work should fill these three functions: "To give a man a chance to utilize and develop his faculties; to enable him to overcome his ego-centeredness by joining with other people in a common task; and to bring forth the goods and services for a becoming existence."[7]

More gets built into that kind of work. It makes sense to continue to use Schumacher's words.

> Wisdom demands a new orientation of science and technology towards the organic, the gentle, the nonviolent, the elegant and beautiful ... We must look for a revolution in technology to give us inventions and machines, which reverse the destructive trends now threatening us all.
>
> ... We need methods and equipment that are
>
> — Cheap enough so that they are accessible to virtually everyone;
> — Suitable for small-scale application; and
> — Compatible with man's need for creativity.[8]

It is not difficult to see what is left out of these calculations. No talk of manager elites and of the masses. They simply have no place when economics becomes a serious affair for individuals. Nor is there the false calculation that large size is more "economical" than small, or the desire to try to quantify the concepts of gentleness, elegance, and beauty.

The way we choose to operate our material relationships, our economics, is a basic question of how we live our lives and how we do our politics. The important value questions we ask for ourselves should be asked of our economics.

If we try tying labor with leisure, producing in a nondestructive way,

7   Schumacher, *Small Is Beautiful*, p. 51.
8   Ibid., pp. 31–32.

making work compatible with creativity, making goods and services accessible in a more equitable way—if we decide on these kinds of values, we can only expect a world radically different (and probably much more wonderful) than the one we have now.

It seems safe to assume that there will be no one best way to answer the new set of questions, no one set of people, no single class or council or committee or board of directors that will give us folks the word. The way we choose to organize and to create should take its directions from our self, our physical surroundings, and our social setting. As each gets mixed in different amounts for different reasons, and as we relearn the uses of our imaginations, our economic dealings and our politics and our lives will line up in ways to make all of those things more interesting.

I can think of no way to make the notion clear and understandable. When there are no single answers, but only sets of multiple answers, one is forced to sacrifice the clarity of dogma.

Let me try it this way: Imagine that instead of General Motors, America had a number of independent, small, beautiful, organic peaceful places making different kinds of transportation vehicles. Instead of General Motors, America would be full of Specific Motors.

# chapter 6

# Politics as Fraud: Liberalism and Voting in America

*While studying liberalism, I came across the following quote which does much to sum up the problem: "The way this business is run," said the lady, "we would have failed long ago if we did not make so much money."*

*[People] have to make themselves predictable, otherwise the machines get angry and kill them.*

—*Gregory Bateson*

*Murray Edleman tells the story of the election-day interview of a Little Old Lady in England.*
    *"Who are you going to vote for?" she was asked.*
    *"Oh, I never vote," she said. "It encourages them so."*

I am a good friend of a fellow whose family never tells jokes. All they say are the punch lines of jokes they told years before. Sometimes one of them will offer a new punch line, and generally the rest of the family will be able to construct an appropriate story around it. In many ways, that is how Americans are about voting. The punch line is always "vote"; only the story changes to make the punch line seem appropriate.

It would be unreasonable to begin with the idea that voting in America is a positive virtue and then continue our study from there. Indeed, given the biases of society—Madisonian people, in an objective world, organized bureaucratically—we cannot understand voting out of its context. It would seem reasonable to argue that considering the way we have set up voting in America, voting is only a trivial distraction to keep the masses happy, to keep them occupied, to keep them powerless.

But that is getting ahead of ourselves. To get to the view of voting that makes it seem worse than irrelevant, there are certain historical and social science things we should know. We should know what our ideology has to do with government and our attitudes toward it. We should know how political scientists, and the general mythology of society, view voting. Finally, we must begin to develop a different way of questioning what voting is all about.

## Liberalism

The United States is a self-consciously liberal country. All our scholars agree, and surely our common sense tells us, that for a long time we citizens of America have held (pretty much) the same view of the world. We believe the same general truths, have the same general kind of ideology; in sum, we are all liberals in a liberal state.[1] It is important to make clear that when I use the term *liberal,* I mean something more by it than that Democrats are somehow "liberal" and Republicans are somehow "conservative." Beneath the common liberal/conservative language of our newspapers lie the classic liberal and conservative political theories. It would be wrong to say that the liberal tradition was the only one in America, that it was the only ideology. We are now in the process of rediscovering the Puritans and the Populists, the Southern Bourbon aristocracy and the Wobblies, the Native Americans, the blacks, and the Chicanos. But, as we shall see, it would be equally wrong to argue that

---

1    The following discussion of liberalism is based on Louis Hartz, *The Liberal Tradition in America* (New York: Harcourt, Brace & World, 1955).

America has been anything other than a liberal state—in the classic sense—or that the vast majority of her citizens were not liberals.[2]

> *There's nothing in the middle of the road but yellow stripes and dead armadillos.*
>
> —*Jim Hightower*

## A Lock(e) on Us

Liberalism, at least in its American manifestation, is in large part the intellectual formulation of the Englishman John Locke.[3] The writers of the American Constitution had read Locke, and his influence on them is obvious. At the time Locke wrote, the medieval world was ending. The guilds and the fiefs and the manors of Western Europe were crumbling, and the nation-states were being built. This change led to a tension in Locke's liberalism, and ultimately to a tension in American liberalism.

There are several ways in which one can view what people were like in a mythical state of nature. Maybe people were noble savages, maybe just savages. John Locke believed that if left alone, most people, most of the time, would get along all right. There would be harmony, but not total peace. This was not to say that government was unnecessary. In fact, Locke wrote that government was important, especially as a counter-weight to the tyranny of the Church, the guilds, and the manors of medieval times. Locke thought that the state should have control over all of them. But Locke was more complex than that. He also believed that, potentially, government could do evil.

So, in his liberal state, government was to act only as a referee, as a judge for the people. This would allow the people to do just about what they wanted to do (privately), while being assured that their property—something tied closely to their lives and happiness—would be protected. But it also did one other thing. It divided the public and the private; and the crease that divided the one from the other was to become a huge split, with the important half of the split being the private.

---

2  Indeed, one of the first—and most important—problems for any minority is to avoid being co-opted by the liberal ideology.

3  It is very instructive to read John Locke, *The Second Treatise of Government* (Indianapolis, Ind.: Bobbs-Merrill, 1952).

*There is not much difference in basic temperament between a good tight end and a successful politician. They both go down in the pit and do whatever has to be done—then come up smiling, and occasionally licking blood off their teeth.*

—Hunter S. Thompson

We Americans both added to and misunderstood Lockean liberalism. Certainly our heritage seems to include the idea that a citizen should be afforded rights. We assume life and liberty and the pursuit of happiness/property. We also think we are guaranteed the right to believe in any religion, a fast trial, and the right to assemble. All these seem to be for the good.

But what we do not assume, what we do not seem to have, is the space in which to act like citizens. While we are given rights, we are not given the responsibility for acting on those rights. This, in many important ways, is a major flaw in our liberalism. The citizen is granted rights, but is given no place to exercise them; each person has potential power, but no place to actualize it. The individual is given political tools, but no area in which he or she may act politically.[4] Surely we have tried to turn things on their heads.

Part of the problem is due to the fact that the American experience was not the European one. Locke was well aware that institutions unchecked by government could be repressive. That was the lesson of feudalism. But America had never experienced feudalism, had never known the tyranny of private realms. So we accepted only half of what Locke argued. We liberals assume that government might be evil, that it might be repressive. What we forget is that government was to be set up to protect us. Because of our fear of government, we set it up to protect us from itself. Further, we have a belief in a "private realm" that we think is best left unregulated.

In essence, we have managed to make liberalism a double curse. The private is continually raping us. We get polluted and paved and built around and torn down in the name of free enterprise. On the other hand,

---

4   This point is most clearly made in Hannah Arendt, *On Revolution* (New York: Viking Press, 1963).

we fear government in part because we have no control over it. Both realms are uncontrolled by the people. We will not control the private because of our faith; and we cannot control our government because of our fear.

As we noted in a previous chapter, Enron Corp. represented the largest bankruptcy in American history, and is a good example of individuals putting too much faith in private bureaucracy. Enron's estimated off-the-books liability was about $690 million, but the estimated loss to employees through 401k's was $1.2 billion. It has been suggested that Enron froze the 401k's so that employees could not sell their shares while corporate bigwigs liquidated their share holdings and a major corporation went under.

Once we were merely scammed by corporations, but now, since we are unwilling to involve the government, private corporations are able to suck us in and bleed us dry. While we picked up the pieces of our checkbooks and looked for a new place to put our faith, the Enron executives gave themselves a bonus for a job well done.

So we are caught between the terror of anarchy and the tyranny of the state. We become immobilized by our beliefs.

Locke wrote that the state was formed by a contract between the people and the government. Each had a duty, each had much responsibility. Locke carefully explained that when the government failed to carry out its responsibilities, then it was the duty of each citizen to break the contract.

That is a serious thought: to break the contract. Regrettably, it is a thought with which we all must come to terms. When we do, when we think about breaking the contract, we find a problem. A real one. We find that our liberalism gives us no hint of an alternative, no idea of anything different. We seem stuck, afraid of more government or of less government, of more freedom or of less freedom. We are wax statues who melt, under the pressure of trying to create.

We seem to be unable to think of change, so we hang our heads and hold our noses, and go to the polls periodically to vote. Once every two years or four years or more, we fool ourselves into thinking that we are saving freedom and protecting democracy by pulling a lever of a voting machine. We are so proud, so self-righteous.

But as we vote, we never think that voting does nothing but condemn us to the status quo. To vote is the ultimate act of futility; it is to pretend change while prolonging stability. Our only act of citizenship, our only public act, turns out to be private farce. As we vote, we simply endorse our own immobility.

Wrong, you say? Imagination, you say? What about Salvador Dali? (Who is Salvador Dali, you say?) Dali was a man of genius and imagination who did some remarkable art during the twentieth century. Here's a story about how Dali did things that we somehow cannot understand or do ourselves.

When he was an old man, he lived in a castle. Nearby, in a neighboring castle, lived his wife, who was a Russian princess. They grew old together, but in a very stylized way. When Dali had a new painting or some such thing to show his wife, he would send her a message to that effect. In return, Dali received a formal written invitation for tea the next day at his wife's castle. He went and, one imagines, they enjoyed themselves. It seemed to be a very workable and satisfactory arrangement.

The point is that as liberal Americans, we understand *neither* part of Dali. He outflanks us on *both* sides. Not only is he more creative than we, he is also more formal, stylized, "conservative" than we. He sees the beauty of the artistic frontier as well as the richness of social form. I am not arguing we should do both, or either for that matter. What seems so striking is that we can't do much of one or the other; even our imagination cuts us off from feeling why Dali can love and do both.

We are dead-center liberals, missing the best of both worlds.

## The Voting Fetish

To begin to truly understand voting in America, we must put the whole discussion in context. We need to know just how it fits into our view of the world. It may be best to discuss it by "pretending." Pretend that we are constructing a state. This state is to be inhabited by evil people; the population is to be motivated by self-interest. The worldview is to be scientific. That is to say, reality and value are to be attributed only to those things that are physical and material, to those things that are countable and quantifiable. Finally, the population is to organize itself bureaucratically.

As good political scientists, as good creators, we would have to deal with a very fundamental problem: How do we keep citizens within the system? How can we give them an illusion of power so as to keep them content? How can we distract them from important questions—and possibly answers—while making trivial behavior important? The answer is deceivingly simple: Make voting a meaningless gesture (both to the individual and to the society), but also make voting a myth of important proportions. Good myths need high ritual to motivate the faithful. Ours have adapted well over time.

Do you know how they voted to elect Davy Crockett to Congress? Seize the poll and publicly call out your choice—a very different ritual. I think I was there at the beginning of our postindustrial ritual, and so was Nixon—the 1952 Republican Convention. There were very few televisions in Utah in those days, but the Republican National Convention was an important event, even for second graders, so a TV was set up at school and we watched the Republicans nominate Ike. As TVs multiplied the ritual moved out of the schools and into the homes of Americans, along with the World Series. Even while it was being rendered meaningless by presidential primaries, the second pillar of the new ritual, spending on hype and the media coverage for conventions increased with each election cycle. In 1960 Kennedy and Nixon gave us the presidential debate, the third leg of the new electoral stool. Our political lives now revolve around these ritual celebrations. With the advance of technology there is talk of integrating voting with the infrastructure of the ritual. With our smart Visa, driver's license, or voter registration card we may soon be wired into our TVs—full participants in the ritual from our living rooms. Primaries will still be a good way to people the conventions, but will they be bound by the results of the past or the will of the people participating from their living rooms? It looks like there will be all kinds of exciting technical problems to solve in the Information Age.

What did contemporary books have to say as the new ritual developed? Virtually nothing directly related to voting! There are chapters on nominations, elections, parties, and the media; but no chapters on voting. Hmm, something is going on here. Why concentrate on, say, the media and not on what it means to vote? There is, of course, some discussion of voting, but the questions asked about it almost always miss the point. To look at how voting is discussed is an exercise in understanding how questions can pre-determine answers. To understand the voting fetish, we must familiarize ourselves not only with the common questions and answers but also begin to ask those questions that seldom get asked.

The idea of voting is important in America, very important. The public schools pump our heads full of the importance of elections, the TV networks spend millions on their coverage, and we social scientists study and restudy elections and electors and the electorate. Before one election has begun, people are making plans for the following one. There seems little doubt that elections—and voting—are the biggest games in town; but do they really mean anything? To put it differently, what does it mean to vote? How does it count?[5]

> *Democracy is being allowed to vote for the candidate you dislike least.*
>
> — *Robert Blyne*

> *He nodded heavily and called for another scotch & soda. "It's a goddam shame," he muttered. "But what can you really expect? You lie down with pigs and they'll call you a swine every time..."*
>
> —*Kurt Vonnegut*

Political scientists have worked hard studying elections. In part, elections are perfect to study if one believes in objective reality. Voting is an objective fact. A vote is something real, something that can be counted, computed, and "played with" in a variety of ways. Further, about the time one batch of votes is used up, there is another election and another batch. So we know a great deal about voting and we are told much about elections. In a political science book, it makes some sense to see what political scientists have to say:

---

5   The argument has been made that the importance of the process lies in its folly. For instance, Herbert McClosky has written, "It is not clear ... that either the parties or the voters want the conventions reformed. Like the circus to which they are sometimes compared, they are among the greatest shows on earth" (*New York Times Magazine*, August 4, 1968).

Elections are the centerpieces of democratic government. In many countries they are a sham ... Only a few countries have elections, which give voters real choices and strong voices in deciding who will govern.

American Presidential elections do not occur under ideal conditions ... At the same time, presidential politics has, on the whole, been quite competitive. Voters have been offered clear choices. They have increasingly shown ability to make choices on the basis of issues rather than mindlessly, irrationally, crassly ... and the electoral system has worked fairly well to assure victory for the most popular candidate and to weaken divisive tendencies in our politics.[6]

It is all there—the myth of voting, that is. Let us examine the findings of those who study voting and elections and see if we can understand the myth more clearly. More importantly, we can understand what they don't ask.

A question then, and a fair one, is this: Why should we be concerned with how many people vote, or why they vote? The simplest answer gets us straight to the myth: To vote is democratic, and those who vote have a say in who governs and—possibly—how they govern.

There is, of course, a much better question. It is this: Does knowing how many, and why, people vote really tell us that much about democracy? In a simpleminded way, we are taught that to vote is democratic and that those who vote will have a say in determining policy. Political scientists are interested in who votes, in part to see which groups choose those who govern.

Let's see just how many people vote.[7] According to the Federal Election Commission (FEC), in the most recent presidential election a record 105 million voters cast their ballots. That might seem like something to get excited about until we realize that there were another 51 million registered

---

6  Samuel C. Patterson, Roger H. Davidson, and Randall B. Ripley, *A More Perfect Union* (Homewood, Ill.: Dorsey Press, 1982), p. 175.

7  Frances Fox Piven and Richard A. Cloward, "Government Statistics and Conflicting Explanations of Nonvoting," in *PS: Political Science and Politics*, vol. 22, no. 3 (Fall 1989).

voters who didn't vote. Only 67.5 percent of those registered to vote actually participated in choosing the president. But those numbers don't tell the whole story—and may not be the most interesting ones. The FEC estimates that there were at least another 49 million citizens of voting age who did not register to vote. That means only slightly more than half of the eligible voters actually voted.

So what does it mean when elections begin with that many people having already decided that the election is not worth their time? For one thing, it means that the winner was chosen by less than 25 percent of the total eligible voters.

If you believe that more people voting is more democratic, then there is clearly a problem. The solution is to get people registered so that they will vote. Why isn't that happening? There are least two reasons—one is Republican and other is Democrat. The Republicans believe that a disproportionate number of new voters will be either poor people or minorities—exactly those people who are likely to vote for Democrats. There is no great Republican support for making registration easier for the opposition.

The Democrats fear those potential minorities almost as much as the Republicans do. The Democrats want to appeal to the mass of white voters and believe that they can't get both groups at the same time. So, in a strange way, we have organized ourselves to discourage whole segments of our population from voting. (Luckily, this does not discourage any politician from constantly telling all of us, all of the time, to get out there and vote.)

Voting studies are popular among political scientists. Generally, the questions asked revolve around probabilities. For example: How many women voted for which party? Or, how many Republicans voted for Republicans? If you ask enough of those kinds of questions, then you get a picture of how people voted. A strange kind of logic then takes over, and you begin working on the idea that if you turn all of those associations around you can say something about why people vote the way they do. A list of answers looks like this:[8]

---

8   The list is from Lewis Lipsitz and David M. Speak, *American Democracy*, 2d edn. (New York: St. Martin's Press, 1989), p. 214.

The more money a person makes, the more likely he or she is to vote.

The higher a person's level of education, the more likely he or she is to vote.

People between the ages of thirty-five and fifty-five are considerably more likely to vote than are younger or older persons.

Men are more likely to vote than women … Whites are more likely to vote than nonwhites …

Because Republican voters are more likely to be college-educated and to earn high incomes, Republicans are more likely to vote than are Democrats.

Persons who identify themselves either as Republicans or Democrats are more likely to vote than those who call themselves independents.

Well, the list is interesting enough, but it doesn't really get us very far.

Now you know that a highly educated, rich Republican white male who is thirty-five to fifty-five years old is more likely to vote than you are. And, that if a person is going to vote, it is more likely to be in a national, high-media-coverage election than in local elections where potholes and school boards might be the main issues. Knowing that, what do you really know?

What if we changed the way questions were asked? Why does a single person decide to vote or not to vote? Or, how does a single person decide to vote or not to vote? There are some answers in "the literature." One political scientist writes:

> Where institutions provide citizens with incentives to vote, more people actually participate; where institutions generate disincentives to vote, turnout suffers.[9]

Another writes:

> When Americans contemplate their own personal situation and that of their families, they find considerable cause for satisfaction. When they consider the fundamental organization of

9   Robert W. Jackman, "Political Institutions and Voter Turnout in the Industrial Democracies," *American Political Science Review*, vol. 81, no. 2 (June 1987), p. 419.

their society, as in the arrangement of government and the economy, they see no valid claim for drastic change. Indeed, they strongly defend the established order. But they believe that the primary institutions of the society, rather than making the most of the generally fortunate situation in which the country finds itself, are through various sundry shortcomings detracting from it.[10]

There are other possibilities, and they might be better. It could be that the less educated, the nonwhite, the young or old, may believe that whoever holds power does not hold it for their benefit. To understand elections in the United States is to begin to understand that those people may well be right.

> *As it turned out, [his] campaign was totally flawed from the start. It was all tip and no iceberg ... The main problem with any democracy is that crowd-pleasers are generally brainless swine who can go out on a stage & whup their supporters into an orgiastic frenzy—then go back to the office & sell every one of the poor bastards down the tube for a nickel apiece.*
>
> *—Hunter S. Thompson*

One basic criticism of elections is that they are not democratic. There is more than some truth in this contention. It is important to understand this point of view and then to understand why it does not get us far enough.[11] To be democratic, elections should fulfill the following four requirements.

First, either the parties or the candidates should offer clear-cut choices to the voters—not a choice of hair color or of speaking style, but of politics and programs. Second, the voters must be concerned with and aware of the choices. Third, voting should somehow indicate how the majority

---

10  Everett Carl Ladd, *Where Have All the Voters Gone?* 2nd edn. (New York: W.W. Norton, 1982), p. xix.

11  Thomas Dye and Harmon Zeigler, *The Irony of Democracy* (Belmont, Calif.: Wadsworth, 1970), p. 174.

feels about the issues. Fourth and finally, when a candidate is elected, he or she should somehow be bound by his or her promises. What we know about elections indicates that none of these conditions is met, or is even in very much danger of being met.

First things first. Are there policy alternatives? The answer is no. People do not run on issues; they run to be elected. Political parties are interested in winning the greatest number of votes, so they try to avoid taking stands that might offend or bringing up issues that seem to deviate too far from the center. When two parties equally intent on winning the election clash, the party that is the most vague about its aims may well triumph. Making the difficult issues clear is simply risky electoral politics. Our parties, our candidates, almost always play follow-the-leader; the funny part is that the leader never gets off dead center.

> *Ambrose Bierce once defined a president as one of two men about whom we know this: Many millions of people do not want him to be president.*
>
> — *George F. Will*

Because the major parties deliberately try not to articulate the choices, the answer to our second condition is easy: The voters cannot be aware of policy alternatives when there are none. I blush at the redundancy of this statement.

If people do not vote on issues, why do we vote? Generally speaking, people join the same party their parents joined. When elections come, most people, most of the time, vote for the candidate of their party. If people vote according to party, then what do the parties do, what functions do they serve?

> *The two real political parties in America are the Winners and the Losers. The people do not acknowledge this. They claim membership in two imaginary parties, the Republicans and the Democrats; instead losers can join imaginary parties. Losers can vote.*
>
> — *Kurt Vonnegut*

Robert Dahl argues that political parties are of great help to the voter because they "present to voters a very small number of alternatives out of the total number theoretically available."[12] So that is what parties do! They help us to make rational choices by limiting those choices to two. They ease our anxiety over right and wrong—or, at least over whom or what to vote for—by limiting our selection to a seemingly identical set of alternatives. Parties make it possible for us to choose between two representatives of the system—and they make the choice relatively unencumbered by numbers.

Is it possible somehow for voting to indicate how the majority feels about the issues? The answer, of course, is no. With two—or three—candidates hedging on the issues, and each taking weak stands on many issues, it is simply naive to believe that a vote can be translated into support for a particular policy or set of policies. Our elections are not organized so that the voter can help decide what the major policies of the country will be. When an individual is elected, all that means is that he or she gets to hold office. Because the campaign promises were vague or silly or both, and because we do not really expect such promises to be kept, policies are not the result of elections.

So maybe that poor black person is right not to vote. What we know is that he or she is not the only person who doesn't. We know that only about two out of three voting-age people take the time to even register to vote. We know that in presidential elections, it is not unusual for less than 55 percent of those eligible to actually vote. The percentage is lower for local elections. The fact is that, even with all of the elections in the United States, people just do not vote very much. Our less than 55 percent is pretty feeble compared to 75 percent in Great Britain, 88 percent in Sweden and Germany, and 92 percent in Belgium.

Why is it so low? Well, there are rationalizations. One wonderful rationalization for the steady hundred-year decline in voting (in 1876 about 80 percent of the eligible voters voted) is that there was so much fraud then. The best example is from West Virginia. In 1888, West Virginia recorded 159,440 votes. Not at all bad for 147,408 eligible voters. Now that is really

---

12  Robert Dahl, *Pluralist Democracy in the United States* (Chicago: Rand McNally, 1967), p. 250.

taking voting seriously: a turnout of 108 percent. The answer, in part, is history. There was an old saying on Election Day: Vote early and vote often. While there was certainly some truth to that, it cannot explain our decline in voting.

There are other reasons why we do not vote. One "accounting" of voting in a typical textbook analyzes the cost and benefits of voting.[13] There is something sadly normal in getting a CPA vision of a supposed political act. Anyway, here are the "costs":

1. Having to register is time consuming.
2. Learning about candidates may be difficult.
3. Voting takes time.
4. Getting to the polling place on your own is trouble.
5. Waiting in line to vote is a drag.

And maybe a point six: Remember, federal elections are in November, when it is often cold and rainy.

> *Two thoughts about voting. H. L. Mencken advised: "Let us hold our noses and do our duty." Gene McCarthy, on being a good Democrat: "I'm voting for Humphrey, and I think you should suffer with me."*
>
> — *Garry Wills*

Well, all is not lost. There are two reasons to vote, two "benefits": the sense of satisfaction that comes from doing your duty, and the one chance in a million your vote will make a difference. But is that really a benefit?

There are, to me, several very notable things that need to be mentioned. In the thirty-nine-page "Elections and Campaigning" chapter of the Standard Textbook, the author made the choice to simply drop this "fact" on us: Voting is our duty. The chapter is full of information about campaigning, campaign staffs, money, and the like. But the key to the whole process—what it means or does not mean to vote—is barely mentioned.

Earlier, we discussed the two levels of communication. The first level is

13 James Q. Wilson, *American Government* (Lexington, Mass.: D. C. Heath, 1980), pp. 195–96.

what is actually said and done; the second level is the context, which is central to the meaning of the action. Voting is the first level of communication, while the reasons to vote are the second level. What is lacking is an intelligent discussion of the reasons. Because these reasons are assumed, we are caught with the feeling that voting is foolish (at best) but must assume that our feeling is wrong.

Consider the costs and benefits we just reviewed. Certainly the costs are very small. We know, for instance, that many people have to go through at least that much (plus pay money) just to play golf or tennis. We might want to consider the proposition that something is wrong when voting is less important to people than either tennis or golf.

According to the two benefits of voting, it is not hard to see why people do not vote. To argue that a person might have to vote in a million elections in order to have one vote count sounds like very bad odds to me. To proclaim that voting is our duty has a way of tugging at our emotions.

What would be nice, as well as helpful, would be an explanation of why it is our duty. (A hint about studying a new subject: You can learn a great deal if you question those things that seem self-evident. "Self-evident" is all too often the code word for underlying bias.) As a semi-serious aside, maybe voting is good because a person is able to label him- or herself. We know there are voting blocs—which mean something to how candidates conduct themselves. Maybe those blocs do more than that.

Periodically, whole new groups of people are discovered. In 1984, Gary Hart discovered yuppies (young urban [upwardly mobile] professionals). While it is accurate to say they were not really discovered by Hart, he certainly popularized them by politicizing them. The election (and it was only a primary) gave a sense of group identity to those among us who eat croissants and kiwi fruit, wear Nike running shoes with their business suits (female or male), just love their Saab (or Volvo or BMW), can't do without their Cuisinart, own at least one Nautilus exercise machine, and "do" quality time with their infants by trying to get them to learn French verbs with flash cards. There are apparently many Americans who are yuppies, and they had felt isolated until the election. Happily, they are finally an identifiable voting bloc and presumably lonely no more.

By the end of the 1980s, however, yuppies were feeling out of favor and isolated. People made fun of them. When the stock market crashed in

1987, some of the upwardly mobile was taken out of the yuppies. To be so precious and self-involved began to look pretty foolish.

There is another fact that seems important. The chapter following the one on elections in this Standard Textbook is about interest groups. As you might recall, interest groups were introduced in the first chapter. What we found was that according to this normal book Americans joined groups at a comparatively high rate because of what the author characterized as a "stronger sense of civic duty."

Why do you suppose we exercise our "civic duty" by joining private organizations instead of voting? Voting, in principle, should be a supremely political action. It seems our Standard Textbook has taken politics and, with ease, has stood it on its head. Turned it upside down. It is *1984*. It is doublespeak.

Public action is not civic duty.

Civic duty is to be done in private.

Public is private.

What's going on here? Certainly it will occur to you that the author does not really mean what I am claiming he means. Maybe he does not; the fact is, if he does not mean that, we can only guess what he really means. (Mythmaker, mythmaker, make me a myth.) Aside from that, the text itself is instructive.

What this Standard Textbook shows, in part, is what I am trying to show in larger part. By taking the same material that we normally read and putting that material in a context that pays more attention to all the facts, we can see the standard biases much more clearly. Public is private. Civic duty is silence.

That makes it easier to understand the fraud of voting.

In the future the definition of an exciting election may change. Instead of being excited about who might win, we might be excited to see if anyone votes. Surely voting must do something, must help someone. Oddly enough, it is not entirely clear just who does gain from elections. The voter may gain psychic satisfaction in knowing that he or she has "protected democracy" or whatever other symbols that citizen was serving. Someone gets elected; so certainly that someone is helped. In honesty, I believe the best we can do, the most we can say, is that voting contributes to the system. It symbolically hooks people to the process, at little or no risk to that process. Systems seek stability, and for us voting has uniquely served the status quo.

## Voting and Politics

Up to here, two distinct arguments have been made. First, that our liberalism keeps us from an active involvement in politics, and second, that discussions of voting only show us that voting in America does not live up to the "requirements" of democracy. We have implied more than that. Certainly it seems possible to understand voting as fulfilling a stabilizing, symbolic function, as a method of keeping people from making important decisions and away from power. Few people ask what voting means if, in a bureaucratic society, most leaders are interchangeable anyway. But even that may not be the most important point.

If this is a book about politics, then it is necessary to ask at least one more question about voting in America. It is important to ask a very obvious question, which is almost never asked: Is voting in America a political action?

We have already discussed politics. To act politically, one must honestly work toward an eventual outcome. That means—more or less—that one must help frame the issues; one works for those issues; and, finally, one must help carry out the results of those issues. Ideally, this is done openly and with others. The argument, stated most simply, is that we make something legitimate, make something moral, by actively participating in it. By being political, we give meaning to what goes on. It is not a simple process of acquiescing; it is action.

In order to understand politics, we must understand what it means to take action. We can get at this by discussing the differences between behavior and action. Behavior is the normal, the routine, and those things that are carefully closed by boundaries. To behave is to do the predictable, to do what has always been done. Pets behave; children "should" behave.

In oddly similar ways, rats behave for scientists as voters behave for the system.

*President Robbins was so well adjusted to his environment that sometimes you could not tell which was the environment and which was President Robbins.*

*— Randall Jarrell*

To take action is to cut across traditional boundaries. It is to invent new methods, create new means, and make new connections. It is to consciously help define who you are by what you do. It is an individual's way of relating to the whole, but in his or her own unique, special way. You are what you do, if you act. You are what you are told to be, if you behave.

In order to act, one must have space. There must be political space provided by the state. Space metaphysically and actually—space in which citizens may come together for creative political action, not simply for normal behavior; the greater the space available, the greater the opportunity for each citizen to act. But people must want political space, they must be willing to fight for it and finally to protect it. It is as much a human property as a property provided by the state. In other words, one of the reasons we have no political space is that it might endanger the system; another is that we are not actively working to get that space.

Briefly, a person must have space in order to act creatively, in order to engage publicly in politics. But just what does that really mean?

For the purposes of our discussion, it simply means this: Voting as we practice it is not a political act. We know that we have no real say in who we vote for. All the candidates look the same. It is like being given a choice between identical twins in a beauty contest. We surely cannot feel creative, nor can we feel we are defining ourselves by what we do. There is no sense of participation.

The way voting has been set up is neither politics nor action. Nowadays especially—with mail-in ballots—it is not even public. It is simply a fact that having three minutes alone in a three-foot-by-three-foot space once every few years neither furthers democracy nor enhances freedom. It is almost all those things we were taught that it was not.

*It is precisely the division of the individual into actor and onlooker, and its extension within the social mind into which we owe the birth of the hero ... This is the division that is insanity. This is the division that is the hero. As there can be no hero without an audience, there can be no insanity without an audience.*

*— Trigant Burrow*

In many places, voting has come to mean behavior in the most confining sense. It is only a method of endorsing those who will keep doing the same old thing, in the same old way, according to the same old rules, under the same old system. It is the meaningless raised to important societal myth.

Is there any way to avoid the numbness, a way to keep voting from being a mere endorsement? Could there be an election that would bring a smile to your lips? Maybe even a laugh? In truth, there may be cause for hope. This little ray of light came from—of all places—one of the grayest of all political states. How many times have you had a good laugh at Russian politics?

In the 1980s the Union of Soviet Socialist Republics finally decided to have multicandidate elections—big stuff for a repressive regime. The elections were for members of a new national parliament. It turned out that a remarkable number of citizens decided, to misuse Nancy Reagan's advice a little, to just say no—an option allowed by the new electoral laws. They crossed out candidates' names on the ballots. The results were sensational: Twenty-seven Communist Party leaders were not elected. The humiliation was greatest for those officials who ran unopposed and still lost because more than half the voters crossed out their names. Can you imagine running against no one—and losing? In all, no one was elected in 168 electoral districts where there were one or two candidates because so many citizens voted against them. Now that's an election.

At the end of a creative political act, people should vote; if not, there should at least be ways of making others understand your displeasure.

*It is best we heed these words of Nietzsche: "I say unto you: a man must have chaos yet within him to be able to give birth to a dancing star."*

# chapter 7

# Politics and Myth:
# The Face in the Mirror

*Each performer had to strike his or her private bargain with make-believe. It is clear ... what Reagan's device would be: he pretended there was no pretense. When he had to, he could will his own innocence ... In photograph after photograph, one finds the same expression, not varied by a centimeter. The mask has been perfected. It takes unsleeping vigilance to remain a ... political chastity symbol.*

— *Garry Wills*

There are many ways to illustrate the ties between our selves and our myths and our voting. One way to do it is to review some fairly recent history.

## Duty/Privilege

Before discussing more current events, I want to be as clear as I can about the mixture in each of us, of voting, and of the government.

It is not at all unusual for an individual to think of the vote as a privilege. During the Cold War it was a way of showing gratitude for not living in a repressive society. Then, as the vanguard of the New World Order, we were proud to be part of a free society. Now with our freedom under attack, it seems that we really do have a reason to vote.

The burden of the argument about voting in the last chapter was that the government deserves gratitude and respect only to the extent that it makes popular sovereignty genuinely real. If voting is a sham; if voting has become nothing more than a symbolic act symbolizing nothing; if it is agreed that the government is out of control, then it is equally our duty not to vote. It becomes our duty (according to the contract that binds us) to go beyond voting in order to get the government back on track.

The government never simply gave us the vote, and it is not our simple obligation to just keep on voting. We have an obligation to ourselves as citizens to make certain that we each have a political voice. When that is no longer the case, it is our obligation to take back what was taken away.

## Elections and the *Preface*

> *For make no mistake about it, if our way of life derives from America's "givenness," Nixon is what will be given us.*
>
> — *Garry Wills*

Let me offer some recent presidential history. Presidents are bigger than life, and we can learn a surprising amount about American political theory and ourselves by understanding our presidents. In all too many ways they reflect us as much—or more—than they lead us. The next few pages will be a short review of presidents in the last half of the twentieth century.

In 1952 we elected Ike (Eisenhower/Nixon) to save us, not from communism, but from the Korean War. Sixteen years later we returned to that presidential ticket and brought Dick Nixon back to save us from the war in Vietnam. The *Preface* was born as the Nixon/Kissinger team was wrapping up the operation in Vietnam to bring us "peace with honor" and win the Nobel Prize for our German-born secretary of state.

Success was short-lived, as it must be if we are to keep "succeeding." Two years after Nixon was reelected, the Watergate scandal forced him to flee from the White House and public life to escape impeachment. This seminal event forced revision of the *Preface*. It remains the formative episode in the life of the book and for the two of us. But many of you now reading this may not have even been born when Watergate happened, or maybe you've never seen Richard M. Nixon ("Tricky Dick") on TV, so how could you recognize him in the mirror? Nixon is history like FDR & Ike or George Washington & Abe Lincoln. No matter: If Garry Wills is right, and he seems to have been, any president we are given will do.

## Daytime TV

Some twenty-five years ago we had a summer of such good TV—we changed presidents; or "horses in midstream" or some such trite phrase. It was interesting and oddly traumatic and regrettably necessary. Regrettable because we might learn things we don't want to know, for in the end, Richard Nixon was one of us. Think about it: He was the one who made it—the Horatio Alger hero of his time.

That summer, people would ask questions of each other about Watergate, and impeachment, and the weather, and "normal" things. It finally made sense to me to try and work out some kind of Watergate Answer. After all, I taught at a Big State University and was being paid to do that. More than that, it is my country and it was important for me to know what the hell was going on.

I composed an answer to the question: What do you say when someone asks you about Watergate? Depending on my mood, the kind of day it had been, who I was talking with, how long we had to talk, and the like, I would do all or part of the following in whatever manner seemed appropriate.

It seemed that I always got to this point: We all had a common stake in what was going on. The stake was a strange one, as almost all the real effect of Watergate was *mood*. Somehow, Watergate is a reflection of ourselves as a funny-shaped sixty-year-old-man. To see that more clearly is to go through levels of American myths, through levels of thoughts in our own heads until we get to the parent myths. It is, in part, to catch a glimpse of how political myths work in ourselves.

There were all kinds of preresignation explanations we all heard, maybe said, possibly even believed. For example:

Conservatives: To save the country, we must save the presidency. We cannot afford to mess around with our hallowed national institutions. If the irresponsible (crummy) liberal Eastern Establishment Press would just stop all of its idle chatter and destructive work, everything would be fine, et cetera, et cetera, BLAH, BLAH, BLAH.

American Civil Liberties Union Liberals: America is really an all-right place; there are just some bad people. So, the Constitution and the courts and the country will be vindicated when the legal system gets finished with the investigation and trial. We all know that no matter how painfully and slowly it works, the majesty of the law always gets the wrong-doer (macho, in legal language and Latin phrases).

Radical: It would be "wrong" to impeach him. Keep him. Neuter Nixon. Let things gently fall apart. Let the corruption and rot show through so that space will be opened up for radicals. Then something constructive could happen. (My nose always keeps running—I think I'll cut it off to spite my face.)

Essentially, the first range of response is as much style as anything. While we can learn something about the person who answers in one of these ways, that fairly narrow range of newspaper-type reasoning won't get us as far as we need to go.

Another way to go about it is to talk about what the "best" impeachment case might be and what the "best" legal case might be. Those wise people among us would say, and rightly so, that if it had ever come to trial—*The United States of America* v. *Richard M. Nixon*—the charges would be decided on "political" considerations.

For example, a very good legal case might have been made against Nixon because of his bombing of Cambodia. It was, after all, secret, unauthorized by Congress, and illegal—fairly impressive causes for a legal case. Evidence? Sure. There were memos, military people who knew, the press who saw it, and on and on. But to bring charges against Nixon on this basis would be politically risky. Why?

Why? In part because of the games played by our elected officials. There is, as a case in point, a congressional committee that is supposed to oversee the military. To bring charges over Cambodia would make those on the committee look like fools, or worse. If they admitted they knew about the bombings, they acted illegally; if they didn't know, they weren't doing their jobs. Either way, it was pretty clear Nixon would escape on this charge.

There could have been charges stemming from the Milk Fund mess. It was only a fair case and, anyway, almost everyone took money from the milk industry. Even Congressman Rodino took $100, and there are remarkably few cows in his part of Brooklyn.

So, it was sensible to believe that the issue would be Watergate not because it was Nixon's worst crime, the most damaging or destructive, but because no one else had done exactly that same one. It is a kind of fun analysis to make, but, like the first set of answers, it ignores most of the interesting and important theoretical points.

## Dummies and Card Games

If part of the purpose of our learning about politics is to see the ties that bind myths, and actions, and our lives, then we should study the relationship of Richard Nixon to the way our heads work. We can talk about Nixon as the ideal American, the Horatio Alger hero of his time.

There are a couple of questions to keep in mind: Was there a Richard Nixon (insert appropriate president) and, if so, do we (you) want to see his face if we (you) look into a mirror?

There are a couple of keys to remember: Playing the game, and proving and re-proving yourself is part of our liberal upbringing.

Garry Wills, in his fine book *Nixon Agonistes,* tells of young Dick as a footballer at Whittier College. There were almost no funds for the football team, and there were few players. Nixon was both small and clumsy, but he was determined even then. For three seasons he and one other man were literally tackling dummies for the first team to practice on. Nixon finally lettered in his senior year.

The important thing is that we have some empathy, if not respect, for that continuing effort—that trying so hard to succeed. There is an American myth that, in part, assures us that if you try hard enough, you deserve to win ... and you will.

An obvious question is: What does the world look like in the myth? The world, for the Richard Nixon in us, is one of a series of starting lines—or of card games—in which you are continually made to prove yourself. The world is seen as countless opportunities to start and restart—high school, college, jobs, and sports—the American vision of competition. Every so often you line up and race to beat your mates.

Politically, the metaphor is closer to a card game than a race. We get the New Deal and the Fair Deal. Somehow, we find ourselves in this amazing game of You Bet Your Life; every once in a while we throw in our cards, which are then reshuffled and dealt. We continually try to win "pots."

Of course, this particular myth lacks substantial evidence in reality. In lots of senses, the rich stay rich or get richer, and the rest of us are always playing for penny-ante pots. But that's what is so fascinating about Nixon: He kept trying. He earned his letter and became president—a kind of perfect/ideal American model. He was the modern Horatio Alger hero.

Who was Horatio Alger? What was this dime-store-novel novelist into?

For Alger, there was sacredness in the running; in showing that, by making the effort, you deserve to win. The important part was on rising, on showing how hard work can mold character. Listen to the book titles: *Making His Way, Helping Himself, Struggling Upward, Bound to Rise.* The poisonous thing wasn't that Alger's heroes aimed at wealth or success; their heroes didn't aim at those things.

The tricky part is that the hero aimed not at success, but at succeeding.

Wills writes that this person becomes "a martyr to duty." The self-made man or woman is the true American monster. If you make something outside of yourself—build a chair, write a paper, grow a garden—that thing comes from the self, but is apart from the self. But the self-maker, the self-improver, is never finished; cannot stand alone; isn't apart from or severed from the self. The person must always tinker, improve, adjust, and start over. There is always the fear your product—your self—will be out of date, or it will rot from nonuse.

Sound too crazy to be true? Amazon.com now lists over 20,000 titles for self-help books.

You always have to go back and begin again. Life becomes an eternal series of botox injections.

You have to have the heat of decisions—of "crises" in Nixon's language—to know yourself. The whole stress, in 1971, was not to be a good president but to be re-elected; the sickness of always competing and of never completing your project—of never really having a self—was eating away at Nixon.

Was there a Richard Nixon? If so, when he looked into a mirror, there may have been blank spaces, an incompleteness of self that he must have understood as moral failure.

When you vote for the Presidential Candidate of Your Choice, I think Nixon's presidency is a good model: one with no vision, or goal, or aims that are really understandable. Because, as a self-improver, he was up to his neck in his need to keep succeeding. Watergate wasn't really immoral. Tricky maybe, but everyone was at the starting line—and the aim was to finish first, and then to start again.

It is enormously destructive to think that Nixon really is our model; not because he made it, but because he is a vacuum. It is in that sense that we really do have *self*-government. We are not monsters, nor are we political. But we're all about the same, all private, and always tinkering with our product, which is our very own self.

So, Students of Voting, there is/was Richard Nixon receiving an amazing electoral mandate. Vote and save democracy. Indeed.

The most grotesque part of Watergate is that we somehow forgot that America is its people; its shared, collective past; noble deeds and good examples, as well as the bad and rotten. We are much more than the institution of the presidency, or any institution I can think of.

There is no defense for Watergate: maybe a lesson or two for us, but certainly no defense.

It is a moral stain.

## The End?

While it is always helpful to have Nixon as a bad example, it is important to remember that he was not the first—nor will he be the last—to show us rotten things.

The next elected president after Nixon was the self-proclaimed Religious Carter. He was self-righteous, morally upstanding, and as interested in being re-elected as Nixon was. In his effort to be renominated, Carter used federal money in the "right" places to get votes; he refused to open his decisions to public debate; he was even ready to use the Iranian crisis to his political advantage.

It is certainly fair to call that politics as usual. To contend that it is not unusual would be correct. It would be truthful to say that others have done the same things.

All this is so, but to say that Carter's actions were normal is not to say that they were either good or right or, in the long run, helpful to anyone but the president.

For years and years Richard Nixon had a terrible reputation. He was seen as ruthlessly ambitious and not altogether moral. Jimmy Carter was different. We did not know he was equally ruthlessly ambitious and not altogether moral until he became president. In our land of redemption, Jimmy Carter has become a wonderful former president, possibly the best former president in our history. He deserved the Nobel Peace Prize that he won.

## Relax

> *"You are a very bad man," Dorothy said.*
> *"No," replied the Wizard, "I'm a very good man. I'm just a very bad wizard."*
> — *L. Frank Baum,* The Wizard of Oz

If nothing else, Ronald Reagan was relaxed. Goofy grin and all, he seemed to give Americans a sense of pride. What a guy! During his crime-ridden administration, he showed us something about the presidency.

It is possible, we now know, to be president without the kind of great tension showed by Nixon and Carter. Reagan vacationed, and napped, and nothing much seemed different. His staff said awful things, and many did things that were outside of morality (and sometimes outside of the law); bad things happened in foreign affairs (the deaths of U.S. soldiers in Lebanon, for example); bad things happened domestically (the worst recession since the 1930s), but everything seemed to be OK.

Even when Reagan was upset, he sounded kind of laid back. You could tell when he was furious, but that didn't last very long. Unlike Carter, he neither dwelled on nor even knew details; unlike Nixon, the corruption around him did not seem to hurt his popularity. And, even relaxed, he was able to pass a lot of legislation the first two years he was in office.

Was Reagan as relaxed as he seemed? Maybe so. Maybe everything was under control. Maybe not. The following is from *Make-Believe: The Story of Nancy and Ronald Reagan* by Laurence Learner. He writes:

> What was so extraordinary was Ronnie's apparent psychic distance from the burden of the presidency. He sat in cabinet meetings doodling. Unless held to a rigid agenda, he would start telling Hollywood stories or talk about football. "He has a habit now," his brother Neil said. "You might be talking to him, and it's like he's picking his fingernails, but he's not. And you know then he's talking to himself."
>
> "If people knew about him living in his own reality, they wouldn't believe it," said one White House aide. "There are only ten to fifteen people who know the extent, and until they leave and begin talking, no one will believe it."

What seems amazing is the amount of remarkable things that went on in the Reagan White House. There was the Iran-Contra Affair (for details, see Oliver North in chapter 10), the fraud at HUD, the scandal at the EPA, the mess with the savings and loans, the crimes at the Pentagon, the immense national debt, becoming the world's biggest debtor nation, and the more than 100 members of the administration who were either convicted of crimes or forced out of their jobs because of scandals.

It appears that Reagan either had a selective memory or had no memory at all. He testified (on videotape) during the trial of his security adviser John Poindexter. He couldn't quite remember about the arms-for-hostages/Contra aid business, nor could he remember things he had announced on national television, or had ordered his attorney general to do, or the things reported to him by a commission he himself had appointed. Our selective-memory former president could only remember this: He had broken no laws. Quite a man.

Yet Ronald Reagan helps us understand something about our politics. He was, after all, very popular, and in the eyes of his supporters very successful. Unlike poor Nixon, he was untouchable—above the law.

What we can learn about is the image of success.

In this century, we have had several presidents who could somehow communicate in special ways. Franklin Roosevelt was one, John Kennedy another. They said the right thing at the right time in the right place. So, too, did Ronald Reagan. What he did well was make speeches. He gave speeches on television to sell his legislative program. He went to Omaha Beach in Normandy (the World War II battlefield) and was simply in the right place at the right time. He summed up our collective grief when the *Challenger* blew up.[1]

The images were terrific, and his popularity was high and long-lasting.

## And So On ...

> *George Bush is "a toothache of a man."*
> —*Jim Hightower*

Upon his election to the top job the first President Bush couldn't do much more than continue the Reagan legacy. Then Saddam Hussein invaded Kuwait and gave George Bush an identity of his own. He became the Commander-in-Chief, protector of democracy, with the highest approval ratings of any president in decades. With reelection less than eighteen months away, the champion of "Desert Storm" (aka Liberator of Kuwait) looked unbeatable; but success is fleeting, and it all faded away before the election that, of course, he lost. He learned what many had believed all along—that our voting really is tied to our pocketbooks.

Robert Eisner, an economics professor, offered the following fable. A very unhappy peasant came to his priest. He complained that he and his wife and their six kids lived in a one-room hut and it was awful.

The priest said: "Tonight, move in the chickens." The peasant did, and came back the next day even unhappier. The priest said: "Tonight, move in the cows." The peasant did, and came back the next day miserable. The priest said: "Tonight, move in the pigs."

The next morning the peasant came back in the worst state ever. He pleaded for help. The priest said: "Tonight, move all of the animals out."

The peasant moved all of the animals out. He came back the next day

---

1  Fred I. Greenstein, "Ronald Reagan—Another Hidden-Hand Ike?" *Political Science and Politics,* vol. 23, no. 1 (March 1990), pp. 7–13.

and thanked the priest. "Thank you," the peasant said. "Thank you for your help. Now we are better off than we were."

There are two important points. One is that during the 1984 election Reagan asked us if we were better off than we had been four years before. What we did was compare our conditions then with those two years before. We remembered when unemployment was 10.6 percent (1982); what we forgot is that Reagan was president then, not Carter.

As with the peasant, during Reagan's first four years, the chickens, cows, and pigs all moved in and then moved out. It felt like we were better off. It felt like we should be grateful. That is one reason why Reagan asked the questions:

"Are you better off now than you were four years ago?"

"Wouldn't you rather have me than Jimmy Carter as president?"

Reagan really did soothe us—perhaps we really are better off if we feel better off.

> *Reagan promised everyone a seven-course dinner. Ours turned out*
> *to be a possum and a six-pack.*
>
> *— Jim Hightower*

## ... And So On

Bill Clinton's victory over George Bush in 1992 was about the economy, but it was also about us. Aside from wanting better economic times, America wanted a change. We wanted a president who was more like the rest of us: one who was younger and more charismatic, and who had a better understanding of the hardships the average American faced each day. Bill Clinton felt our pain.

We learned over the next eight years that our first baby-boomer president was in fact very much just like us—maybe too much so. We also found out that he was not very different from the presidents who preceded him.

Bill was a Democrat who made us feel like Republicans were guarding the purse. Economic times were really good. It was Reagan again, but no imagination was required. While Ron had to make us believe, Bill just let us enjoy while everyone tried to take credit. Ron's deficit turned into a surplus and everyone wanted a share. It looked like we had really returned to the good old days.

Tangled in a web of war, deficit, and danger, Ronald Reagan was able to sidestep impeachment ("Irangate") in a situation that seemed far more perilous than the one facing Nixon, but a decade later Bill Clinton with no deficit, no war, and a booming economy became the second president in history to be impeached. What's going on here? Since the *Preface* was published, they've tried to impeach every president who's been re-elected.

Maybe it takes more than four years for investigative reporting to produce results. In the Reagan case maybe there was just too much real stuff happening. But the Clintons became the news early on.

The problem was putting the pieces together. They played with the shady Little Rock real estate ventures (Whitewater sounds like Watergate), Vince Baker's suicide, and Hillary's luck in the futures market, but nothing came together. Bill was re-elected in spite of the mid-term Republican sweep in 1994 and their "Contract with America."

Clinton's problems or successes (sometimes it's hard to tell) with women had been background music for the whole show—charges, suits, and really "good" stories gave us something to talk and laugh about. Then there was Monica the intern. Mature women in hotels are one thing, but students in the White House? Definitely a "high misdemeanor." A special counsel was appointed to do the paperwork and the Republican majority in the House flexed its muscle. When the tedium ended Clinton had been impeached for lying. There were not, nor had there ever been, the votes in the Senate to convict him, so he was still president. Everyone looked foolish—the nation's mirrors were covered. Had we looked at ourselves, we would have seen a clown's face.

So here we are. Stuck somewhere between the extremes of an aging veteran of World War II whose wife wore "respectable Republican cloth coats" lying about a break-in, and a young, charismatic "man of the people" lying about sex. Different men on different roads wound up with the same address and similar fates. What if George Washington had lied about that cherry tree? Would he have gone on *60 Minutes* with Martha to explain?

Imagine if you can, a Dali painting of these two Horatio Alger heroes.

## Exceptions: Koop

Politics is appearing. It is being seen and being heard.[2] It is seeing and hearing. Politics is, in part, the ability to articulate the right thing at the right time. Politics is doing. Good politics holds things together. Now and then, people who are good at politics come along. They are exceptions to what we know as normal: They are exceptional.

My nomination for the person who was best at politics during the last quarter-century is a pediatric surgeon (one of his specialties was separating Siamese twins). The guy is anti-abortion, a devout Christian, and a genuine political conservative. When he was nominated to be surgeon general, the *New York Times* called him "Dr. Unqualified." It seems strange that this guy would be one of my favorites. Ah, but one of the secrets of politics is the unexpected, things you just cannot anticipate. Dr. Charles Everett Koop was a grand surprise.

It took eight months for the Reagan administration to bully Congress into accepting the Koop nomination. Koop, at sixty-four, was just about everything the liberal Congress did not like. Eight months to get into a job that, up to then, carried almost no weight. In case you didn't know, the Office of the Surgeon General has a small budget, a small staff, and almost no power.

All that the surgeon general can really do is speak up: be seen and be heard. The surgeon general is little more than a symbolic leader.

During the eight months that Koop was waiting for his nomination for this weak position to be confirmed, he studied what needed to be done. He says that the wait was the best thing for him: He learned what it was possible for him to do. The first thing he did was put everyone under his statutory authority (the Commissioned Corps of the Public Health Service) in uniform. As Reagan began to dismantle public health, Koop's people began to feel revitalized: They began to feel that they were doing something important. They dressed up.

What happened then is not at all strange in politics: Issues found the person.

---

2  I believe the person who was best at presidential politics since FDR was Bill Clinton.

The three most interesting issues were smoking, AIDS, and abortions. Smoking first. Most surgeon generals since the sixties have said that smoking is bad. They said, "Don't do it." Koop's attitude was this: "People asked me, 'Why not just stick to saying smoking is bad for you?' I say if you want to do the job well, you do it all." So, he began to work for a "smoke-free society" by the year 2000.

Koop supported smoking restrictions in federal buildings, favored a total smoking ban on all airline flights, challenged tobacco marketing aimed at the young, and attacked sales of cigarettes to Third World countries. He didn't make friends in the administration. The White House pushed the sales of cigarettes overseas and wanted Koop to keep his mouth shut. They didn't want Koop to testify before Congress, but backed away from having it look like that. Koop went to the Hill and talked before a full house.

One tobacco-state congressman thought that banning advertising would be wrong. Did Koop have any other ideas?

Let them keep advertising, he answered—only let the government have equal space. So, if on one page you had a hunk or a beautiful woman lighting up, on the other page would be the reply. Koop imagined the other ad: It would be a pretty scene, with a cottage, and a white picket fence, and two cute kids playing on the lawn, and a mom standing in the doorway, and a daddy dying of a coronary on the front steps.

Neither the White House nor the Congress really liked Koop's stance, but that did not seem to matter. "If a health issue is given to me to solve, I don't feel I have to necessarily take the administration's point of view. I really think the public would be very disappointed if I were part of the team in that instance …"

We saw some of how Koop handled AIDS when he sent his report around the cabinet. When he was asked by the administration to issue a report, it was believed that it wouldn't be much. After all, Koop seemed to be homophobic, and too much of the right wing believed AIDS was a gay sickness that the government shouldn't bother about. President Reagan thought that AIDS was like the measles for gay men.

What Koop did was listen and talk to twenty-five medical, religious, and political groups. The most skeptical was the AIDS Action Council, a confederation of gay groups. The head of the group, Jeff Levy, describes

Koop as "very formal. A very stiff person, who quite frankly we didn't think would listen. We thought we were there just to go through the motions. But in the course of the meeting, he did seem to be listening ..." At one point, the council requested that Koop avoid the prejudicial term "high-risk groups" for the more neutral "high-risk behavior." People recall Koop listening, then nudging his assistant and saying, "Make a note of that. That's important."

Koop issued a thirty-five-page report that could be understood by an eighth-grader. It presented AIDS as a public health issue—nothing more. He arued that education was the only way to stop the spread of the disease, and that there should be sex education at "the lowest possible grade."

It made the administration crazy, especially Education Secretary (later Drug Czar) William Bennett. They all felt betrayed. "The conservatives assumed a lot of things," said Koop. "But one of the problems people don't understand is, if I were sitting here talking to you (as a private citizen), in my living room and I worked for Xerox or some private company, I would talk to you in a totally different way. I would tell you how I, as a person, feel about certain things."

Finally, Reagan asked Koop to write a surgeon general's report about the impact of abortion on women. At last, the conservatives thought, Koop would come through. After all, he had spent most of his medical career saving the lives of those babies people might reasonably want to abort. He is strongly anti-abortion.

Koop, upon given the assignment, prepared this report like he did the AIDS report. He researched. He listened. He thought about it. This was his conclusion: There was not sufficient material to write anything that could not be picked apart by the scientific community. There was nothing good enough to deserve the imprimatur of a surgeon general's report.

Outrage again. The Conservative Caucus called Koop a moral wimp. One of the bottom lines was that Bush accepted Koop's resignation when the new administration took over.

Koop said that not only was the data thin, but that the women he had talked to about abortions gave him different views. Some said that it was the worst thing that ever happened to them; others said that it was the best thing. Conservatives, Koop explained, were only interested in listening to those who had bad experiences. I was surgeon general, he said, of the other women, too.

After reading about him, it is unclear if I would get along with him. One whole wall of his office, for example, is filled with pictures of himself. I certainly do not share many of his privately held beliefs.

But that has never been the point. Politically, he is in my highest category. He stood up and said and did exactly what he thought was right for the people he served. He said that his job was to be "America's family doctor," but if you look carefully he was more than that. He turned out to be one of America's premier political actors of his time.

# chapter 8

# Politics as Loneliness and Pressure (Or, What Holds America Together?)

*How else do things work always unless by imitation bred of the passion to be liked? All the processes of society are based on it, all individual development. For some reason, it was something that we seemed to have a conspiracy to ignore or not to mention, even while most single-mindedly engaged in it. There was some sort of conspiracy of belief that people—children, adults, everyone—grew by an acquisition of unconnected habits, of isolated bits of knowledge, like choosing things off a counter: "Yes, I'll have that one," or "No, I don't want that one!" But in fact people develop for good or for bad by swallowing whole other people, atmospheres, events, places—develop by admiration. Often enough unconsciously, of course. We are the company we keep.*

*— Doris Lessing*

*One of the guarantees of freedom in a planned society will be the maintenance of the individual capacity for adjustment.*

*— Karl Mannheim*

We are all here. All together in the same country, products of more or less the same culture. We are mass-produced Americans. The nation in which we live is seemingly vital. Like a huge machine or a giant hungry animal, it continues to produce and grow, grow and produce.

But what does that really mean? What does it mean to be a part of America, to be American? More specifically, what holds the machine together? Why doesn't it fall apart? Why does it cohere; what is the glue that holds us as parts of the system, and in turn holds the system together?

To begin to answer these questions—even to get wrong answers—there are several steps we must take. The punch line of this chapter will be the suggestion that, just possibly, the system is held together at our expense. That by sacrificing some of our rights and powers, the system continues to run. To get to that point, however, it is first necessary to understand more about what a system is and is not, and what that has to do with politics and with people.

## Systems

The system. Just what is The System? What is a system? It's an old idea with some new meanings. We use the term for almost everything, so it doesn't mean much of anything. For the last four hundred years it has described things people have been interested in. Lately, it has become a word to describe us.

Remember this: A system is an idea. It is a way of thinking about how things, people, anything, fit together. It is a useful idea when we want to pay attention to certain kinds of connections.

The important parts of a system are easy enough to describe. A system has a boundary that separates what's inside the system from what's outside the system. It has some kind of communication network, some way of holding the parts together. It has inputs, processes for working on and changing those inputs, and finally it has outputs.

Systems have purposes, and even goals. People who use the idea of systems to understand politics emphasize the need of systems to grow and survive.[1]

---

1    The classic statement of systems analysis is to be found in David Easton, *The Political System* (New York: Knopf, 1953).

We have a system in the United States; more precisely, we know that parts of our society can be understood in terms that describe a system. It seems equally obvious that what we call the political system cannot be separated from most social and economic goings-on. Social scientists tell us that a political system must have methods of formulating issues, deliberating them, resolving them, and finally finding solutions for them. What they do not tell us is that most issues are political ones and that many are "resolved" in less than open, political ways.

In other words, the system may work well in its own terms. It may stay together, function normally and smoothly, yet never really be a "political" system. The high school as an institution is a political system in which the students are rarely given a political voice. The "experts" within the system decide the important questions: the teachers, the principal, even the school board. Students are simply an "input" into the system. At the end of a few years, the students leave school, thereby becoming "outputs" of the system. In systemic terms, nothing has basically changed. The only thing that has really been affected is the student, who has been exposed to what it means to be a "citizen" of the system. It will not come as a big surprise to learn that college is not very different. There appears to be more freedom, and maybe there actually is. There should be, because by the time a person has spent thirteen years in public schools, his or her imagination should be sufficiently limited so that he or she can be trusted with a small increment of freedom. In systemic terms, a functional output is one that will continue to support the system. It is clear that our educational system, in spite of signs encouraging to some, continues to produce functional outputs.

While the school system enables us to understand more about systems in general, it does not help enough. One of the critical deficiencies of systems analysis is that it is blind to both change and values; it cannot really tell us about ourselves and can tell us only a very little about our surroundings. A systems analysis seems to assume that whatever is functional is good and that whatever is dysfunctional is bad; but to know that is to remain completely uninformed about the nature of either good or bad. It is simply to know what makes a system stable, to know what might affect the status quo. We must know more than that. What we are most interested in is what the system means to us; how, essentially, the system holds itself together, with us in it. One way to begin to understand what our system does is by studying what it does not do. More accurately, we can begin by discovering what is not included in the system.

From James Madison, writing in *Federalist* No. 10, we learned that ours was a rational system, one that was set up to run almost in spite of people. Power was separated, balanced, federated, and, some believe, pluralized. What about the relationship among politics and the people and the state? To get at those questions, we may begin by asking these:

1. Do we have any idea of what it means to have a political community?
2. Do we have any idea of political obligation?

## Community

> ... *suburbanites who philosophize over their back fence with complete sincerity about their "dog-eat-dog world," and what-is-it-all-for, and you-can't-take-it-with-you, and success-doesn't-make-you-happy-it-just-gives-you-ulcers-and-a-heart-condition would be enraged should their children pay serious attention to such a viewpoint ...*
>
> *We seek a private house, a private means of transportation, a private garden, a private laundry, self-service stores, and do-it-yourself skills of every kind.*
>
> — *Philip Slater*

It is possible to relate to some of the concepts of a "political system" simply because we are surrounded by its words. "Community" is different. The idea of a system and the idea of a community are very different. Different in almost every way, from the way each is set up to the way it feels to live in one.[2] Let us begin with how each is created.

There are several theories about how governments, or political entities,

---

2  For analysis of the difference between community and what we now have in America, see Robert Nisbet, *Community and Power* (New York: Oxford University Press, 1962). Another approach to the problem can be found in Perry Miller's brilliant book on the Puritans, *Errand into the Wilderness* (New York: Harper & Row, 1958).

are created. For example, there are those who believe that God chooses someone to rule: hence, a divine right provides legitimacy to the leader, to kings and queens and such.

Our tradition does not recognize divine right. In a society infatuated with law, it is no mistake that we believe that governments are founded by contracts, by people banding together and agreeing to the conditions under which the state will function. For our purposes, there are at least two ways in which this contract can be drawn up. The first way is for all of the people individually to give their support to one source, for each person to make his or her own pledge and to have his or her private compact. This kind of contract leads to a "political system" as we know it. There is no community, for everyone operates solely as an individual; no politics, for each has his or her own private interests; no power other than that of the state, for everyone is isolated. As we shall see, this is the contract of individualism.

The second kind of contract binds each to the other. Each citizen becomes responsible for every other citizen. The bonds among people are personal, visible ones. Identity comes from membership and participation in the actions of the community. Decisions are reached communally and openly and, hopefully, for the good of those concerned. Power resides in the group, in the many. In theory, power is held by all, in common.

Ours is a political system, not a political community; ours is a society created by 280,000,000 single contracts, pledging support to an impersonal system. As we shall see, the illusion is individualism, the reality political isolation; the hope is equality, the truth much different.

In place of community in America, we have interests. Of course, interests may be greater than any single individual, but interests are not communities. Our interests are private. Further, our interests are either social or economic, and in America these are generally the same.

We serve our interests because we are on the make, not because there is a better vision of the world. The calculus is precise: We are driven into the public realm only to the extent that we must protect our private interests. Our business is predominantly private, very often selfish, and has the long-run effect of leaving us isolated. By substituting the idea of interest politics for political community, we have put business in the place of brotherhood. Of course, we have good friends, and some of us even have an idea of what a nice neighborhood is, but these are difficult to achieve. If they exist, they exist in spite of, surely not because of, our system. These things speak more to the urges of people than to the dynamics of the process.

Interest politics is a popular (and rightfully so) subject in books about American politics. We are well acquainted with the argument that private interest groups—pressure groups—often exercise a great deal of influence on national, state, and local policy.[3] We also know that the most effective of these groups are generally well organized, wealthy, and white. What I would like to argue is that the system is set up to reward these groups, while teaching that we are each an individual, each with a contract with the state, each equal in power—or powerlessness. The reality of most private interests and of politics based on them is privatization. Privatization is not a bad thing, if one does not care about those major decisions that affect one's life.

## Have We Any Idea of Political Obligation?

Do we really have any political obligations? Does the system encourage us to be political? Some things seem clear. It appears that we have a war obligation to the state. We must also assume a tax burden. There is pressure to vote—but little pressure to understand what that means. After all, voting has come to mean that apolitical act we go through from time to time to choose a person already selected by the system to serve the purposes of that system. We seem to have a greater obligation to the system than to the body politic, to the private sphere than to the public, to the anonymous than to the known. In an important sense, the essence of our political obligation is simple: We are taught that one should not talk about income, religion, or politics in polite company.

One argument is that people being political may hold the system together. In its most simple form, the logic is this: If privatization makes us vulnerable by way of powerlessness, then politics—openness and publicness—is the solution. But instinctively we know that a true plurality of

---

3   For a fine treatment of interest-group politics, see Grant McConnell, *Private Power and American Democracy* (New York: Knopf, 1966). A further discussion of interest groups is found in this book, chapter 10.

interests would be unpredictable. We know that when presented in a public, political way, plurality looks like chaos, and chaos is dysfunctional to a willful, self-protective system. The combinations of isolation and representation, individualism and Madisonian liberalism, seem to pull us further and further away from any positive, healthy sense of the political. It pushes us toward behavior that is best understood as systemically functional.

I am not arguing that the potential for politics has never existed in America. Just the opposite: The sense that politics was a way in which the individual could interact with the many and ensure personal freedom and individualism was expressed most clearly during the 1830s by a Frenchman named Alexis de Tocqueville. Tocqueville, an Old World aristocrat, well understood the tensions between liberty and equality, between individualism and isolation, and believed that the best way to guard against the triumph of equality/isolation was through politics. In *Democracy in America,* we can find an analysis of the potential problems and solutions in the then new democratic state of America.

The following passage is from the first volume of his two-volume work. It describes, in Tocqueville's terms, "Political Associations in the United States":

> In no country in the world has the principle of association been more successfully used or applied to a greater multitude of objects than in America. Besides the permanent associations, which are established by law under the names of townships, cities, and counties, a vast number of others are formed and maintained by the agency of private individuals.
>
> The citizen of the United States is taught from infancy to rely upon his own exertions in order to resist the evils and the difficulties of life; he looks upon the social authority with an eye of mistrust and anxiety, and he claims its assistance only when he is unable to do without it. This habit may be traced even in the schools, where the children in their games are wont to submit to rules that they have themselves established, and to punish misdemeanors, which they have themselves defined. The same spirit pervades every act of social life. If a stoppage occurs in a thoroughfare and the circulation of ve-

hicles is hindered, the neighbors immediately form themselves into a deliberative body; and this extemporaneous assembly gives rise to an executive power which remedies the inconvenience before anybody has thought of recurring to a pre-existing authority superior to that of the persons immediately concerned. If some public pleasure is concerned, an association is formed to give more splendor and regularity to the entertainment. Societies are formed to resist evils that are exclusively of a moral nature, as to diminish the vice of intemperance. In the United States associations are established to promote the public safety, commerce, industry, morality, and religion. There is no end, which the human will despairs of attaining through the combined power of individuals united into a society.

I shall have occasion hereafter to show the effects of association in civil life; I confine myself for the present to the political world. When once the right of association is recognized, the citizens may use it in different ways.

An association consists simply in the public assent, which a number of individuals give to certain doctrines, and in the engagement, which they contract to promote in a certain manner the spread of those doctrines. The right of associating in this fashion almost merges with freedom of the press, but societies thus formed possess more authority than the press. When an opinion is represented by a society, it necessarily assumes a more exact and explicit form. It numbers its partisans and engages them in its cause; they, on the other hand, become acquainted with one another, and their zeal is increased by their number. An association unites into one channel the efforts of divergent minds and urges them vigorously towards the one end that it clearly points out.

The second degree in the exercise of the right of association is the power of meeting. When an association is allowed to establish centers of action at certain important points in the country, its activity is increased and its influence extended. Men have the opportunity of seeing one another; means of execution are combined; and opinions are maintained with a warmth and energy that written language can never attain.

Lastly, in the exercise of the right of political association there is a third degree: the partisans of an opinion may unite in electoral bodies and choose delegates to represent them in a central assembly. This is, properly speaking, the application of the representative system to a party.

Thus, in the first instance, a society is formed between individuals professing the same opinion, and the tie that keeps it together is of a purely intellectual nature. In the second case, small assemblies are formed, which represent only a fraction of the party. Lastly, in the third case, they constitute, as it were, a separate nation in the midst of the nation, a government within the government. Their delegates, like the real delegates of the majority, represent the whole collective force of their party, and like them, also, have an appearance of nationality and all the moral power that results from it. It is true that they have not the right, like the others, of making the laws; but they have the power of attacking those that are in force and of drawing up beforehand those that ought to be enacted.

If, among a people who are imperfectly accustomed to the exercise of freedom, or are exposed to violent political passions, by the side of the majority which makes the laws is placed a minority which only deliberates and gets laws ready for adoption, I cannot but believe that public tranquility would there incur very great risks. There is doubtless a wide difference between proving that one law is in itself better than another and proving that the former ought to be substituted for the latter. But the imagination of the multitude is very apt to overlook this difference, which is so apparent to the minds of thinking men. It sometimes happens that a nation is divided into two nearly equal parties, each of which affects to represent the majority. If, near the directing power, another power is established which exercises almost as much moral authority as the former, we are not to believe that it will long be content to speak without acting; or that it will always be restrained by the abstract consideration that associations are meant to direct opinions, but not to enforce them, to suggest but not to make the laws.

The more I consider the independence of the press in its principal consequences, the more am I convinced that in the modern world it is the chief and, so to speak, the constitutive element of liberty. A nation that is determined to remain free is therefore right in demanding, at any price, the exercise of this independence. But the *unlimited* liberty of political association cannot be entirely assimilated to the liberty of the press. The one is at the same time less necessary and more dangerous than the other. A nation may confine it within certain limits without forfeiting any part of its self-directing power; and it may sometimes be obliged to do so in order to maintain its own authority.

In America the liberty of association for political purposes is unlimited. An example will show in the clearest light to what an extent this privilege is tolerated ...

In 1831, when the tariff dispute was raging with the greatest violence, a private citizen of Massachusetts proposed, by means of the newspapers, to all the enemies of the tariff to send delegates to Philadelphia in order to consult together upon the best means of restoring freedom of trade. This proposal circulated in a few days, by the power of the press, from Maine to New Orleans. The opponents of the tariff adopted it with enthusiasm; meetings were held in all quarters, and delegates were appointed. The majority of these delegates were well known, and some of them had earned a considerable degree of celebrity. South Carolina alone, which afterwards took up arms in the same cause, sent sixty-three delegates. On the first of October 1831 this assembly, which, according to the American custom, had taken the name of a Convention, met at Philadelphia; it consisted, of more than two hundred members. Its debates were public, and they at once assumed a legislative character; the extent of the powers of Congress, the theories of free trade, and the different provisions of the tariff were discussed. At the end of ten days the Convention broke up, having drawn up an address to the American people in which it declared: (1) that Congress had not the right of making a tariff, and that the existing tariff was unconstitutional; (2) that the prohibition of free trade was prejudicial to the interests of any nation, and to those of the American people especially.

It must be acknowledged that the unrestrained liberty of political association has not hitherto produced in the United States the fatal results that might perhaps be expected from it elsewhere. The right of association was imported from England, and it has always existed in America; the exercise of this privilege is, now incorporated with the manners and customs of the people. At the present time the liberty of association has become a necessary guarantee against the tyranny of the majority. In the United States, as soon as a party has become dominant, all public authority passes into its hands; its private supporters occupy all the offices and have all the force of the administration at their disposal. As the most distinguished members of the opposite party cannot surmount the barrier that excludes them from power, they must establish themselves outside of it and oppose the whole moral authority of the minority to the physical power that domineers over it. Thus a dangerous expedient is used to obviate a still more formidable danger.

The omnipotence of the majority appears to me to be so full of peril to the American republics that dangerous means used to bridle it seem to be more advantageous than prejudicial. And here I will express an opinion that may remind the reader of what I said when speaking of the freedom of townships. *There are no countries in which associations are more needed to prevent the despotism of faction or the arbitrary power of a prince than those which are democratically constituted.*[4] In aristocratic nations the body of the nobles and the wealthy are in themselves natural associations that check the abuses of power. In countries where such associations do not exist, if private individuals cannot create an artificial and temporary substitute for them I can see no permanent protection against the most galling tyranny; and a great people may be oppressed with impunity by a small faction or by a single individual.

The meeting of a great political convention (for there are conventions of all kinds), which may frequently become a necessary measure, is always a serious occurrence, even in America, and one that judicious patriots cannot regard without alarm. This was very perceptible in the Convention of 1831, at which all the most distinguished members strove to moderate its language and to restrain its

4  Emphasis added.

objects within certain limits. It is probable that this Convention exercised a great influence on the minds of the malcontents and prepared them for the open revolt against the commercial laws of the Union that took place in 1832.

It cannot be denied that the unrestrained liberty of association for political purposes is the privilege, which a people is longest in learning how to exercise. If it does not throw the nation into anarchy, it perpetually augments the chances of that calamity. On one point, however, this perilous liberty offers a security against dangers of another kind; in countries where associations are free, secret societies are unknown. In America there are factions, but no conspiracies.

The most natural privilege of man, next to the right of acting for himself, is that of combining his exertions with those of his fellow creatures and of acting in common with them. The right of association therefore appears to me almost as inalienable in its nature as the right of personal property. No legislator can attack it without impairing the foundations of society. Nevertheless, if the liberty of association is only a source of advantage and prosperity to some nations, it may be perverted or carried to excess by others, and from an element of life may be changed into a cause of destruction. A comparison of the different methods that associations pursue in those countries in which liberty is well understood and in those where liberty degenerates into license may be useful both to governments and to parties.

Most Europeans look upon association as a weapon, which is to be hastily fashioned and immediately tried in the conflict. A society is formed for discussion, but the idea of impending action prevails in the minds of all those who constitute it. It is, in fact, an army; and the time given to speech serves to reckon up the strength and to animate the courage of the host, after which they march against the enemy. To the persons who compose it, resources, which lie within the bounds of law, may suggest themselves as means of success, but never as the only means.

Such, however, is not the manner in which the right of association is understood in the United States. In America the citizens who form the minority associate in order, first, to show their numerical strength and so to diminish the moral power of the majority; and, secondly, to stimulate competition and thus to discover those arguments that are most fitted to act upon the majority; for they always entertain hopes of drawing over the majority to their own side, and then controlling the supreme power in its name. Political associations in the United States are therefore peaceable in their intentions and strictly legal in the means, which they employ; and they assert with perfect truth that they aim at success only by lawful expedients.[5]

Tocqueville gives us a vision of what he believes should be an idea of politics, a form of association that would not only protect individuals from tyranny but also actively involve them in the making of decisions. It is the poetry of our democracy; it is the image of what we have never become.

To return to one of our central questions: If we are to use Tocqueville as a model, it becomes clear that our system is not being held together by the kinds of creative political activities he describes. This is true, in part, because the ideology of the system encourages neither political community nor political obligation.

## Things and Symbolism: What Does Hold Us Together?

> *The truth isn't news, and the news isn't true.*
> — *Jon Winters*

To know that politics does not hold us together gets us just so far. It gives us one less thing to worry about—we can check it off our list—and it gives us something to aim for. But the point is we still don't know what holds us together. We might get closer to an answer by trying to understand what seems to be really important, what we seem to believe, and how that affects staying together. Maybe material objects hold the system together. It is possible, if one were cynical enough, to argue that in this land of electric can openers and vibrating beds, possessions are far more important than

5   Alexis de Tocqueville, *Democracy in America,* Vol. 1 (New York: Vintage, 1945), pp. 198–206.

politics. Houses and cars and big bikes and boats really do count. People work very hard to be able to buy and to own. In the end, we may have to conclude that "things" hold us together, tie us to the system, and ensure the status quo.

Of course, built into our technology are amazing social values. I have two things for you to consider. The first is the "call-waiting" service provided by the phone company—the little thing that, while you are talking on the phone, tells you that someone else is calling. It clicks in, intrudes on your conversation, and lets you know that you have another option.

What does it mean when you are talking to someone who is "clicked" and who answers the clicker? What goes through everybody's head? Who knows? Oh, says one person. Another call. Maybe it will make me rich and famous. Maybe it's Mr. or Ms. Wonderful. Maybe, maybe, maybe. Oh, says the other person. I am second best to whoever clicks into this conversation. It could be anybody, and I'm stuck, holding a dead phone. It might even be worse than never having talked in the first place.

Clickers, then, are an amazing social invention. They feed on fantasy (the ideal of the perfect call), and feed into the isolation that a phone caller might be trying to get rid of.

The other invention, less intrusive, has to do with television sets that let you see more than one channel at a time. Now that's amazing. You can get a big picture and at the same time a little picture in the top corner. More is better. Got to have it all and see it all. Just look at that.

One of the results is that you can never see one thing well. The old symbolic "big picture" is literally eaten away by the litter of little pictures. For a fast-moving, kind of sloppy society, this multiple-image television is all too perfect. The viewer can be a seer of all and master of none.

There are other equally important products of the system. There is the violence of television sports or the gooey-ness of the ice cream from the local parlor. Somehow, these things are important. We do identify. Maybe it is ice cream that holds us together. Sweet and sticky, available and fattening: Prisoners of Ice Cream.

But the ice cream image can easily be strained and overemphasized: While true, its truth is not inclusive enough. Besides, ice cream either has too many calories, or has too much cholesterol, or both, or tastes funny because it's made with strange stuff. No, we have to try something else.

What about television?

In a discussion of what holds us together, how could we not talk a little about television? It forms the core of much—probably way too much—of what we now have in common. We experience national events together in an odd way. If something important happens (the Super Bowl, a national election, the shooting of a president, the collapse of the Twin Towers, a war on the other side of the world), we can all be expected to go home, watch television, and "experience" it.

We know that watching something, that being an observer, and not actually being at the event puts us in an interesting position. We can see only through a mechanical eye, we can hear only a mechanical voice, and we are at the will of technicians who aim those eyes and ears.

As a nation, we are both tied together and passive. In the old days, it took months for news to travel from one part of the country to another. We would never stand for that today. We want to know now, and to be done with it.

But to talk about the "main events" of our national life is to miss the point of our electronic ties. It is important to remember our faithfulness. How religiously we watch our favorite soaps, our favorite prime-time fantasies, our favorite games. The truth is, in an everyday way, our schedules are held together, in part, by television programming. *The Osbournes* is a specific event for millions. Doesn't that qualify for holding us together?

If ice cream has the drawback of calories, heart attacks, and potential pimples, then television may be even more dangerous for our public health. The passive part of television probably dominates everything else. Never mind the violence, the giveaway/survivor shows, and the general moronic level of much that is shown. Think about what happens when you watch television.

You have choices: You can stand, sit, or lie down. If you are serious, you will not stand. You can eat, or drink, or smoke, or none of those things. I guess you can knit, if you do not have to watch what you are doing. Put a little differently, there is nothing you can do with another human being.

The television set receives the picture and sound and transmits it to you. You are the true receiver. You look and listen. You absorb.

Nothing is left to your imagination. If you simply listen to music, your imagination is free to fantasize. If you simply listen to music, you are free to associate it with whatever is going on. If you *watch* music (for example, MTV), then you are tied to what you receive.

So we are receivers. We are tied together not so much in the particulars of what is shown as much as in the specific way we have given up social activities for passive ones.

There is one other way to learn about the system that I want to present. By discussing words, and understanding some of our language, we can see another way in which the system is held together.

## The Use of Words

> *To know the reality of politics, we have to believe the myth, to believe what we are told as children.*
> — *Norman O. Brown*

We all know that systems are dependent, in part, upon the use of a common political language. Common language carries common myths. These words, these myths, are crucially important for any system—for any set of related institutions—since they provide the subtlest, most economical method of self-maintenance. It is critical for the government to set societal rules through language, through the words it uses, in order to keep order.[6]

As a simple example, we are taught that we have a representative democracy. Those are the words used; they frame our ideas of what is. It takes little insight to know that what we have is only marginally related to representation and that it has even less in common with democracy. The words only represent our official institutional myth. They are part of the symbols that work well to keep the system going. What I should like to argue is that much of our symbolic glue works at our personal expense, at the expense of the citizenry. If we examine two more myth-laden words, perhaps that thought will be clarified. The two words *equality* and *justice* are as familiar as they are misunderstood, as

6 Words? George Carlin gives us the clue to "Our Creator." Think about it: Carlin tells us that God had his/her choice of *any* name and took the very best one.

they are systemically effective. Because they are words that are so common, words that we seem to understand implicitly, it is important to try to figure out their implications.

As we know, the Constitution was written as if all men (to be sure, white Protestant, propertied men—the framers did mean *men*) were equal. What that was to mean, what we have understood it to mean, is that no individual was entitled to more rights than another. Each person—in the public realm—was to be treated equally by the system of rules to which all were equally subject. It is difficult to fault such a formulation. Equal is equal.

Justice came to mean equality of rights and equality of treatment. Moreover, justice was equated with fairness. A just or a fair decision was one that had no objective standard of reason or justice, or even passion; it merely meant a decision lacking bias. Again the formulation is a standard, everyday definition of what we feel/know to be true. What we must do now is to put the two words together.

By merging the myths of justice and equality, the system is able to overlook many kinds of inequalities. In the process, the system helps protect itself. It works in a simple enough manner: In our alikeness, we become alone. A "fair trial" can overlook the money, connections, color, and cultural background of the defendant. We all become bleached white; we all look the same—each alone, each the same, no matter what. Justice comes to mean the equality of everyone, equal or not. When we try to band together to work out our public problems, whether we become Black Panthers or militant PTA'ers, we learn that equal rights and equal treatment mean simply this: equal dependence and equal subjection.

Let me put it a little differently: To put equality together with justice, yet ignore such things as politics, community, and culture, results not in interesting kinds of individualism but in mass conformity.[7] What I have been suggesting is that the system is held together—and this may seem a paradox—by the very fact that each of us is alone. The system coheres—and coerces—because the one has no defense against the mass. Even

---

7   In a sense, this is the logical extension of the public–private problem of liberalism that was discussed earlier in connection with bureaucracies. The point here is that private advantage is often overlooked in public alikeness.

though it can be demonstrated that some people control much more wealth than others, that some make much more wide-ranging decisions than others, the fact remains that people don't think of America or of themselves in very meaningful class terms. The point is that those who hold "real power" are well limited by the boundaries of the system. (Indeed, one wonders if power is worth the price paid to get it.) It is the unique, the challenging—in a word, the *political*—that is mistrusted. The "real power" is the power of the guardian, and the guardian is as limited in creative political terms as those he or she "watches over." The powerful and the powerless are equally susceptible.

Most of us think of ourselves as some variation of middle class; and it is arguable that our imaginations are as limited as our self-definitions. The seeds of our powerlessness lie in the isolation of being the same. We turn again to the writings of Alexis de Tocqueville to understand the problem he identifies as the "Tyranny of the Majority."

> A distinction must be drawn between tyranny and arbitrary power. Tyranny may be exercised by means of the law itself, and in that case it is not arbitrary; arbitrary power may be exercised for the public good, in which case it is not tyrannical. Tyranny usually employs arbitrary means, but if necessary it can do without them …
>
> In general, the American functionaries are far more independent within the sphere that is prescribed to them than the French civil officers. Sometimes, even, they are allowed by the popular authority to exceed those bounds; and as they are protected by the opinion and backed by the power of the majority, they dare do things that even a European, accustomed as he is to arbitrary power, is astonished at. By this means habits are formed in the heart of a free country that may some day prove fatal to its liberties.
>
> It is in the examination of the exercise of thought in the United States that we clearly perceive how far the power of the majority surpasses all the powers with which we are acquainted in Europe. Thought is an invisible and subtle power that mocks all the efforts of tyranny. At the present time the most absolute monarchs in Europe cannot prevent certain opinions hostile to their authority from circulating in secret through their dominions and even in their courts. It

is not so in America; as long as the majority is still undecided, discussion is carried on; but as soon as its decision is irrevocably pronounced, everyone is silent, and the friends as well as the opponents of the measure unite in assenting to its propriety. The reason for this is perfectly clear: no monarch is so absolute as to combine all the powers of society in his own hands and to conquer all opposition, as a majority is able to do, which has the right both of making and of executing the laws.

The authority of a king is physical and controls the actions of men without subduing their will. But the majority possesses a power that is physical and moral at the same time, which acts upon the will as much as upon the actions and represses not only all contest, but also all controversy.

*I know of no country in which there is so little independence of mind and real freedom of discussion as in America.*[8] In any constitutional state in Europe every sort of religious and political theory may be freely preached and disseminated; for there is no country in Europe so subdued by any single authority as not to protect the man who raises his voice in the cause of truth from the consequences of his hardihood. If he is unfortunate enough to live under an absolute government, the people are often on his side; if he inhabits a free country, he can, if necessary, find a shelter behind the throne. The aristocratic part of society supports him in some countries, and the democracy in others. But in a nation where democratic institutions exist, organized like those of the United States, there is but one authority, one element of strength and success, with nothing beyond it.

In America the majority raises formidable barriers around the liberty of opinion; within these barriers an author may write what he pleases, but woe to him if he goes beyond them. Not that he is in danger of an auto-da-fé, but he is exposed to continued obloquy and persecution. His political career is closed forever, since he has offended the only authority that is able to open it. Every sort of compensation, even that of celebrity is refused to him. Before making public his

8  Emphasis added.

opinions he thought he had sympathizers; now it seems to him that he has none any more since he has revealed himself to everyone; then those who blame him criticize loudly and those who think as he does keep quiet and move away without courage. He yields at length, overcome by the daily effort which he has to make, and subsides into silence, as if he felt remorse for having spoken the truth.

Fetters and beadsmen were the coarse instruments that tyranny formerly employed; but the civilization of our age has perfected despotism itself, though it seemed to have nothing to learn. Monarchs had, so to speak, materialized oppression; the Democratic republics of the present day have rendered it as entirely an affair of the mind as the will, which it is intended to coerce. Under the absolute sway of one man the body was attacked in order to subdue the soul; but the soul escaped the blows, which were directed against it and rose proudly superior. Such is not the course adopted by tyranny in democratic republics; there the body is left free, and the soul is enslaved. The master no longer says: "You shall think as I do or you shall die"; but he says: "You are free to think differently from me and to retain your life, your property, and all that you possess, but you are henceforth a stranger among your people. You may retain your civil rights, but they will be useless to you, for you will never be chosen by your fellow citizens if you solicit their votes; and they will affect to scorn you if you ask for their esteem. You will remain among men, but you will be deprived of the rights of mankind. Your fellow creatures will shun you like an impure being; and even those who believe in your innocence will abandon you, lest they should be shunned in their turn. Go in peace! I have given you your life, but it is an existence worse than death."[9]

---

9   Tocqueville, *Democracy in America*, Vol. 1, pp. 269–72.

## Uniformity and Individualism: The Politics of Our Very Own Tyranny

*Imagine a mass of cancerous tissue, the cells of which enjoyed consciousness. Would they not be full of self-congratulatory sentiments at their independence, their more advanced level of development, their rapid rate of growth? Would they not sneer at their more primitive cousins who were bound into a static and unfree existence, with limited aspirations, subject to heavy group constraint, and obviously "going nowhere"? Would they not rejoice in their control over their own destiny, and cheer the conversion of more and more normal cells as convincing proof of the validity of their own way of life? Would they not, in fact, feel increasingly triumphant right up to the moment the organism on which they fed expired?*

*— Philip Slater*

To understand how the system is held together, it may help to think of a huge machine. The machine, when healthy, seems almost organic. Looking inside the machine, one could see the hundreds of thousands of political associations Tocqueville described in the first reading in this chapter. While there could be no single "rational" plan of action for that kind of system, neither could there be an ongoing tyranny of the individual by the many.

Now imagine the same machine sick. Indeed, imagine those political associations gone, the insides of the system rotted. The system is then dependent not upon the politics of the citizens but upon the strength of the state, the oppressiveness of the cover of the machine. As the inside weakens, the outside gets strong. As the population becomes isolated, the force of the state goes unchallenged. As we become less interested in joint action, in politics, we become more susceptible to oppression.

The tyranny of the majority, the terrible conformity and confinement of which Tocqueville warns, is as important as it is obvious. Each of us is, at one and the same time, both the tyrannized and the majority. Our instincts drive us into private life, while the majority determines our choices in that life. It may be instructive to anticipate that discussion here.

When I was growing up, there were four of us in the family. The usual assortment: a mother, father, older sister, and myself. One day my sister (I think she was maybe fourteen or fifteen) brought home the fifth member of the family. We took in They Say.

You know They Say. "Why do you have to do that?" "Well, They Say," or, "Is it really important that you do that?" "Well, They Say." or, "How do you know that?" "Well, They Say."

Put differently, we can name—can actually see—the pressure of the faceless majority that comes right into our homes. That majority can walk right in and be a faceless power and force in how we think and act. The tyranny of the majority is as real as They Say, and carries the weight of all those around us.

What is so magical is that everyone seems at the mercy of They Say. Equally true, it always seems that everyone else is a member of They. It comes to this: The power of being part of the They does us no good, while being at the mercy of the They all too often hurts.

## Nationalization of They Say?

I'd have probably been happier had They Say stayed away. As individuals, we like to believe that there are a series of choices—important ones—we will have the opportunity to make. We fret not only over the make of the automobile we are going to buy but also over its color. In weaker, less guarded moments, we realize that these decisions are not really critical ones; indeed, they are not even important. These insights rarely mean that we will stop worrying over such matters of consumption. To review the chapter on voting is to begin to understand that doing things alone does not necessarily lead to individualism, and that doing things in association does not automatically eliminate it.

Symbolically, voting is American democracy at its height, the apex of political participation: The common person, spending a few minutes every two or four years, alone in a small booth, choosing between two individuals who were selected by people he or she does not know, to make decisions that individual should be able to participate in. Behavior is our substitute for action, psychic satisfaction our substitute for power.

Our concerns are those of the majority, those the system prescribes for us. When we make a choice, and then take an action, we generally do it alone. Our choice is the same others make, our behavior the same as theirs, too, but somehow we convince ourselves that it is unique and that we are individuals. Philip Slater describes the phenomenon thus:

> When a value is as strongly held as is individualism in America the illnesses it produces tend to be treated by increasing the dosage, in the same way an alcoholic treats a hangover or a drug addict ... withdrawal symptoms ... The desire to be somehow special inaugurates an even more competitive quest for progressively more rare and expensive symbols—a quest that is ultimately futile since it is individualism itself that produces uniformity. This is poorly understood by Americans who tend to confuse uniformity with "conformity," in the sense of compliance with or submission to group demands. Many societies exert far more pressure on the individual to mold himself to fit a particularized segment of a total group pattern, but there is variation among those circumscribed roles. Our society gives far more leeway to the individual to pursue his own ends, but since it defines what is worthy and desirable everyone tends, independently but monotonously, to pursue the same things in the same way. The first pattern combines cooperation, conformity, and variety, the second, competition, individualism, and uniformity.[10]

One must agree that there is irony in the great traffic jams that occur when hundreds of thousands of vacationers all leave for home early in order to "beat the traffic."

Maybe the system is held together—and continues to function in lockstep precision—because of the symbolic value we give to, and what we ironically call, individualism.

*The more peaceful a community has become, the more cowardly the citizens become; the less accustomed they are to standing pain,*

10  Philip E. Slater, *The Pursuit of Loneliness* (Boston: Beacon, 1971), pp. 7, 8–9.

*the more will worldly punishments suffice as deterrents, the faster will religious threats become superfluous ... In highly civilized peoples, finally, even punishments should become highly superfluous deterrents; the mere fear of shame, the trembling of vanity, is so continually effective that immoral actions are left undone. The refinement of morality increases together with the refinement of fear. Today the fear of disagreeable feelings in other people is almost the strongest of our own disagreeable feelings. One would like ever so much to live in such a way as to do nothing except what causes others agreeable feelings, and even to take pleasure in nothing more that does not also fulfill this condition.*

—*Friedrich Nietzsche*

# chapter 9

# Politics and Freedom: Freedom To and Freedom From

Albert Camus writes of the myth of Sisyphus, a Greek who was condemned by the gods to push a giant rock to the top of a mountain. Once at the top, the rock would roll back to the valley of its own weight, and Sisyphus would walk down and again begin pushing the rock up. The fate of Sisyphus is the ceaseless rolling of the rock up the mountain.

Camus argues that Sisyphus experiences a kind of silent joy. "His fate belongs to him. His rock is his thing." He experiences joy—but not simply when the rock is at the top, when his task is "completed." Camus writes:

> "I leave Sisyphus at the foot of the mountain! One always finds one's burden again. But Sisyphus teaches the higher fidelity that negates the gods and raises rocks. He too concludes that all is well. This universe henceforth without a master seems to him neither sterile nor futile. Each atom of that stone, each mineral flake of that night-filled mountain, in itself forms a world. The struggle itself toward the heights is enough to fill a man's heart.
>
> "One must imagine Sisyphus happy."

*If everyone has the right to express his will ... what does this right mean if their will is merely an echo of the chorus around them?*
— *John Schaar*

## On Freedom

It is a tricky thing to be free, and awfully hard. One would guess that there are a lot of people who want to be free—but surprisingly, there are many who do not. We know that there are many people who think that they are free, and that there are very few people who really are.

In this chapter, we can only begin to understand why there is so much confusion about being free. There will be a short essay, and some explanation, and a few excerpts from literature to help show us how hard it is to arrive at a meaning of freedom. As a topic, it is pretentious. I admit that. But it seems so sloppily defined, so misunderstood, yet so often assumed to be an important part of life that it seems reasonable to spend some time thinking about it.

Out of all of our literature, out of all of American letters, it seems natural to begin with Henry David Thoreau. Maybe he wrote about freedom. Maybe we all want to go to Walden Pond to commune with nature, with the ghost of Thoreau. Or to the mountains or to the ocean or to an island to just be away. To just be free. To do whatever we need to do, alone. Do it by ourselves, to ourselves, and for ourselves.

But is that being free, or is it simply being separated from others, experiencing anomie or being alienated? Thoreau might be a part of the American Dream, but is he truly part of the legacy of freedom?

Get away. Now that is a good idea. Most Americans are impatient types. There has always been a West, and somehow freedom was always there. So, with covered wagons, or iron horses, or some exotic van or bus or camper or God-knows-what, we all move West to get free and get rich. Americans move and move and move.

Those in the East move west. People go from the South to the North, and from small and middle-sized towns to big ones, from big ones to bedroom communities. Some of us even go to villages (now electronic) or even to the country. But we all move. We are restless. We are in search of the perfect place or the perfect job or the perfect neighborhood. We are, in the end, looking for ourselves; we are looking to be free.

We run to any place, going nowhere. Nowhere people living in a nowhere land. Is it really freedom, to move from but never to?

As we go, we waste one place after another. The pattern now seems to be well established. In our restlessness, we buy, destroy, buy and destroy. Our home is only where our investment is. As soon as the river is polluted, or the land is barren and the winds carve out a dust bowl, or all the trees are down and the land will not support even animal life, then we move on. We move west. We move free.

We consume and, in doing so, destroy; then we restlessly move to more consumption and destruction. We do this as a free people, yearning to stay free.

But if we have no freedom in our physical "homes," then are we free in our beliefs? Doesn't it seem logical that we all might believe in the same thing; in other words, that in our similar moral beliefs and actions we could find a kind of freedom?

For example, the Puritans believed that they had a covenant with God and that by working together they could build the New Jerusalem in the New World. It would be a model community that would stand out as a beacon against the depravity they perceived in Europe's Christian community. What I would like to suggest is that in fact the Puritans had a kind of freedom that we no longer possess. That, despite their "Puritanism," they were tied together by a vision of the kind of world they wanted to create.

Can we define our own freedom in any kind of positive terms? Are we truly naive enough to claim that what we call freedom includes the ideas of building or creating? Do we even have any kind of binding belief that might lead us to the freedom that comes from shared visions?

Of course the questions are rhetorical. It seems impossible for us to understand freedom as truly something positive. We have a terrible time trying to distinguish between freedom from (running away) and freedom to. What we need is freedom to; what we have is freedom from. One of the most frustrating things is that something so normal as attending college in order to get a good job may not end up what it appears to be.

The fact seems to be that we work hard, that we move from place to place, looking for Walden Pond, looking to escape. We continually prove our freedom from by running away as fast as we can. We are bound by nothing, tied to no one. And we call the isolation and destruction freedom, and defend it with our very selves.

> *Free men and women never need to be told of their good fortune ...*
> *repressed men and women do not need to be told of their repression.*
> —*Larry Spence*

## The Ideology of Our Letters

> *He slept on the straw with the groom, and memories weighed heavily on his chest; he awakened many times. Scattered and infertile, the scenes of his life stretched out behind him, rich in magnificent images but broken in so many pieces, so poor in value, so poor in love! In the morning, as they rode away, he looked anxiously up to the windows. Perhaps he could catch another glimpse of Julie. A few days ago he had looked just as anxiously up to the windows of the bishop's palace to see if Agnes might not appear. She had not shown herself, and neither did Julie. His whole life had been like that, it seemed to him. Saying farewell, escaping, being forgotten, finding himself alone again, with empty hands and a frozen heart.*
> — *Hermann Hesse*

There are, as indicated above, different ways to think about freedom. In the rest of the chapter, I will discuss, in turn, freedom and how it has been interpreted in American letters, freedom and economics, freedom and psychology, and freedom and politics.

To begin with Thoreau is to begin with the classic statement on being free by being alone. He makes one case all too well: What we must do is to get away; discover ourselves by being alone; find freedom by experiencing nature. Thoreau was a poet, a spokesman for that urge in us that tells us to ignore society and relearn primary associations, and to learn to commune with nature.

Sketching in Thoreau's experience at Walden and understanding some of it in his own words can best make the point of our common past. He was born in 1817 and did what the bright, white sons of New England citizens did in those days: He went to Harvard College. For a time after he graduated, he wrote, opened a private school, and was friendly with people like Ralph Waldo Emerson. He made a little trouble (he was fired as a schoolteacher for refusing to administer discipline) and had problems deciding on a vocation, but he was generally regarded as a promising scholar. On July 4, 1845, Thoreau went to live at Walden Pond. There he kept a journal.[1]

"The real attractions," Thoreau writes of Walden, "were: its complete retirement, being about two miles from the village, half a mile from the nearest neighbor, and separated from the highway by a broad field."

So he is set. In the wilderness, near a town, indeed, only a field away from a highway, but by himself. For what?

"To enjoy these advantages I was ready to carry it on; like Atlas, to take the world on my shoulders—I never heard what compensation he received for that—and do all those things, which had no other motive or excuse but that I might pay for it and be unmolested in my possession of it." That is what he wanted: to enjoy the benefits and to be unmolested. Certainly we understand that. He knew what that meant, and counseled "my fellows, once for all, as long as possible live free and uncommitted."

To examine Thoreau's Walden thoroughly is not the object of these paragraphs. But it would be unfair not to glimpse his "day" at the pond; it would be a loss to miss his perceptions.

> Morning is when I awake and there is a dawn in me ... The millions are awake enough for physical labor; but only one in a million is awake enough for effective intellectual exertion, only one in a hundred millions to a poetic or divine life. To be awake is to be alive. I have never yet met a man who is quite awake.
>
> I went to the woods because I wished to live deliberately, to front not only the essential facts of life, and see if I could not learn what it had to teach, and not, when I came to die, discover that I had not lived. I did not wish to live what was not life ... I wanted to live deep and suck the marrow of life ... to drive life into a corner, and reduce it to its lowest terms ...

1 Henry David Thoreau, *Walden*, ed. Sherman Paul (Boston: Houghton Mifflin, 1960). The following quotations come from the chapter "Where I Lived, and What I Lived For."

Our life is frittered away by detail … simplicity, simplicity, simplicity! I say, let your affairs be as two or three, and not a hundred or a thousand, instead of a million count half a dozen, and keep your accounts on your thumbnail … Simplify, simplify … the nation itself, with all its so-called internal improvements, which, by the way are all external and superficial … If we do not get our sleepers and forge rails, and devote days and nights to the work, but go to tinkering upon our lives to improve them, who will build railroads? And if railroads are not built, how shall we get to heaven in season? If we stay at home and mind our business, who will want railroads? We do not ride on the railroad; it rides upon us.

Of course Henry is right. What American could disagree with that? Just to have two problems, to simplify and to be awake. But, of course, to be only half-awake is at least to be aware that the world has some problems. Are we Americans—or is anyone who has decided to live in a world with anyone else—perhaps too complex simply to be simple? More importantly, at least practically, what do we do if there are not enough ponds to go around?

In other words, Thoreau's powerful experience and equally powerful prose are limited in their helpfulness. We are not much farther along in understanding ourselves in a world full of people. We cannot understand who we are in terms of social or cultural interactions. We are no closer to the idea that freedom might be contained in commitment, or that being free might include something more than ourselves.

## Freedom as a Highway

What remains of the ideology is the quest. The search. The Open Road. What the pioneers helped start and Thoreau romanticized, Walt Whitman described, and D. H. Lawrence analyzed.

In a remarkable essay, D. H. Lawrence took Walt Whitman to task for what Lawrence saw as an empty quest. What follows, in order, is a passage from Whitman's *Song of Myself,* and what Lawrence writes about this noted American poet.

I tramp a perpetual journey, (come listen all!)
My signs are a rainproof coat, good shoes, and a staff cut from
    the woods,
No friend of mine takes his ease in my chair,
I have no chair, no church, no philosophy,
I lead no man to a dinner-table, library, exchange,
But each man and each woman of you I lead upon a knoll,
My left hand hooking you round the waist,
My right hand pointing to landscapes of continents and the
    public road.

Not I, not any one else can travel that road with you,
You must travel it yourself.

Thus Whitman; now Lawrence:

The Open Road. The great home of the Soul is the Open Road. Not heaven, not paradise. Not "above." Not even "within." The soul is neither "above" nor "within." It is a wayfarer down the open road.

Not by meditating. Not by fasting. Not by exploring heaven after heaven, inwardly, in the manner of the great mystics. Not by exaltation. Not by ecstasy. Not by any of these ways does the soul come into her own.

Only by taking the open road. Not through charity. Not through sacrifice. Not even through love. Not through good works. Not through these does the soul accomplish herself.

Only through the journey down the open road.

The journey itself, down the open road. Exposed to full contact. On two slow feet. Meeting whatever comes down the open road. In company with those that drift in the same measure along the same way. Towards no goal. Always the open road. Having no direction even.[2]

2  D. H. Lawrence, *Studies in Classic American Literature* (New York: Viking, 1966). The passage comes from the chapter "Whitman." Larry Spence insisted that the reality of Whitman not be ignored. I am once again indebted to his thoughtfulness.

As you might have noted, I described the Lawrence essay as "remarkable." Notice that I did not say accurate. The fact is that the essay is very well written, very funny, often very insightful, and just as often, very wrong. Most people believe that the part just quoted has everything to do with Lawrence and not very much to do with Whitman.

Whitman, more than most, had a vision of the American people that celebrated the possibility of individualism in an American community. There is a real appreciation of the variety of lives that has made us who we are. The use of Lawrence is really to show, in almost parody form, what he understood to be the urge to run away that is so common among us. That he misused Walt Whitman is a shame.

There are other examples. We can read these words from Henry Miller's *The Air-Conditioned Nightmare:*

> America is made up, as we all know, of people who ran away from such ugly situations. America is the land par excellence of expatriates and escapists, *renegades,* to use a strong word. A wonderful world we might have made of this new continent if we had really run out on our fellow men in Europe, Asia, and Africa. A brave, new world it might have become, had we had the courage to turn our back on the old, to build afresh, to eradicate the poisons which had accumulated through centuries of bitter rivalry, jealousy and strife.

But the desire to keep moving, to be left alone, is just one way to handle freedom. Deep down, it may be the one with which we have most sympathy; it is certainly a most obvious one. It is going to Europe to get away (for one summer); it is traveling cross-country just to count the miles you are away from where you started. At some point, the quest for some thing—for some meaning somewhere—changes into the simple idea of leaving, of getting away, of movement. Whitman is Thoreau on the road. It seems both legitimate and necessary to ask if either gives adequate advice about freedom.

We have already raised problems connected with this approach. But we are not yet ready for an "answer." It would be premature to present a full-scale retort or even to tentatively offer a different approach. There are other ideas, other circumstances and approaches that must be dealt with before we get to politics and freedom.

## Freedom as Material

> *Instead of being primarily concerned over right and wrong, men would learn, while fighting over these issues, that political arithmetic could be substituted for ethics, that they could live more peaceably by a calculus of forces than by the spirit. At the end of the seventeenth century, the medieval synthesis, in which all activities were gradations within a coherent organization of existence, was broken apart. Into this new world of reason and commerce, Virginia was prepared to enter as early as 1624; it was stripped of its medieval notions and was started on the road which led from teleology to competition and expedience, where the decisive factor would be, not the example from the Apostles, but the price per pound of tobacco.*
>
> — *Perry Miller*

There is buried in us—maybe deeply, maybe close to the surface— an idea that somehow freedom is tied to material things. Certainly there are impressive advocates of such a position. The argument is that people who are free from material wants are free from oppression; they are, in fact, free to be themselves. There is little doubt that the advocates of material freedom have a point. It is neither intelligent nor sensible to argue that people are best off when they are hungry, or have no shelter, or are in poor health. That is not what I wish to defend.[3]

I want to argue that we have connected freedom and materialism in extreme ways. That we have probably long since passed the point where we could all be fed and housed and medically treated. Yet we still pursue a material goal. We pursue that goal without realizing its costs.

If the preceding sections about Thoreau and Whitman—ideas about

---

3 For a fine argument that people can be more than their material surroundings, see John Schaar, *Escape from Authority: The Perspectives of Erich Fromm* (New York: Basic Books, 1961). To quote: "Some part of the mystery and grandeur of human beings lies in the fact that they make paintings on the walls of miserable caves and write poetry and philosophy in the midst of hunger and filth."

us—are right, then we should expect to find some evidence somewhere of the pursuit of goods. There should be some evidence in our history that points to a moving toward freedom from the past. Moreover, that moving might have economic overtones.

There is evidence, and it lies right in the middle of one of our nicest, most romantic myths, the myth of the yeoman farmer.

Remember the yeoman farmer? The brave and noble pioneer who moved west to settle the land? To find roots? To be self-sufficient, to be away, to be hard-working, and to be free? Had we just been born in the nineteenth century, then we could have known the land. Then we could have communed with the stuff of our primordial past—with nature."[4]

There is no doubt that the myth of the yeoman farmer stems from the facts. There were those who went west and felt free. There were some small towns where a communal spirit existed; where each person took an interest in the other; and where citizens personally got together and personally helped their neighbors. Rural America, with the Noble Farmer, is a part of our collective past worth remembering—at least in that vision.

The facts about the farmers seem much closer to our assumptions than our myths: They moved a great deal, wanted to be "free," and were interested in the land primarily for the money they could make from it. Not much romance in that. Richard Hofstadter, in *The Age of Reform,* tells us:

> The predominance in American agriculture of the isolated farmstead standing in the midst of great acreage, the frequent movements, the absence of village life, deprived the farmer and his family of the advantages of community, the chances of association and cooperation, and encouraged that rampant, suspicious, and almost suicidal individualism for which the American farmer was long noted ... The characteristic product of American rural society was not a yeoman or a villager but a harassed little country businessman who worked very hard, moved all too often, gambled with his land, and made his way alone.[5]

4   For a fine example of the restlessness involved in moving West, see Ken Kesey, *Sometimes a Great Notion.*

5   Richard Hofstadter, *The Age of Reform* (New York: Random House, 1955), p. 45.

Not very noble, that vision of freedom. The vision of the small isolated farmer continually moving for profits, relating to the land primarily for the economic reward, communing with an investment while thinking about future riches. But that is the past, a past buried almost as deeply as our treatment of the Indians, who really did have a home in the land.

We have not lost the idea that wealth is important, that it is "freeing." We move from our civilization—from our problems, from our cities—to the suburbs. Money or at least mortgages physically remove us from social responsibility. To be free in a tract home. But we know that enough money will also buy us power, will enable us to control.

The terrible split between the haves who can move, and the have-nots who are stuck, is all too clear. The suburbs get good schools, repaired roads, fine services; the inner city gets gun fights, drugs on the street corners, overburdened school systems, and the homeless sleeping in doorways. Money moves you away from parts of American reality; it puts physical distance between sweet comforts and those who live the hard life. Or at least it used to. Our freedom from is slowly revealing how tied down we really are. Neglect of social responsibility is catching up; gunfire in school is happening in suburbia.

Back to power. There is a whole literature in sociology and political science telling us where power is, who possesses it, and why they have it. A nice example of such a book is *Who Rules America?* by G. William Domhoff.[6] Domhoff tries to prove what many people suspect:

1. That there is an upper class;
2. That it owns a disproportionate amount of the country's wealth and receives a disproportionate amount of its yearly income;
3. That it—along with its high-level executives—controls the nation's major banks, corporations, elite universities, and largest mass media;
4. That its control extends to the executive branch of the federal government;
5. That it merely influences the Congress, most state governments, and most city governments.

6  See G. William Domhoff, *Who Rules America?* (Englewood Cliffs, N.J.: Prentice-Hall, 1967).

That is a big job for any group of people. I suppose one could conclude that this is no mere idle rich. But there are more important implications. If power and freedom are tied together (whoever heard of powerlessness being freedom in America?), then the message is clear: Get rich. Money is power, power is freedom. We work out a perversion of this every day. Instead of being rich, we can at least appear rich. So we earn small and buy big. We give ourselves the charge of power by charging what we buy.

I am not happy to leave the analysis at that. Too many things are forgotten, too many things are assumed. We forget that people really do need food and shelter and medicine, and that we are skilled enough to provide everyone with all these things. We are, if nothing else, a productive people. We also assume that to have money is to have control, is to be free. I am unconvinced. I am simply unsure. Henry Kariel hints at the problems:

> But freedom from want and for leisure is not enough… Abundant resources may themselves be produced by means utterly indifferent to the values of political freedom. In point of fact, abundance is made possible by large-scale technology and a sweeping division of human labor, which have already entailed the subordination of personal interests… Men must be free, therefore, not only from the necessity of finding the means for sustenance but also from the presumed imperatives of technology…

In short, it matters how material abundance and the amenities of life are provided.[7]

What Kariel implies is that there are hidden costs to our overabundance, real prices we must pay in order to buy our way to freedom or power or both. Let us list some of the costs. In our search for freedom we have lost our home. While developing the skills of speculation, of buying and then selling for profit—in other words, developing the skills of a "developer" who does not stay on his or her development—we have lost touch with the land. We have sacrificed any meaningful relationship with our surroundings by thinking of them in terms of debits and credits. It is

7   Henry Kariel, *The Promise of Politics* (Englewood Cliffs, N.J.: Prentice-Hall, 1966), p. 39.

simply a ledger-book relationship where wheat and grass have come to mean money and possible independence. Maybe even freedom.

As we are beginning to find out, this kind of dynamic can go on until we have destroyed our surroundings. There are just so many trees to be cut, animals to shoot, lands to ruin, oceans to muck up, and lakes to kill. We produce things by destroying other things. The price of material freedom is paid, in part, by breathing our own air. Taxes seem cheaper.

That, of course, is the common argument, the easy one. Part of what I would like to suggest is that even if we had cleaned up everything—air and water and minds—we might not be much better off. The problems of "clean" are certainly solvable. Ralph Nader knows that.[8] What is at stake is our freedom. Do we really have power? Can money give us the control to make us free? As argued earlier, I think not.

There are at least two ways to get at the problem of money and power leading to freedom. The first way is to look at those at the "top"— the rich, the executives. The whole idea of dealing with this group is obvious. These are the envied, the ones who have won, the ones, we suspect, who might be free. But the point is painful for the belief. These people, as much as or more than any others, are in many ways the prisoners of bureaucracies.

They are where they are because they have best learned and acted out the money/production/freedom ethic. That is their morality, the defining limitations of their imaginations and actions. They are different only because they push bigger buttons from more comfortable offices. Given a choice between comfort or discomfort, money or poverty, buttons or no buttons, most of us would choose comfort, money, and buttons. But that set of choices may mask the real issue of freedom: the freedom to act together, the freedom to define oneself by one's actions.

The second way to get at the problem is by looking at those who have not "made it," those who are outside the ethic. It seems clear that things other than money can lead to freedom, if money is not the principal value.

---

8  The whole Ralph Nader/ecology problem is in itself a problem. Nader promises cleanliness but not really reform. If he is successful, it will merely mean that we can live in the same system—which we have made stronger—without the pollution. We will soon find out that there is much money to be made from ecology and that lawyers have found yet another way to funnel public problems through the courts.

Minorities that have not been allowed to participate equally in the pursuit of materialism may be freer than some of those at the top. The militant minority may have understood more about freedom than the executive. Still, money would be nice.

All I want to suggest is something that I believe most of you already suspect: Materialism as an ideology may not lead us to freedom. Materialism, no matter how much we invest in it and attribute to it, is not the entire answer to our dreams. Further, those we consider "economically disadvantaged" may be able to teach us valuable lessons about the costs of financial success—and the power of ideology.

## Freedom and Time

Time, in many ways, turns out to be a very political topic. In an earlier chapter, we understood time as a piece of organization theory, but here we are interested in time as a kind of cage with invisible but very real bars. More and more, the technology of time is constraining us. This is not without irony; technology is supposed to set us free, to save us from dirty hands and dreary jobs. What we are coming to see is that the cost of clean hands might be pretty high.

Before we get to nanoseconds (time in the short), let's begin with a couple of examples of the politics of time. Doesn't, after all, time just go by?[9] The most obvious political playing with the calendar was during the French Revolution. In 1792, Year One by the new French calendar, everything was changed. It was a scientifically based calendar: Twelve months, each with thirty days, each month divided in three ten-day cycles called decades. A day had ten hours, an hour had a hundred decimal minutes, and a minute had a hundred decimal seconds.

This rational calendar cut the number of rest days from 180 to 36. It was a remarkable attempt to change time, and not very smart. Would you like your vacation cut by 75 percent? The new French calendar was doomed from the beginning; it lasted thirteen years.

Did you know that the Benedictine Order invented schedules in the sixth century? St. Benedict believed that "idleness is the enemy of the soul," so there was to be no "free" time. They then invented the clock (the

9   Jeremy Rifkin, *Time Wars* (New York: Touchstone, 1989). This, and the following argument, come from Rifkin.

first ones didn't have any hands, just bells on the hour) so that the monks knew when it was time to do the next activity. Now children in preschool are taught to listen to the bell. They, too, are taught that the sound of the bell means "it's time" to change their activity. It is not until they graduate from high school that they will be freed from bells—freed from bells by their own wristwatches. It's hard to imagine a world without schedules and clocks.

The point is that the things we take for granted are the result of political decisions and technological developments. The argument here is that the new technology robs us of our own freedom. We seem, in many ways, to be at the end of clock-time. Hours and minutes and seconds—measures that we could see and understand—are giving way to computer time. The new measure is the nanosecond.

The new time, put differently, is something that we have no way of experiencing. It is beyond us. Just too fast. Since almost all of the workers in the country use electronic terminal equipment, that means almost all of our workers are now tuned into and somehow driven by faster-than-human speed. It is a world where training, in part, comes from the game platform and joystick at home. Video games set the tone for the world you are about to enter. You have to somehow gear up in order to keep up with whatever game, or program, is in front of you. And, as we know, that is not an easy thing to do.

For example, there was a study about the effects of our new and speeded-up processing of information. In the program studied, the processor had to respond to the data on the screen in seventeen seconds, or the data disappeared. It turned out that "from the eleventh second they [the operators] begin to perspire, then the heart rate goes up. Consequently they experience enormous fatigue." People who work with computers often have "electronic supervisors," programs that constantly monitor the work that is being done. The programs are described as an "unwinking computer taskmaster," and computer work is sometimes seen as "electronic sweatshops."

The field of ergonomics, which originated during World War II to reduce performance failures due to human error in operatiang high-tech defense systems, is now used to minimize the health problems associated with computers. Instructions are given on the kind of lighting, posture, and workstation design that can best reduce the risks of computer-related health problems such as eyestrain and repetitive stress injuries like carpal tunnel syndrome.

There is even a medical condition that describes "computer compulsives." These are the people who are best able to keep up with the computer rhythm and nanosecond pace. They are, it turns out, remarkably unsocial people, who avoid normal human interaction. They demand brevity and understand conversations as merely data-gathering times. Humans, for these particular compulsives, are just too slow.

The technology of time is, at best, a very mixed blessing for freedom and politics. While it allows us to "see" almost anywhere in the world, to "see" demonstrations and revolutions and wars, it is not at all helpful in teaching us how to do politics. Politics requires reflection and consideration. It requires being seen and heard and responding—personally—to what is going on.

In a nanosecond world, the best one can do is attempt to keep up with the program to play out a predetermined future. And we fall behind. The stock market crashed, in no small part, because computer programs did what they were programmed to do faster than common sense could stop them. Our missile system has, of course, everything to do with programmed responses.

Where is the politics in all of that? Where is the freedom?

## Freedom and Psychology (With a Word About Dope)

> *"Everything else in this world is being turned on and off—lights, television sets, refrigerators, stoves, fans, phonographs, vacuum cleaners, and so on—so why shouldn't we want to be turned on too?"*
>
> — *Leslie Farber, quoting a young student*

There are times—all too frequent—when it occurs to me that freedom is a used-up, unrealistic problem. Most people do not consider it for long enough to count; they are able to "common-sense" it out, to come to terms with it, and then to let it go. Essentially, Who Cares? There are other times—almost as frequent—when it occurs to me that that is part of the problem. We act as if we know what freedom is, without working on it. We accept what we are told, or what we observe, and leave it unquestioned.

If freedom is an important concept that ought to be acted upon, then it makes sense to try to figure out what it means. Further, if freedom has something to do with other people, then it should be properly studied as a topic of politics. It is possible that we—"we" being an ill-defined group of people who are either young or "hip," or "punk," or "rad," or simply identify with now—have gone beyond some of the preceding American definitions of freedom. While the Open Road (the Real World, after all, is a road show) may still be attractive; materialism may not be quite so alluring. While nature may be attractive, maybe obvious destruction has lost some of its appeal. But while some science seems to have lost its appeal, other science has taken its place. It is this latter science, the science of people's behavior and people's minds that now purports to have insight into a new freedom.

The new scientists—the behavioral psychologists, for example—are serious people who make serious claims about our lives and our freedom. It is only fair to take them seriously.

Behavioral scientists are capable of formidable magic. They can train animals to run the right way or to salivate on cue; they can teach pigeons to play Ping-Pong. These scientists are even able to make human beings feel good or bad, angry or happy, by running electric currents to certain parts of the brain. No sense in being frightened or outraged or anything else, it is simply a scientific fact: Scientists can make us feel and do certain things they want us to. They put their faith in determinism: the belief that each act is caused by something, or a series of somethings, and that if one can only determine the stimulus, then one can predict the response.

That, of course, is science and determinism reduced to simplest terms. But the kernel of the belief is there: That it is theoretically possible to understand every action by discovering all the things that have gone into determining the action. Given this assumption, freedom—standing by itself—is a nonsense concept. If we learn what to do, how we act and react, then the behavioral sciences are surely right. In the book quoted at the beginning of this section, *Requiem for Democracy,* arguments for "freedom" are presented and then discussed.

For example, we are told it is foolish to believe that people can be free in the absence of "scientific behavior control." The authors write: "We cannot deal rationally with the behavioral sciences until we realize that control *per se* is not even an issue. From the scientist's viewpoint, all human actions follow laws and patterns, just as physical events do, and are, in that sense, controlled... The real question is not, 'should [people] be controlled?' but 'how should [they] be controlled?'"[10]

The words used seem so reasonable, so value-free, so ... scientific. It is as if rationality really were the basis of the world, and that we know what that rationality is. It is as if physical events are controlled by laws and patterns that we know—and so, too, human actions. There is no hint of Einstein's descriptions of the relativity of perception; there is no recognition of the phenomenologist Hussurl's idea that rationality has its roots in subjective thought. What we get is "value-free reason" run amuck, a belief system in behavioral science clothes.

All of this is not lost on our politicians. There are labs where people are hooked up with wires to measure their responses to certain words. A pretty simple and harmless activity. Speechwriters look at the results and craft speeches around the words that have the greatest emotional impact. It almost seems that the political issue involved is which candidate has hired the best behavioral psychologist.

Back to the argument. Andrews and Karlins continue by assuring us that the scientific control of behavior is not evil ("An atomic reaction can light a city or burn it") and that it does not appear, at this time, as if an elite corps of scientists or a tyrannical government could use behavioral control technology to regulate human conduct. There are, of course, some potential problems noted by Andrews and Karlins, which they formulate as follows:

| Effective behavior control technology | + | Alienated individual | = | Conditions conducive to formation of a psytocracy |
|---|---|---|---|---|

---

10  Lewis M. Andrews and Marvin Karlins, *Requiem for Democracy?* (New York: Holt, Rinehart & Winston, 1971), p. 39.

To put it another way, we may be more easily controlled by the technology of the behavioral sciences if we persist in being alienated from our fellow citizens. In part, this is a good insight. But the avoidance of a psytocracy does not mean that we are not determined, does not mean that we are "free."

According to the behavioral scientists, "If man's sense of freedom is to be restored, it must be expressed within the framework of science."[11] It is as simple as that. Freedom is determinism. Science makes us free. Not only is it science that frees us, but also it is, more particularly, the mind. The process-people (those who accept determinism but think it is complicated, those who think the key lies in the "highly elaborate information-processing organ," the brain) believe that we are determined. But determined in a special way. That way involves our thought: "*The quality of thought is not a given; it is a product of training and experience*."[12]

So this is where behavioral science takes us, to where we can be free, to where we can determine our own quality of thought. Some scientists assume that is freedom, the ultimate freedom. Certainly the ultimate if one accepts that freedom is bound by the rules of science. The human condition is pretty easy to understand if we just believe. The struggle to be free has taken a new form.

The problems raised by the behavioral scientists are not easily answered. We should not accept their pronouncements without understanding their biases. But, if "more is better" in grade school, certainty now seems to be best in college.

What has become of serendipity?

Students now want frequent quizzes on the material that was just learned. They want study questions for exams: cut-and-dried, black-and-white questions and answers, which require no real understanding of what was discussed, and no development of what the material means. They want certainty. They want to be told and then they want to repeat it. They want the truth on CD-ROM.

Being a student and being a citizen have certain things in common. Both require a sense of what is going on, an idea of what needs to be done,

11  Ibid., p. 103.
12  Ibid., p. 116. Emphasis added.

and enough self-respect and autonomy to do something well. In school, we have progressed from a hard rap on the knuckles to a warm hug by an incompetent to a seemingly great desire on the part of students to avoid being educated. It is not hard to see that whatever good education might do, and however good education might help encourage an interest in politics and freedom, we have—on the whole—messed up.

## Dope: Drugs and Drinking

> *"Better Things for Better Living Through Chemistry." So reads one of the prominent hippy buttons, quoting E. I. DuPont. But the slogan is not being used satirically. The wearers mean it the way DuPont means it.*
>
> — *Theodore Roszak*

It may be helpful if we examine a small part of our behavior-changing science, a real-life, and everyday offering of our new "freedom." Like most offerings, it is a very mixed blessing. Like most, it carries with it a distinguishable idea of freedom. The example is of dope, of drugs. Of course it would be foolish to condemn scientists for the tremendous abuse of drugs. I do not mean to suggest it, and have no intention of doing so. What I would like to suggest is that, if understood in a certain way, the drug head and the scientific mind have something in common—and something to teach us.

Certainly drugs are not new. They have a distinguished history—from Indians of this continent to the great religions of the East. They have religious meaning, hold the key to certain kinds of magic, and can help cure the sick. There are those in our time—people like Aldous Huxley—who have combined science and intellect and knowledge with drugs, and have increased our shared knowledge. Drugs have broadened our worlds and have helped increase both our understanding and our perception of the things around us. Moreover, we have medical drugs—for every ill from headaches to ulcers—that will help us to live longer and with less pain. Drugs are simply not all bad, unless one likes pain. Even the stuff we call "dope" (marijuana, cocaine, and so forth) is not all bad; but we will get to that later.

Most of the following discussion is about things other than alcohol. I do not mean to suggest that alcohol is not a popular way to go. In fact, younger people are drinking more than ever before. There are very young alcoholics; there are more drinking problems than drug problems on college campuses; there are far too many automobile deaths caused by drinking.

Alcohol is not the topic here because it rarely leads to the kinds of experiences that will be discussed. Alcohol is a depressant. Maybe it is the drug of choice now because it so mirrors much of what is going on: an hour or so of feeling good—with something socially acceptable—then becoming depressed and, maybe, hung-over the next day. In truth, the reason we drink is a real topic, but it is not the current one.

Alcohol is the number one killer drug in the United States. While it is a depressant, it also makes some people very violent. It has long-term effects on family life; we know that there are many children and adult children of alcoholics in therapy groups. And alcoholism is something that one never gets over. One is always a recovering alcoholic. It is a drug that is able to permeate through many generations.

But this is not about drinking. It is about the dope user, the individual who is seeking something and finds drugs. Part of the seeking, of the pursuit, is for freedom. It is that part that is in the tradition we have been discussing. Philip Slater writes that drugs "promise a return to pure experience, to unencumbered sensation."[13] Not only that, it is just the way the behavioral scientists would want it: through the mind. Drugs extend freedom, in that particular sense. We find our new solutions by willingly changing our minds. We determine our own response by our own artificial stimulus.

The body simply becomes a kind of machine. It becomes our "property," our "asset." We can use it; we can direct it through drugs. Freedom to be ourselves, as long as it does not harm anyone else. That is apple-pie American. But what I want to argue is that it has become self-destructive. There seem to be too many of us to have visions of Walden Pond, to think of freedom as physically escaping, to believe that science has our answers to social problems. As the businessman farmer used the land, so the drug

13 Phillip E. Slater, *The Pursuit of Loneliness: American Culture at the Breaking Point* (Boston: Beacon, 1970), p. 93.

abuser uses him or herself. The doper is used up and then destroyed. It is solitary and mental and "freely" done.

The politics of dope is more complex than that. It fact, many people seem to have learned something from dope. Indeed, just taking an illegal drug and finding out that one does not become some kind of mad-dog-drug-freak makes one wonder about the value of the "official" pronouncements. But there is the question of the end of the experience. If we all took dope, would we all become better people and revolutionize the world and live in love forever after? There is no reason to guess at an answer to that question until we ask just why we do dope, and what it means.

Isn't it possible that freedom is the issue, that freedom is the value, but that instead of freedom we get drugs? Maybe we have created a world in which we just cannot live, so we escape, or, at least, we learn to regulate ourselves according to a new pace, a different drummer. We can make ourselves speed up, slow down, go to sleep, be mellow, or wake up. Could it be possible that the union of people and science has become an unhappy one? That we are not suited—in any kind of natural way—for the "freedom" of science or the society it has built? In that case, we need to rethink society and science and ourselves.

But, Theodore Roszak asks, what if we, on drugs,

> [s]uddenly find ourselves blessed with a society of love, gentleness, innocence, and freedom? If that were so, what should we have to say about ourselves regarding the integrity of our organism? Should we not have to admit that the behavioral technicians have been right from the start? That we are, indeed, the bundle of electrochemical circuitry they tell us we are—and not persons at all who have it in our nature to achieve enlightenment by native ingenuity and a good deal of hard growing.[14]

14 Roszak, *The Making of a Counter Culture: Reflections on a Technocratic Society and Its Youthful Opposition* (Garden City, N. Y.: Anchor, 1969), p. 177

To seek freedom through drugs is at once to misunderstand freedom and to give in to the very dynamic that is causing many of the problems. Drugs—dope—can provide extraordinary experiences. They can lead one to startling flashes of insight, to moments of altered perception. But there are at least two important points that should be made.

First the visions, the flashes, the moments must be prepared for to be fully understood. It's only another Open Road if you are not ready to look for something. Read Aldous Huxley's *The Doors of Perception* or, better yet, Carlos Castaneda's writings to begin to understand elaborate preparations, intelligent perceptions, and potential dangers.

Second, momentary insight changes nothing unless one works at what the insight means. To rely on drugs to keep you in a more or less constant state of "insight" is to be little more than what Roszak suggests: a "bundle of electrochemical circuitry." Dope can be fine. It can point you in the direction of hard work—but little more.

There is at least one more use of drugs: They may be an escape. Several years ago, a middle-class, white male writer for *The New Republic* named Jefferson Morley went to live in the ghetto. He wanted to find out about just how much the drug culture had taken hold and what was going on with crack. In his research, he smoked crack. What he wrote made many people very angry.

He wrote what we all should know, that living in a ghetto with no money and no chance for a better life was terrible—something just unimaginable for the majority of citizens. What he wrote next seemed to follow logically: "If all you have in life is bad choices, crack may not be the most unpleasant of them." For $10, he wrote, people could get away for a while; could go to a better place. A neighbor of mine calls it a "poor man's vacation."

What I want to argue is that freedom is a positive concept that involves people's relationships with one another. And that Thoreau, and Lawrence's Whitman, materialism, behaviorism, and drugs only help show us why we think as we do.

They do not give us clues to politics, hints about how we might make freedom a part of our world. Changing our ideas of freedom would be hard; to explain such a concept may be impossible. The best we can do is to explore one possibility of freedom. To stay as we are is to leave power—and powerlessness—and the possibility of real change un-touched. Freedom is safely out of our reach if we continue on our current ideological path. We will remain unfree, busily involved in the politics of self-deception.

## Freedom To

*He breathed deeply the moist, bitter-scented air of the park and at every step it seemed to him that he was pushing away the past as one who has reached the shore pushes away a skiff, now useless. His probing and his insight were without resignation; full of defiance and venturesome passion, he looked to the new life, which, he was resolved, would no longer be a groping or dim-sighted wandering but rather a bold, steep climb. Later and more painfully perhaps than most men, he had taken leave of the sweet twilight of youth. Now he stood, poor and belated in the broad daylight, and of that he meant never again to lose a precious hour.*

— *Hermann Hesse*

The heading "Freedom To" is full of promise. Freedom to what? To the Revolution, or to the Movement? Freedom to have a fixed income, or freedom not to go to school? Freedom to grow up, or to continue, as we are now—freedom to hurry from the cradle to perpetual adolescence? There is no doubt that there are many things I did not mean to suggest when I wrote the words "Freedom To." What I propose to do is to make some suggestions about a place where we might be free, and to explain the thoughts behind it. The discussion is taken, in part, from Hannah Arendt's *The Human Condition,* a book whose ideas deserve much thought.

Instead of beginning with the assumptions of the behavioral sciences, with the belief that we are determined to be, it seems sensible to start again. In the final analysis, it seems impossible to "explain" human nature. Certainly the words of our surroundings do not explain us. We know that words like life or mortality, love, or home can never fully answer our questions about who we are. This is not to deny that we may be in part de-termined, nor is this to argue that there is a God who created the heavens and the earth. It is simply to say that the problem of human nature seems unanswerable.[15]

That we have no final answers does not mean that we cannot solve at least parts of ourselves, especially those parts that have to do with being free. A possibly helpful model offered by Hannah Arendt has to do with the Greeks. In particular, it has to do with the Greek idea of what is involved in freedom.

For the Greeks, political life was important. A particular kind of politics and organization. For them, it was the polis, a place where people—as equals—could get together, make common decisions, and take actions. It is important to understand that the political realm was not the household, that the polis was not private. The household dealt with those things necessary for survival. The household, in Arendt's words, "was born of necessity and necessity ruled over all activities performed in it."[16]

But the polis was the realm of freedom. It was a public realm, where individuals met as equals. In one sense, freedom meant neither to rule nor to be ruled. It ignored the kind of material and "power" differences that so characterize contemporary "politics." What freedom—and, hence, politics—formerly included was a common world of thought and action. In this commonality existed a kind of freedom that is hard for us to understand. Everyone became involved with the same object, with the same cause, with trying to figure out how to define the same thing.

We might pay attention to Pericles: "We differ from other states in regarding the man who holds aloof from public life not as quiet, but as useless; we decide or debate, carefully and in person, all matters of policy, holding not that words and deeds go ill together, but that acts are foredoomed to failure when undertaken undiscussed."

It was this sharing, this tugging at the same object in order to give it meaning, that helped limit the chances of being tyrannized. When people are isolated, when they are alone, when they have no common vision, then no one can agree with anyone else. But by ignoring everyone else—all

---

15  I think it is important to recall the earlier discussion on phenomenology. We do seem to be social, and we can understand consciousness as a form of reaching out to the world. This carries with it the importance of understanding the relationship between the individual and the world he or she lives in.

16  Hannah Arendt, *The Human Condition* (Garden City, N. Y.: Doubleday, 1958), p. 159.

other seeing and hearing and insights—each becomes dependent upon some central source to define a common world for everyone. To put it differently, without deciding on common things, we become terribly susceptible to the tyranny of conforming to the perceptions of some other force. We accept another's vision; we accept it as a chorus of strangers, unable to communicate felt differences.

In this public world, this political world, people were defined by their acting and their speaking. To act is to do the unexpected, to begin, to initiate, to lead. It is through speaking and acting that one becomes distinctive, one begins to define self. In the polis, people publicly, in sight of their peers, answered the question of who they were by taking positions and taking actions. To quote Arendt, "In acting and speaking, men show who they are, reveal actively their unique personal identities and thus make their appearance in the human world, while their physical identities appear without any activity of their own in the unique shape of the body and sound of the voice. This disclosure of 'who' in contradiction to 'what' somebody is—his qualities, gifts, talents, and shortcomings, which he may display or hide—is implicit in everything somebody says or does."[17]

In creating and revealing, an individual experiences freedom. It is far from an easy thing; there are surely costs one must pay. The future becomes uncertain, unseeable, and an individual is no longer the unique master of what he or she does. But that is the price of freedom, the price of citizens being equals, and of reality being a shared experience. Certainly the struggle of creation, of action, the possibility of understanding one's self and of helping to make important decisions in a public way are rewards in themselves. They are, indeed, the stuff of freedom.

*The people who are not bigoted are the people who have no convictions at all.*

---

17 Ibid., p. 159.

# chapter 10

# Justice: Free Last Meals Next Door

*Trout's favorite formula was to describe a perfectly hideous society, not unlike his own, and then, toward the end, to suggest ways it could be improved. In 2BR02B he hypothecated an America in which almost all of the work was done by machines, and the only people who could get work had three or more Ph.D.'s. There was a serious overpopulation problem, too.*

*All serious diseases had been conquered. So death was voluntary, and the government, to encourage volunteers for death, set up a purple-roofed Ethical Suicide Parlor at every major intersection, right next door to an orange-footed Howard Johnson's. There were pretty hostesses in the parlor, and Barca-Loungers, and Muzak, and a choice of fourteen painless ways to die. The suicide parlors were busy places, because so many people felt silly and pointless, and because it was supposed to be an unselfish, patriotic thing to do, to die. The suicides also got free meals next door.*

*—Kurt Vonnegut, Jr.*

*A fact: Lightning strikes the earth about eight million times each
day and kills about a hundred and fifty Americans every year.
For the land of the free, the greatest delight of every man is getting
the better of the other man.*

—*D. H. Lawrence*

## The Problem of Justice

*Law 'n order, law 'n order. No culture without order—no order
without law. Do you hear?
Is that clear? Rules and regulations/regularity/judges and judgments.
Trial by jury/Trial by peers. It is a trial to see you/it is a trial to
hear.
Justice is process/the evidence is in. Obedience. Be objective. Know
the law/weigh the facts/judge from other judgments.
The Truth—is the rule—is the law—is Our Order. Lets get to-
gether/have a trial/go to Court/fight it out.
How can you see/Blindfolded?*

The question is obvious: Does all this have anything to do with justice, or
is it simply the ideology of our leaders, the beliefs of those in power?

The "title" of this section is "The Problem of Justice." A simple, misleading set of words. The word *problem* suggests that there is a solution. I
am firmly convinced that there will be no clear solutions to the problems
we discuss. The word *justice* is just as misleading. To write about it is to assume a definition of it—something that is not necessarily the truth in this
case. This chapter will consist of thoughts in search of a definition, of ideas
and phrases that try to capture an illusion. Maybe justice is simply an illusion. Maybe this section should be titled: "The Unsolvable Problem of an
Illusion."

So much for accuracy. What about justice? What about law?

Most of us have a great respect for the law. At least, a respect for the *idea*
of Law. We are taught to think that our system of law is only natural and
normal, well and good. What we do not question is the respect. Moreover,
we rarely ask about the law itself. We seldom seem to think about the basis
of the law, and we think even less about justice. Let us begin by trying to

understand what we might assume about the law.

I think that most of us assume that there is a kind of perfect order that exists somewhere. A world where all forms are perfect; a realm, possibly, of thought that is uncorrupted by anything material. We seem to believe that from the perfection of such a world, we might get an idea of some ultimate order, an idea of the perfect working of things. It is also from this world that we seek our definitions of justice.

The world of thought is untouched and perfect. In our heads, there might be an idea of justice. From our heads, we get our laws. From our laws, we assume we are just.

The idea that law and justice are mental, that they are an ideal, is neither new nor unique to the United States. Plato, of course, presented the argument most clearly. He thought, silly ancient that he was, that a world of perfect forms really did exist. That because we are but imperfect reflections of that world, we must spend our lives striving to think perfect thoughts, to be perfect.

His arguments were—and still are for many— compelling for the mind, for the world of the perfection of thought. We can conceive of a perfect circle; we cannot make one. Plato wrote an allegory about a cave. It is helpful to understand it.

Imagine a huge cave. In the cave sit many people facing a wall. They are chained and can neither move nor turn away from that wall. There is light coming in from behind them. There are people constantly moving between that light and those chained, and shadows are cast upon the wall. Those casting the shadows carry puppets and other objects, which make interesting and bizarre images on the wall.

The prisoners, having been exposed to nothing else, soon understand the shadows on the wall to be real. It becomes their shared life: They know and recognize the images; they converse and argue about the shadows.

What Plato argues and what we often believe is that our reality is simply a reflection. That there is a true order of things and that we must strive for this order intellectually. The Republic of Plato is nothing more than a society striving to that order, and by doing so have that society be in accord with the justice of the universe.

There are powerful social implications in the neat arrangement of

Plato's *Republic*. The divine order included, indeed depended on, a rigid social scheme. Plato tells us of the intelligent and the less intelligent, of the warriors and the farmers, of the bureaucrats and the merchants. There was to be a right place for everyone, and everyone was to be in his or her place.

From the world of perfect forms came the idea of perfect order. With a great deal of schooling and training, the intellectuals of the Republic were to understand better the world of perfect forms. We are asked to assume that their rule would be just, that it would lead to harmony in the society.

Find the right order; get the right law; the result would be justice.

Of course, that formulation of justice has its shortcomings. We shall involve ourselves with different views of justice later on and, in doing so, reply to the *Republic*. But it may be helpful to anticipate some of the obvious problems. To believe that, ideally, there is a universal definition of justice is to avoid something important. It is to avoid much of reality. To put it simply, intellectual abstraction can be a way of bypassing unpleasant forms of reality. To base a legal system on a particular form of mental process means that the enforcement of that law will be but an attempt to force unwanted reality out of existence.

To posit a perfect order, a mental realm of universally "right" ways of acting, may be to deny our essentially confused, chaotic selves. I do not intend to argue that there is no room for idealism, but I hope to avoid the mistake of making an individual a slave to his or her mind.

Let us shift the discussion a bit and make it a little more personal. What do we feel about justice? What does it seem like when we are involved in it? What are our thoughts when we think about justice? We might think about justice in this way: We will try to make people do what we think is best for them. To put it another way, we judge other people by imposing our standards and desires on them, and then we decide what is best for them.

This approach to justice is many-sided. It might be the basis of a system in which all people would be given food, or it could support something quite the opposite. Let us now worry about only two of the possibilities implied by this approach to justice.

The first part of the formulation would go something like this: "If we were they, this is probably what we should do." But what does it mean if justice is to judge matters that way? Doesn't this approach mean that we assume a great deal? Aren't we saying that we can be objective and, moreover, that other people will want what we want?

It strikes me that at its heart this is a very pompous attitude. Can we know? Should others want what we want? There may well be a place in justice for the mingling of people's ideas, for a sharing of and deciding on wants. But to truly know one another takes a kind of intimacy, a kind of knowledge that one must spend a great deal of time and effort developing. Even then we rarely know for sure, and what we do know may not be the basis for justice.

The point is simply that it is both necessary and important that we have an idea of what is right and that we try to make others understand that idea. But we must also understand that to translate our ideas into the world of real people, with real ideas and feelings and situations, is difficult. The problem of how this can be done is the other matter we must discuss.

The second part of the formulation ("We will try to make people do what we think is best for them") assumes that justice has something to do with judging from above. It is to impose. To regulate. To set ourselves over others, and to demand that they do what is right. But is this justice, or is it the rule of the strong parading under a different label, under a nicer name?

To sit in judgment of another may be many things, but it is not necessarily an essential element of justice.

What I would like to argue is that there are dynamics at work in our conceptions of law that may have nothing to do with justice. It seems clear that we rarely get too far from the idea of perfect images, from the enticing pictures of the mind. We link justice with ideas that are drawn from an independent, unearthly existence. We try hard to suck from justice a vital, human element. We try to make it the reflection of something we are not: perfect. Or we believe that if we can impose something on those less powerful, we are just.

With these elements at work, it is not surprising that some consider us a nation of law and order that lacks the soul of justice.

D. H. Lawrence writes: "Anger is just, and pity is just, but judgment is never just."

## The Normal View

In earlier chapters we described and discussed liberalism and, in appropriate cases, dismissed it as harmful or unhelpful. We must return to liberalism, for it is almost impossible to write about justice and law in America without coming to terms with its liberal framework. Liberalism represents the rules of debate for most of what we consider justice.

It seems appropriate to begin once again with the writings of John Locke, since they were extremely influential in the drawing up of our Constitution. Locke believed that the natural state of human beings was peaceful and reasonable enough. He thought that most people, most of the time, could be counted on to cause little or no trouble. In fact, there was almost no reason for government to exist—almost, but not quite.

According to Locke, sometimes there were disputes; some people did break the rules. Therefore, there was a need for impartial magistrates, a need for fair judges who would settle arguments and punish wrongdoers. In a sense, it was government-as-referee, an idea that should not sound entirely strange to us. In many ways we have simply taken this formula of Locke's and turned it into an elaborate belief system.

The rules of our debate about justice (*sic*–law) have become the rules of intricate processes and definitions of "impartial" judgment.

The liberals want to make the debate on justice easy: All we must know is how fair and impartial judicial decisions seem to be; then we can measure justice. If we can spot trends in court rulings, then we can determine whether we are becoming a more- or less-just nation. It is the way judgments are made, the process, that is important. Because we always debate within the framework set by these rules and assumptions, it is necessary to understand more fully what the liberals are talking about so that we can at least know what we are missing.

The liberal argument as written by a liberal:

> In essence, the distinction between civilization and savagery is the willingness to settle disputes by other means than force. We say that we are governed by the rule of law, which means that we accept decisions by impartial courts rather than by force of arms. If we are going to remain civilized, we must continue to

accept the decisions of our courts, whether we agree with them or not."[1]

The liberal continues by offering proof that those impartial courts are deciding cases justly. During the last half of the twentieth century, for instance, the Supreme Court made decisions that seemingly widened our freedom. After all, "one man [person], one vote" is only right. Since 1954 it has been illegal to have racially segregated public school systems. Later, bathrooms, drinking fountains, motels, lunch counters, seating at ballparks—well, almost everywhere—became desegregated.

Further, people accused of crimes must be told of their rights (they cannot be forced to incriminate themselves), and an attorney must represent individuals brought to trial. Who could argue with these decisions? Who would challenge them? The system seems so reasonable. Laws are made, and then impartial justices decide whether they are constitutional or unconstitutional, good or bad.

There are ways in which it is hard to fault much of what the Supreme Court decided. It's still uncomfortable to advocate segregation although in the "war on terrorism racial profiling in some cases may be a necessary tool." But what about wiretapping and other eavesdropping that had been curtailed or ruled illegal by the court? Enter the USA Patriot Act. Clearly, a government fighting terrorism must have expanded powers of surveillance. Now "intelligence wiretaps" allow the government to tap into your communication (by reading your email or listening to your conversations) with secret authorization but without probable cause. How will the court stand on homeland security—our security? Now that the decisions of the last fifty years are giving way under the pressure of events, where do we stand? Obviously, we have not given up "civilization for savagery" in adopting or abandoning these positions, but there is something about our rule of law—the biases of the framework—that leave us stuck between the security and savagery.

---

1   The quote is from Erwin Griswold, and was found in James Clayton, *The Making of Justice* (New York: Cornerstone, 1964), p. 7.

## Doing Justice

> *You can't get away from this.*
> *Blood-consciousness overwhelms, obliterates, annuls mind-con-*
> *sciousness.*
> *Mind-consciousness extinguishes blood-consciousness, and con-*
> *sumes the blood.*
> *We are all of us conscious in both ways. And the two ways are*
> *antagonistic in us.*
> *They will always remain so.*
> *That is our cross.*
>
> <div align="right">—<i>D. H. Lawrence</i></div>

It should be obvious that laws and trials mean something. They carry with them a way of looking at the world, a way that permits some people to control the actions of others. What has been argued is that the law, as Americans conceive of it, leaves out some important elements. Our law and "justice" seem an attempt to impose our mind over our other reality. In a sense, it means that justice is something thought, not something actively done; something imposed, not something shared.

The Bible admonishes us to "do justice, and love mercy." Part of justice, it seems to me, is to be done; it is something a person does. Justice is not necessarily created in a void and then imposed on others. Maybe it is more an action than a judgment, more an activity than an idea. In a sense, I mean to suggest that justice may include more than a proper judicial process; it may include, but go well beyond, equality of procedure.

I am not saying that process and procedure are necessarily evil in and of themselves. I am suggesting that justice is much more complex than that; and although one might have a sense of security in knowing that a lot of money can buy a good attorney who will assure a "fair" hearing according to our laws, there is no reason to equate security with justice. Indeed, there is a real question about "fair" to whom and "impartial" to what. There are weaknesses in our liberal idea of justice; there are built-in biases.

First, property is protected. More precisely, private ownership is protected. That makes sense to us, but we rarely think of it in terms of justice.

Sometimes private property—a lot of it—is defended as having been "earned" by a hard-working, intelligent person. We know this means, more precisely, that the person has a marketable skill that he or she is willing to sell. We also know that people can acquire property by inheritance. But all this is obvious. The point is that built into our legal system is the idea that private property is sacred; yet relevant to justice may be the fact that some people go without food or clothing.

Back to John Locke. He believed that many problems in a pre-governmental society arose out of disputes over property. One reason for instituting government was to protect that property, to protect the fruits of an individual's labor. When our Constitution was written and the public and private realms were split, it became the duty of the public to protect the property of the private. The business of government was to protect private business. Contracts bound the relationships.

The case is easily documented. It was the Supreme Court, in the *Dred Scott* case of 1857, that ruled that slaves were property and that property was protected by the Constitution. Indeed, in its history the court has struck down laws that attempted to regulate the hours per week worked by children and the age at which they were permitted to begin work. A long series of rulings during the early 1930s held, essentially, that government could not regulate wages or prices. It was, primarily, the *principle* of the thing that mattered; the principle being that property was to be protected. The social costs of child labor and low wages seemed to be an entirely different matter.

Second, our system is built on the premise that in every case there is an innocent and a guilty party. It is an adversary method—one against the other. Neighbor versus neighbor doing battle in the court of law. One must be right, the other must be wrong; one is praised, the other blamed. In the end, one often gets a cash reward. We never consider the possibility that a problem might extend way beyond the two who are actually engaged in the proceedings. This particularized, personalized liberal justice makes almost no attempt to incorporate the principle of collective rights, or the idea that a people might collectively be wronged. The law is blind to groups of people. Everyone looks alike, single and alone.[2]

2  This is too important to be left unexamined, so we shall return to it at the end of this chapter.

Third, the system leaves us at the mercy of those who know the law. Our instincts for justice are exchanged for the expertise of the attorney. Lawyers are simply an elite. Their backgrounds are generally upper-middle class, their educations particular and expensive, and they possess the power to shape real events into a form unrecognized by us, but recognized by our system. They are the agents of the process, no matter which side they take. Theirs is a profession that is almost exclusively involved in adherence to rules. We, in turn, are dependent upon them.[3]

To stay within the liberal structure of the debate is too limiting. We will forever be forced to talk about process. Think back to the "advances" made by the court. Most had to do with the process itself. To understand the court as a biased, elite-oriented part of the system is to understand that *even if* the process were to become "perfect," we might still be no closer to justice than we are now.

Of course, the Mother of All Cases—at least involving American politics—was about a presidential election. In a totally unbiased decision, the five conservative members of the Supreme Court (some put there by Daddy Bush) voted to elect Baby Bush president. The written opinions were, basically, high humor from the High Court. They distributed their decisions late at night, as if embarrassed by what they had written.

If justice is nine people (appointed and approved for life by an elite) whose decisions generally favor what white, upper-middle-class people favor, then ours is a system of justice. There is a less complicated way of saying the same thing: American "justice" sings the song of the upper-middle class. A brief history should be helpful. According to the account given by Thomas Dye and Harmon Zeigler:

> Before the Civil War, the Supreme Court was spokesman first
> for the Federalists under John Marshall and later for Southern
> planters and slaveholders under Roger Taney ... Following
> the emergence of industrial capitalism in the second half of the
> nineteenth century, the Supreme Court became the spokes-
> man for the prevailing elite philosophy of Social Darwinism.
> The Court struck down the federal income tax; prevented

3  For a beautiful account of this, see Alexis de Tocqueville, *Democracy in America* (New York: Vintage, 1945).

prosecutions of corporations under the Sherman Antitrust Act, while applying this Act against labor unions; and struck down child labor laws and laws limiting the work week. The Court gave such a restrictive interpretation of the interstate commerce clause that it prevented federal regulation of the economy. It interpreted the "due process" clause of the Fifth and Fourteenth Amendments and the contract clause of Article II, Section 10, in such a way as to protect business enterprise from almost any form of government regulation.[4]

The time the court was in greatest trouble was when it "failed to respond swiftly to changes in elite philosophy ... In a four-year period, 1933–37, the court made the most active use of the power of judicial review over congressional legislation in its history, in a vain attempt to curtail the economic recovery programs of the New Deal. It invalidated the National Industrial Recovery Administration, nullified the Railroad Retirement Act, invalidated the National Farm Mortgage Act, and threw out the Agricultural Adjustment Act. Having denied the federal government the power to regulate manufacturing, petroleum, mining, agriculture, and labor conditions, the court reaffirmed the notion that the states could not regulate hours and wages."[5]

During the 1960s, the court seemed to be most interested in civil liberties. Certainly "progress" was made. But the fact seems to be this: Essentially, nothing has changed. The court is still a group of individuals with the biases of stability and security. Even as liberals work hard to purify the process, justice in America is still only judging. Rhetoric aside, justice's proverbial "blindness" to differences, the "majesty" and "sacredness" of the law, and the "equalness" of due process, remain confining and biased concepts.

Justice is greater than any sum of judgments, generally more inclusive than two arguing individuals, and should be accessible to more people than the few who know the "secret" language. In a sense, justice is too important and too immediate an activity to be left in the hands of only a few.

4   Thomas Dye and Harmon Zeigler, *The Irony of Democracy* (Belmont, Calif.: Wadsworth, 1970), pp. 458–59.

5   Ibid., p. 259.

It is too far-reaching to be limited to laws as interpreted by a minority.

The history of the Supreme Court comprises more than its rulings. It is the history of a people openly able to avoid justice under the label of law; the history of a few judging for the many; the history of the law following the times, with only a passing nod to the doing of justice. The liberalism of Locke called for the government to be a referee when the private affairs of individuals came into conflict. It did not offer many useful guidelines as to what it means to practice politics or to do justice. It is possible to understand our reliance on the Supreme Court as a justification for the individual to be uninvolved in justice. Our judicial system has inherited the weaknesses of Lockean liberalism.

As we know more about the weaknesses of liberalism, we also know more about the very human weaknesses of liberals. Let me give an example.

## Brief-ly

I would like to introduce the example with a new category. It is the "Is nothing sacred?" category, and we can now put the Supreme Court and its justices in it. We found out that no particular president is sacred, when Richard Nixon was dissected in the newspapers, on television, and on the radio. Psychologists and handwriting experts, in addition to reporters, lawyers, and next-door neighbors, told us much more about the man than we wanted to know.

Neither the president nor the presidency is now sacred. With Bob Woodward's book *The Brethren* we get the story of the Supreme Court in general, the justices in particular, and the chief justice for example.

While there is an amount of injustice about briefly characterizing a long book, there are some general lessons to be learned. The short of it is this: The Supreme Court acts about the way we would imagine it would act. Some justices are brighter than others, some more careful legal scholars than others, some better athletes than their colleagues, some more interested in power than their brethren.

What the court decides on any single issue is our rule of law. The rule of law, as we learn, has to do with decisions made by a majority of the justices, and majorities may be the results of deals made, bargains struck, favors granted, and the like. Lawyers negotiate; Supreme Court justices are lawyers supreme. The argument is not that the deals, negotiations, and such are bad; the argument has to do with the mystique of the Supreme Court.

Basically, the mystique tells us that those nine justices are the nine wise and fair people of our land. That they embody the good about us, and their concerns are for justice and fairness. They are impartial, nonpolitical seekers of the truth about a controversy. *The Brethren* is a book about that mystique—and how it is wrong.

In a way, the argument of the book finds its best symbol in then Chief Justice Burger. Have you ever seen a picture of him? There he was, white hair and distinguished looks: The man *looked* like a chief justice. Much of the book is about how those looks masked a relatively incompetent judge. He was not all that careful or smart. He bumbled things. Put differently, the mystique of the looks really hid the works of the man.

We can understand the same lesson in more substantive ways. The mystique of the court hides the very human-ness (indeed, liberal/capitalist/lawyer human-ness) of how the court works.

They really aren't perfect?

Is nothing sacred?

But to know that biases exist—and that justices are sometimes fools—doesn't necessarily mean that we will change. Indeed, most people still think that this system is the best we can do. There is the fear we are taught that if we had a system of people, it would simply become a tyranny. One person's whim would control other people's activities—certainly an unhappy situation. Another possibility is that a system of people would turn into chaos, into anarchy; it would mean that the worst of us would be unchecked. It would mean that we could not walk the streets after dark. But does it?

## Biases Shown

While it is not much of a surprise to find out that the law is biased, it is occasionally comforting to see the argument worked out. In that spirit, it is interesting to take a short look at a book by Morton Horwitz titled *The Transformation of American Law, 1780–1860*. It is an interesting book because it documents, clearly and carefully, changes in how the law has been understood and how it has functioned since the constitutional period. Let me repeat two basic arguments of the book.

First, Horwitz shows us that, as commerce and industry developed, they had clear effects on the law. As merchants and entrepreneurial groups gained political and economic power, they became closely allied with lawyers to advance their interests.

Many basic doctrines changed. The old understandings of property were done away with, and laws that seemed to hinder commerce were destroyed. As Horwitz puts it:

> Legal relations ... were increasingly subordinated to the disproportionate economic power of individuals or corporations ... law once thought of as protective ... and above all, a paramount expression of the moral sense of the community, had come to be thought of as a facilitative of individual desires and as simply reflective of the existing organization of economic and political power.[6]

By 1850 this shift in the law had pretty well been completed. We were, legally, a product/market-oriented society. Not just in our earning a living, but also legally. Industry and industrialists were blessed. So were lawyers. Workers, consumers, farmers, and basically the rest of us were made to play by the industrial/legal rules.

Having the bias set up like that is really not enough. There is a second thing that happened that was necessary for enforcement of the bias. During this time—from 1780 to 1860—there was an effort to make the law seem objective: different from and above politics. An effort was made to change the meaning just a little, toward what is called formalism.

Laws and legal doctrines became increasingly general in order to include more and more areas. Sometimes it seems everything we do is connected to our legal system. In addition, and in a really amazing way, there is a great increase in the number of rules surrounding the law. There was a time when legal rules—prescribed conduct—were set up to help protect moral principles. Now the rules *themselves* have become moral principles. The rules *are* the morality. Lawyers and the legal profession have become

---

6  Morton Horwitz, *The Transformation of American Law, 1780–1860* (Cambridge, Mass.: Harvard University Press, 1977), p. 253.

the knowers and keepers of the faith.

To just barely overstate the case, the lawyers are viewed as above politics, above citizens, above restriction. Again, Horwitz: "A scientific, objective, professional, and apolitical conception of the law ... now comes to extend its domain and to infiltrate into the everyday categories of adjudication."[7]

What we know from the evidence is that "everyday ... adjudication" has a specific economic bias. Put simply, what Horwitz—a Harvard Law professor—is arguing is that the fix is in. He tells us there was a fight over what the law was going to be about. More than a hundred years ago, the fight was effectively over. Now, today, the spiritual descendants of the winners are still winning, and the others are still losing. If our law is supposed to be unbiased, I wonder what biased would look like.

## A Head Job

> *It is said that to every generation ten just people are born. No one knows who those people are.*

There is more than a little reason to believe that many of the people who read this book will want to become lawyers. Some for fairly standard, greedy reasons: money and power. Others will study law because of pressure from parents, and still others in order to do "good" work. You know about "good" work: work within the system to change it ... and who knows more about the system than lawyers? (Rhetorical questions are wonderful. While the *answers* are always clear, the *implications* of the answers are seldom considered and are often very strange.)

I want to spend some time with the do-good-lawyers among you. Anybody may read this section, since it has to do with all of us; but the people who might want to take notes are the future do-gooders. They are often blind to the fact that law cuts at least two ways: (1) It is the aggressive carrier of our particular brand of liberalism; and (2) its first victim is the law student/lawyer. The lawyer becomes the law, the state becomes the person, the person becomes the lawyer becomes the state. Law changes you. It does a head job. You don't have a chance. Not only is it silly to assume *you,*

7   Ibid., p. 266.

as a lawyer, are going to change the system: it is especially wrong-headed to believe you will escape being changed. They'll get you. Count on it.

Law is something that is done; and, in the twentieth century, the fact seems to be that you are what you do. More than that, what you do you're responsible for. In the end, law—that "neutral" arbiter of our society—is built on a whole set of attitudes and results in a prescription for how each of us is *supposed* to relate to the world. Law goes to our heads, and our heads have a lot to say about what we do.

In an interesting piece of research, Jacqueline Smethurst looked into this problem by studying women who went to law school. [8] She talked to them before they studied law and then again after they became lawyers. One of the underlying questions was this: Now that women were lawyers, would they be different from their male counterparts? After all, there are many concerns (like having children) that have traditionally been women's. Also, there has been new research indicating that there is a women's way of thinking that is more integrative and less combative than men's way of thinking.

What Smethurst found was that lawyers were lawyers. That more women became lawyers meant that there were more women lawyers. Now, it is nice that there is more equality of opportunity, but it seems foolish to think that things will change. In the law, it is ambition against ambition, brain against brain, hard work against hard work, push against shove. What difference does it make, in the long run, if either or both or neither of the pushers and shovers are men or women? Our system of law will easily assimilate people that the law school educates and who are able to pass the bar.

To believe you will be different is fantasy of the highest order. A second way to get a view of the law (get a view of ourselves) is to look at how lawyers structure and do their work. The case in point deals with some ideas that seem so commonsensical as to be almost foolish to discuss. It may well be that it is these commonsense ideas that will give us the best mirror to see ourselves. Our mirror image, I must warn you, may not be our self-image.

The case has to do with how "radical" lawyers understand the problems of Native Americans, and how they try to solve those problems. It is

8   See Jacqueline Smethurst, "Women Becoming Lawyers: A Process with Implications for Public and Private Spheres" (Ed. D. diss., Amherst, Mass., 1984).

important not to get too far from the fact that answers are built into questions, and that we have about as much to learn from the answers the lawyers give as from the questions they ask. The following comes from a dissertation written by Linda Medcalf. The details of the lawyer/Indian interactions are not fully explored here, since the *Preface* is not the place for the full lesson. But there are things that we can learn.

## The Case: Ongoing Shame

Almost since the time of Columbus, the Europeans who came to live here have treated the Native Americans cruelly. That is simply a very terrible, shameful fact. There has been everything from early germ warfare (Lord Jeffrey Amherst suggested giving Indians disease-infested blankets that would kill them and make old Lord Jeff even more wealthy), to broken treaties and promises, to forced marches from swamps to dust bowls, to simple murder.

To understate, Liberal America has not done itself proud in its dealings with the natives of this land. Before settlers started mucking around and moving and murdering the Indians, Native Americans seemed to live as they wished. Their tribes were strong communities; their relationship to the environment was one not of control but of respect; they had their wars, but many of the tribes were peaceful.

To fast-paced, alienated, bureaucratized, controlling, standard Americans, the Indian—both in fact and myth—seemed to be more whole and together than we are.

They were, in odd combination, a good example, and because of that, a threat. We have gotten rid of almost everything but the myth.

In an effort to "make things right," there has been a move to provide tribes with aid. Regrettably, it has generally been legal aid. Well-intentioned attorneys have done their best with Native Americans, made real attempts to do what they understood as necessary for a group of people who have been systematically abused.

As a group, the Indians are a little different from other minorities:

1.  They own about 2 percent of the land in America, and the land is in large enough blocks so that they do not need to integrate into mainstream city or suburban living.

2. The land they occupy is rich in natural resources—water, timber, oil, and fish—to be used if and how they wish. And federal law now enables casino gambling—big money.
3. They have done things in accordance with our law, and the courts of the United States regularly uphold their claims.

For attorneys, the Indians are often "difficult" to relate to but are certainly "good" clients. The attorneys believe the problems of the Indians they represent can, in a rough way, be understood as (1) the poverty of the individuals; (2) their lack of power—both personally and tribally; and (3) the lack of education and skills of the people. These are all problems we can relate to; after all, we sort out much of the world with those very categories. Lawyers are trained to solve these problems in very specific ways, and we know that their training doesn't stop at the reservation gate.

The problems—poverty, power, and education—are so interrelated as to be inseparable in any real way. When a lawyer makes an attempt to solve one of the problems, he or she is also working on the other ones. The changes, the solving, go on in the context of an ongoing tribal life that the attorneys are committed to keep. Keep, and make better. Those are the words they use.

In an attempt to keep the form of the tribe, the lawyer makes it over into a corporation. The tribal member becomes a shareholder. Of course, the corporate style—the *needs* and *aims*—of a corporation are a little different from those of a tribe. The reorganization is built, in part, on the premise that to be strong and to avoid poverty, all those natural resources on the reservations must become economic assets. They must be well managed to bring in more money, and new opportunities must be sought and exploited to achieve economic sustainability.

That means, naturally enough, some different qualities in the Chief (Chairperson of the Board?) and his or her legal advisers. Instead of carrying and refining the traditions and wisdom of the tribe, the Chief now has to have the skills of a corporate manager.[9] There's more. In order for the shareholders (that is, the tribe members) to be good citizens/capitalists, they must become educated in the ways of liberal America. The America that most of us learn in school. The one that demands that people see the

---

9   The language being used is ours.

world and make arguments in the form and language of a liberal/individual/competitive style we know as normal.

No more "passive" Red People. No more "submissive" aboriginal tribes. If the lawyers have their way, strong tribal (entrepreneurial) leadership and a powerful (wealthy) tribe will be the result of a vigorous, intratribal politics based on economic self-interest.

## Right(s)?

Once you get to that point in the logic, it seems sensible that people need some protection. It becomes necessary and logical and seemingly normal to make certain that every person in the tribe be granted *rights*. After all, the individual has certain duties and responsibilities as well as some "freedom" from repression. Rights form a basis of much of our political thinking, and it *seems* good that everyone has them. I mean, *what could possibly be wrong with rights?* The answer, if I understand it correctly, is plenty. The concept of rights is a cultural one. There is nothing universal about it. Rights as defined by the lawyers for and to Native Americans are wholly culturally based. The rights that seem so natural to us are built on the assumptions of individualism, which require certain kinds of aggressive actions. To quote: "A human being is not a bundle of legal rights; it is a much richer complex of emotions and mind and interaction with others and the environment which has very little resemblance to the bare contractual outline individual rights gives. To reduce human relationships to one of rights and responsibilities, one against the other, is to render the human relationship possibilities barren, to make of human relationships an 'irreducible minimum' before they become nothing at all."

Rights divide and liberalism/legalism conquers.

Let's go back and judge the lawyers, judge those who have power to ask the questions, define the problems, and then solve those very problems. In fact, many tribes now have a great deal of money. They are becoming (in the most mainstream way) viable economic actors. The lawyers "did" the law and were successful at it.

The real question is: Successful at what?

Think about the triad of Economics, Education, and Power. Sound familiar? Once those things take on our definitions, and once they become the central issues, the rest simply flows. Corporations, competition, individualism, efficiency, rationality, rights: We've *Americanized* Native Americans. Franz Kafka spelled it Amerika. Looks different, doesn't it? And the do-gooders? The lawyers? What they do is the law. Of course there are well-intentioned, nice, good lawyers. It just seems a crime that we are forced to live in a world that they help create and perpetuate because of the very structure of *their* thought and activity. What is so "American" to Lockean liberals may well be "Amerika" to those with different cultures. Different, and maybe a little sinister.

Our legal system divides and conquers. It slices life into a million different issues and decisions.

## Justice and Politics

Thus far, we have struggled with justice but have not really gotten much closer to it; we have worked through some of the problems without getting much closer to the solutions. We have done something. We no longer need trouble ourselves with the idea that law (our "justice") is impartial. No law is impartial; probably justice is not, either.

Laws are set up to help and protect certain people and certain things. Police make sure that some of the violators are caught, and our judicial system enforces the laws. Now, if one is white and middle class that may sound a great deal like justice. Police protect "us" against "them." Laws are designed to help "us," not "them." It may be with that us/them formulation, in that space between security and terror that we might begin to understand justice.

While it is not terribly successful to argue that there are social classes in America (almost everyone considers himself or herself part of the middle class), it is undeniable that there are those without power, status, or wealth. If not a lower class, at least a class apart, a class outside the benefits of society. This group of people includes, roughly, the blacks, Chicanos, Native Americans, white poor, and those who "drop out." Possibly most dropouts don't count; after all, they can drop back in. The white poor, the white dropout, may "miraculously" reach the middle class. But the others are outside, subject to a "justice" that does not seem to include them.[10]

10  There are, of course, middle-class people of every color. We still get stories on the news about police who, for example, mistake a middle-class black for a "criminal" poor black. Put differently, racism can conquer economic class.

The white middle class ultimately thinks of the police as friends. Indeed, they are. Police catch criminals, control traffic, and in many ways help people. More exactly, white people. The police are the "thin blue line of protection," so the saying goes. And certainly they are. But they are much more than that. An example of ghetto justice may help show why.

James Baldwin tells the story of a black salesman in Harlem. One day, after he had left a customer, there seemed to be a great deal of activity in the street.

> People were running from the police. Other people, in windows, left their windows, in terror of the police because the police had their guns out and were aiming their guns at the roofs. Then the salesman noticed that two of the policemen were beating up a kid:" So I spoke up and asked them, 'why are you beating him up like that?' Police jump up and start swinging on me. He put the gun on me and said, *'get over there.'* I said, 'What for?'
>
> An unwise question. Three of the policemen beat up the salesman in the streets ...
>
> As of my last information, the salesman is on the streets again, with his attaché case, trying to feed his family. He is more visible now because he wears an eye patch ... His tone is simply the tone of one who has miraculously survived—he might have died; as it is, he is merely half-blind ... It is a dishonorable wound, not earned in a foreign jungle but in the domestic one—not that this would make any difference at all to the nevertheless insuperably patriotic policeman—and it proves that he is a "bad nigger." [11]

It is not easy to find justice in this example. Whites expect the police to protect them—and this generally happens. The person in business expects to carry out his or her white-collar crime, or illegal gambling, uninterrupted—and this generally happens. Anything beyond that is of little

---

11 James Baldwin, "A Report from Occupied Territory," in Laurence Veysey, ed., *Law and Resistance* (Harper & Row, 1970), pp. 318–19; it originally appeared in *The Nation*, 203 (July 11, 1966), pp. 39–43.

concern; beyond that it is someone else's problem. So the police are left to deal with the problems of poverty and race hatred and decaying cities. Somehow whites expect social injustice to be solved by force, stopped by violence. Between the "us" and the "them," the white middle class and the black ghetto, justice does not seem to exist. There is security for the whites, injustice for the blacks, and in the impossible middle—unrestrained and powerful—stand the police.

The black is colonized in white America. The black is trapped. How can he or she act "justly"? Maybe justice is treating a person the way he or she deserves to be treated. If that is the case, one can understand the logic of Frantz Fanon. Fanon writes of the colonized black in Africa. He writes about violence, and the justice of it:

> For the native, this violence represents the absolute line of action. The group requires that each individual perform an irrevocable action. In Algeria, for example, where almost all the men who called on the people to join in the national struggle were condemned to death or searched for by the French police, confidence was proportional to the hopelessness of each case. You could be sure of a new recruit when he [or she] could no longer go back into the colonial system ... To work means to work for the death of the settler. This assumption of responsibility for violence allows both strayed and outlawed members of the group to come back again and to find their place once more, to become integrated. Violence is thus seen comparable to a royal pardon. The colonized man finds his freedom in and through violence.[12]

Perhaps violence not only is necessary but may also even be justice in the case of the American black. But possibly justice is more than treating a person the way he "deserves" to be treated. Justice may involve more than that; it may be a reflection not only of the action of the one, but also of the action of the other. What I am suggesting is that a "punishment" may reflect the one doing the punishing. One does justice, but also loves mercy. It is possible that forgiveness is as much a part of justice as vio-

12 Frantz Fanon, *The Wretched of the Earth* (New York: Grove Press, 1965), pp. 85–86.

lence. Both may be doing justice, and both may involve freedom for the individual.

## Political Trials and People

Part of what I am suggesting is that there are many elements in justice, which at their core have little to do with laws. These elements have to do with people trying to live together in some sensible manner. I am not saying that there should no longer be judges or juries or laws. What I am suggesting is that we examine these things and try to figure out a better method of getting at justice.

We Americans seem hesitant to believe that any—much less many—trials are political ones. In fact, scholars in this field are trying hard to reach agreement on just what a political trial is. Let us stay on the fringes of scholarship and seek some commonsense understanding of what political trials are and what they might mean.

In the most obvious sense, a political trial involves people who have been charged with treason against the state, or some such crime. We have very few of these. We can understand the desire of a state to protect itself. There is a history of political trials as old as the history of trials. Both Socrates and Jesus were perceived as great enough threats to the state to be brought to trial. In a sense, political trials have a noble past.

Yet we deny political motivation. When one is arrested for protesting environmental problems or for antipoverty activity—and those things are surely political—the likelihood is that the charge will involve something like marching without a permit or disrupting traffic. In other words, we require trials that never get to the issues involved. People intensely involved in acting on what they believe to be right are denied their validity as moral beings. They are denied any chance of having their principles dealt with justly.

## Politics and Blind Justice

A series of political trials took place at the end of the 1980s. The most interesting of the series involved that basement warrior, the ace of the shredder, the Marine Cowboy, Oliver North. He was not the only one who went to trial for lying, cheating, and generally breaking laws; but he was the best known, and an example to us all. The driving question, of course, revolves around what kind of example he is.

There he was, on television. Full uniform, sitting up straight, the good soldier, and watery blue eyes. Articulate. A real conservative. A patriot. Some guy.

Before he was caught, he apparently did not think too much of the laws of the land. He broke them. Ah, but then he was caught. Lawbreaker. The first move was a natural liberal move; it seemed as normal as breathing, it was all-American: North hired a lawyer. We need to note, he hired a very high-powered lawyer at that. One that he really couldn't afford, but he hired him anyway. Speaking fees and friends would foot the seven-figure bill.

So just what was North supposed to have done? Some of the things were pretty big. It seems that he was involved in selling arms to Iran (something the United States pledged not to do), then took the profits and gave them to the Contras (something which the Congress had banned). Here's where a good lawyer comes into play: These charges were dropped on "national security" grounds. So North is off the big hook, and so, it seems, were the then president and vice president: Relief for Reagan and Bush.

But there were twelve more counts against North. Did he lie to Congress? (Yes, but he didn't know it was against the law. The jury found him not guilty on five counts.) Did he lie to Attorney General Meese, who conducted an inquiry, in order to "conceal or hide the facts" from the Congress and the public? (Yes, but that was all right. Two more not guilty votes.) Did he defraud the IRS in the way he raised money for the Contras through tax-exempt organizations, and did he take $4,300 for his own use? (The IRS charge seemed picky to the jury: innocent. North said that the money was reimbursement for funds of his own that he used. Sure, said the jury. Another not guilty.)

Up to now, let's see just where we are in this political trial. Here we have an intensely political person, a person who felt strongly enough about his beliefs that he broke some serious laws to advance the cause. And how does American justice deal with this most political man? He was found guilty of accepting money ($13,800) for a home security system, and guilty of shredding documents and altering documents when the investigation began to look serious.

The title of this section has to do with blind justice. I meant it in two ways. The first way has to do, in this case, with the jury. The trial court had to find jurors who had not heard or read about what had gone on or what North had said, a difficult task because North had testified before Congress.

A kind of mission-impossible jury. Washington, D.C. revolves around government. Certainly Oliver North's peers were up to their eyeballs in Iran-Contra news. But to be an informed citizen, in this case, kept a person off of the jury. So, blindfolded Ms. Justice picked twelve black jurors who did not follow the news, and assumed that they were the white marine's peers. And why not?

The second thing that justice seems to be blind to is politics. Or, to put it another way, if you buy into liberalism then your deepest beliefs have to do with process. What we can see with North is that he was willing to be a liberal when confronted with his wrongdoings. It would seem that a remarkable number of us are willing to stand up for what is right. But, when confronted with American law, we readily hire the best American lawyer available.

What if a person does the "right" thing, politically, but it is illegal? Even if it comes to trial, the political reasons cannot be heard. North believed in the Contra cause, but that was never a legal issue. Political beliefs, when tried, literally get shredded.

There are truths beyond process, but the law is all process. Society is full of human beings doing human things. Some are politically motivated; some are the stuff of being alive. All of it, according to our legal system, gets washed out in the process. Some are willing to go to jail because they believe that their political cause is right. One need only think of Martin Luther King to remember a good example.

Finally, there are trials that on the surface seem to have nothing to do with politics. The prostitutes who periodically get arrested, the tenant who refuses to pay his or her rent until something is repaired, and the foreigners, gays, and minorities are automatically guilty. The law is the law. What I want to suggest is that these cases could be handled differently, in such a way that they would take on a political meaning. If this were done, there might even be a chance that justice would emerge.

There are, in different countries, something like people's courts. They seem to me closer to a just method than what we have been discussing. An idealized description may help. Essentially, these courts are neighborhood-centered. The people in the area choose the judge. The judge is a respected, well-known member of the neighborhood, though not necessarily a lawyer. The judge must simply be a fair, just person who understands the aims of society, the aims of a revolutionary people.

The cases that come before the judge are local ones. They are heard in public; in essence, this means that those neighbors who know of the case or the defendants or those who were close to what happened attend. Often, many attend and are part of a case. The catch is this: The audience may be somehow guilty of the crime of the defendant. Guilty for not stopping an argument, guilty for not helping right a wrong, guilty for not helping someone who needed help.

Maybe that is what justice is about. Midway between "an eye for an eye" and "turning the other cheek," we are groping for justice. But the point might be that we should not necessarily wander alone. The People's Courts are one way to begin to understand that to be part of society is to assume some responsibility for what goes on, and that this responsibility reaches into the realm of justice. Not a justice of lawyers and complex legal procedures, but somehow of the doing of justice.

# chapter 11

# About Groups

*It was my destiny to join in a great experience. Having had the good fortune to belong to the League, I was permitted to be a participant in a unique journey. What wonder it had at the time.*

*... we League brothers traveled throughout the world without motorcars or ships; as we conquered the war-shattered world by our faith and transformed it into Paradise, we creatively brought the past, the future and the fictitious into the present moment.*

— *Hermann Hesse*

*"There are going to be times," says Kesey, "when we can't wait for somebody. Now, you're either on the bus or off the bus. If you're on the bus, and you get left behind, then you'll find it again. If you're off the bus in the first place—then it won't make a damn." And nobody had to have it spelled out for them. Everything was becoming allegorical, understood by the group mind, and especially this: you're either on the bus ... or off the bus.*

*—Tom Wolfe*

## Groups, and Social Science Past

There are times when we want to settle back, when we want to be surrounded by a kind of primordial ooze of companionship. We want the ease of wine or religion or dope. Sometimes we want the womblike comfort of a group.

Groups have a long—if not noble—history in American politics. From the time James Madison wrote about factions, group theory has tried to mirror group action in America. We know, too, that Alexis de Tocqueville wrote about groups, "voluntary associations," which to him seemed the backbone of the republic. Because groups seem to have something to do with our reality, we should try to understand them both as a social science discovery and for what they mean in the real world.

At one time or another small groups have been seen as the basis of just about everything. The king had his advisers, the pope his inner councils of close friends, the president a kitchen cabinet, and, most recently—but for rather different reasons—the rock bands have had their groupies.

But even with all those groups around, even knowing that they have had something to do with why things happened as they did, it is hard for us to truly understand the nature of groups. It is difficult mostly because we do not really want to hear about them. As students, we seem to shy away from an understanding of groups because it might be painful. In the end, it may turn out that we are all "groupies" of one kind or another; yet we do not know a thing about groups.

It seems reasonable to approach this section historically so as to better understand ourselves as an extension of what was. Around the turn of the twentieth century, groups were rediscovered in American society, this time by an academic named Arthur Bentley. A seductive theory, his. The idea, in a somewhat bastardized form, was that small groups were the oil that kept society running smoothly. One could look around—casually or carefully—and see that neighbors and corporate executives, army generals and important senators all formed themselves into groups. It was thought all that was needed was to understand how people were brought together, what they did when they were together, and how the different bunches of them interacted; then we could understand all the important things about society.

Just think group, think small, and all answers would be clear.

The understanding of groups did not stop there; indeed, it has been continued, updated, revised, and revitalized by those people who study large organizations. What the investigators found, while a bit of a surprise to them, should be no surprise to us. They found that people who worked in organizations tended to gather in groups. That people in these little groups did things pretty much alike. That they worked at about the same speed, thought about the same thoughts, said about the same things. In sum, members of groups became almost indistinguishable to those outside the group.[1]

In terms of historical importance we can shift from the 1930s to the 1950s, from looking at groups in organizations to groups in society, from the Hawthorne studies to the studies of David Truman. It is through Truman that we can begin to understand some of the basic issues of groupist ideology.

## Ideology and Groups

It is clear that when any "reality" is described, when any theory is presented, it carries with it a bias. Sometimes more pronounced than others; sometimes involving a whole worldview, other times simple prejudices. Those who write about groups are certainly carriers of bias; they surely have a particular view of society to present.

The point is not that group theorists have biases—that is quite normal; the point is to understand what those biases are. We need to examine the implications of their views to know whether we can share them. We must compare what the roles of groups in society are said to be with what they really are; we must know who groups help, and how; finally, we must try to figure out where group theory might be leading us. Maybe then we can begin to make sense out of our group selves.

Groups, according to David Truman, represent the multiple interests in a society. Our diversity is reflected—indeed, represented—by the groups to which we belong. Further, if there is a "national interest," it is

---

1   These were the Hawthorne studies. One major finding resulting from them was that people being studied were more productive then people not being studied. For a first-rate article on modern working groups, see Elinor Langer, "The Women of the Telephone Company," *New York Review of Books*, March 26, 1970.

only the sum of the interests of these groups. In other words, an individual belongs to a group, the group represents the interests of the individual in the public sector, and the sum of the interests of these groups is the "national interest."[2]

Now certainly that makes sense. Indeed, it is wholly reasonable until one begins to think about it and question it. What I want to argue is that Truman fails us in very basic ways, and to understand his failure is to begin to understand one of the meanings of groups.

One "sin" of Truman is simply this: He assumes unquestioningly that leaders do in fact represent the group interest. He does not ask how they do so, or to what extent they do; he just assumes that leaders represent their groups. If Truman is correct, then the system of groups seems fair enough. It means that we can join a group and have a voice in what goes on. Regrettably, however, Truman does not appear to be right.

Theoretically, the internal workings of groups, and therefore the interests they come to represent, are complicated. Groups (for example, labor unions) inevitably come under the leadership of people who are insulated from the rest of the members. Worse, leaders begin developing interests of their own: the desire to stay in power, the desire to form friendships with other group leaders or with powerful, prestigious persons. Much of their behavior can be understood in bureaucratic terms.

In other words, the desires of the leader are often different from, or even in conflict with, the desires of the membership he or she represents. The leader has aims and goals, which, in the last analysis, are conservative. His or her vision becomes limited to a particular position in the system, so that the key to policy must be to keep the system stable. There is no reason to believe that stability is the goal of the membership of the organization; there is little evidence to show that the interests of the group are represented by the leadership.[3]

Group theory in the 1950s, then, was interesting but certainly not democratic. What Truman described was a system run by an elite of group leaders. The elite was responsible for the safety of the system and for its stability, but did not really concern itself with the democratic workings of the group. By definition, the interests of the leadership were thought to be

2   See David Truman, *The Government Process* (New York: Knopf, 1951).

3   Ibid., pp. 132–33.

the interests of the group, but that assumption was only partially correct. As defined by the leadership—by the elite—group interests were represented only if they did not endanger the smooth workings of the system, only if they did not endanger the security of the elite.

When viewed in this light, two things become more understandable. First, at the level of the example itself, it is clear that business and labor *can* agree on many things, because business leaders and labor leaders perceive that they have much in common. The dynamic that pushes the one pushes the other.

Second, it becomes obvious that Truman's theory of groups contains a particular view of the individual. The view is impersonal and material. The individual is to be materially taken care of by the group. That is in the person's interest and in the public interest. Yet, in an important sense, a political sense, the individual is not much better off than he or she was before joining the group. The individual is not really represented by anyone, is not a member of a group that democratically decides the interests of that group; is not in control; is powerless.

Such are the individual costs of this group theory, of this "public interest." They represent, in part, the social and political costs of our system of groups.

## New Groups for Contact

David Truman worked in the 1950s; we are living in the new millennium. The pace of life has become faster. Some of us feel we have to take speed to stay even. Organizations have become bigger. We have become smaller cogs in bigger machines. Much smaller, and much, much bigger.

Somehow society has tried to push us apart organically—and together mechanically. By that I mean that we are less and less able to understand ourselves as human beings, but more able to define ourselves as pieces of social machinery. We are more tool-like; we are more machine-like; we are more pieces of production than ever before.

Where does that leave us? Surely our social science theories would n consciously deny us our own humanity.

Of course they don't. No, social science would not do that. What i do is what it has tried to do for years—tie us neatly together in groups of powerless people. It happens at two levels: personally nizationally. In one sense, this theory of small groups makes the world very recognizable. The United States is made up of millions of little groups. These groups—in car pools, at work, at school, in the neighborhood, people who come together to hunt or play bridge—give humanity and, finally, provide a kind of self-definition to an individual.

In a sense, the theory might be right. We seem to yearn for our own close groups. Yet even these groups have been changing and so too has our involvement in them. Groups in the brave new world now seem to have two distinct qualities: temporariness and great intimacy. Together these traits can be tyrannizing.

Of course, one of the interesting things about the United States is that many of its citizens seem stuck in time. Some are still fighting World War II, with the same enemies and allies, while others need to keep Communists away from our borders ... even though the Communists aren't coming.

Ronald Reagan, for example, seemed to be stuck in the movies of the 1940s, and Trent Lott never quite got over the segregation of the 1950s. Ouch.

We can see old hippies playing out the 1960s, yuppies playing out the 1970s, and people in high school putting the finishing touches on who they might be for the next sixty years.

As we go through generations, we also go through varieties of group experiences. In our ideal past, the family—an extended family at that—was the group that provided the very best support. Grandparents, and nutty aunts and uncles, and all kinds of cousins helped each person in the family through life. And, importantly, they were all accessible. The family lived pretty close together.

But families not only broke up, they became potential problems themselves. (Parents were drunks, or abusive, or divorced, or worked all the time, or whatever.) So, there was a time when we did group therapy. One professional and an assortment of troubled people, together for an hour and a half of group work. Then there were encounter groups, some wholly artificial and temporary. The people in the office went off for an encounter. If you had the time and the money, you could do it for a weekend.

The United States is littered with groups. Some are more interesting than others. There are, for example, two motorcycle groups around here. They take some politics seriously, and they are on different sides.

One group hangs out at a biker bar called the Top Hat. They ride chopped Harley-Davidson motorcycles. Hogs. Made in America. Some are mechanics, some sell dope, some you just don't know about. But they do agree on their bikes. Not too long ago they got on their hogs and took a trip to the state capital. They went to the legislature and testified for their freedom: No mandatory motorcycle helmet law for them. They made their point.

The other bikers ride "Made in America" Golden Wings. Far from chopped, their bikes are fixed up with stereos and bumpers, and some can even pull a trailer. They travel. The youngest members are fifty; some of the others are much older. They are for the mandatory helmet law.

The United States is a great country for groups.

Parents run sports leagues for kids; churches sponsor all kinds of events for everybody; the PTA helps put on the events that sometimes make schools tolerable. At their best, these groups not only provide public services, they also provide places for people to be seen and heard. Too bad we can't find a way to do those same things politically.

Back to our little history of groups. By the 1970s a lot of people had discovered Alcoholics Anonymous, and used that model of a group to attack a whole batch of different problems. In a sense, these groups are coming closer to what we lost when we lost the family.

There are ways in which the circle seems to be closing. All these groups might add something to our lives. Therapy groups can help, and so can encounter groups. But if we turn to political change, to any substantive action, then they seem to influence nothing. These groups provide human contact, which is an important, and neglected, need of our times.

## Groups for Speed

If we now know the important themes about groups, it is necessary to develop them in some detail. In this and the following sections we will deal with the coerciveness of groups, with leadership and participation in groups, with the multitude of new groups, and with groups that will get you places you didn't know existed.

It seems sensible to begin with speed, and with coerciveness.

Maybe death can provide a good example of how speeded up we have become. How long can we mourn a death? What, to be tacky about it, are our bereavement policies? In 1927, Emily Post reported that the formal mourning period for a widow was three years. By 1950, that time had been cut to six months.

Time flies.

More than nine out of ten American companies grant some official time off for bereavement. It is three days. Seventy-two hours and it's back on the job. Not only that, you get to grieve officially only for immediate family members—spouse, children, parents. Anyone else—grandparents, in-laws, aunts and uncles, close friends—are out. Excluded. No time for them.

Our world moves much faster, and the time we have for almost anything is shorter and shorter. I'm dead right about this.

There are ways in which speed genuinely limits a person's power. So, too, can groups. By studying the setting of groups—how they are arranged and managed—and group dynamics, we will get closer to understanding how an individual group member may become powerless. First, the setting.

If I understand the trend correctly, we are moving toward a society in which work groups, and hence all others, are becoming temporary. There is another book, *The Temporary Society,* that focuses on moving itself.[4]

The argument of the future is roughly this. Society, especially the technical one, is experiencing more and more problems. To get to these problems quickly, to solve them fast, we must change our living patterns. We must be able to move around quickly—move to the problems—meet new sets of coworkers, and form together to solve the problem.

Then, move again to solve the next problem.

This is more than just a way to organize (or to reorganize); it is a whole ethic, a whole way of understanding society and ourselves. We become people without a home, without permanence. We become a permanent part of an ever-changing environment, perpetual strangers in a group of strangers. To meet the new requirements, we must continually change

4  Warren Bennis and Philip E. Slater, *The Temporary Society* (New York: Harper & Row, 1968).

homes, towns, work groups, and friends. Above and beyond what was discussed in connection with the Open Road, the implications of this style are enormous.

First, and most obvious, power in such a system lies in the ability to move people around. In other words, there is something at the center finding problems and moving people. Those who move become wholly dependent upon their bosses. They have no other stable reference point. It is possible that the military is the forerunner of temporary America. Every year or two the military family moves. From city to city, from base to base. They are thrown into new work groups and a new social life. Only if they are lucky do they see old friends, that is, people from other one-year stays at other military bases. The military person is loyal to— and dependent upon—the United States government (whoever that is). Loyalties are rarely to the location from which he or she is about to move.

The point is clear: In a world of temporary groups, power flows to those who control the moves. Corporations utilize the idea of task teams, grouping together the best people and sending them out to complete an assignment effectively and efficiently, giving no consideration to the effects on their personal lives.

We can approach it in a different way with this question: Where do we look for strength if not in our phenomenal surroundings? While I am not certain there is an agreed-upon answer, let me suggest one that seems reasonable. As we become less attached to the real (material) things around us, we become more attached to the ever-present symbols that are common to us all. We rely on our commitment to the symbolic values we carry with us rather than those things we know in our immediate surroundings.

The second point about temporariness involves the kind of person who will fit. The question is this: Who will people the Temporary Society? Who will survive? We can speculate.

The young will survive the moving and adjusting. They are healthy enough for all the hassles. But the survivors must be more than young; they must be technical experts, too. A young person with technical expertise might not merely adjust to such a regimen; he or she could possibly thrive on moving from place to place, continually solving problems of a technical nature. The young could somehow handle the ever-changing groups of people, as long as there is work to do.[5]

They will survive, but for how long? "Young" is not a permanent condition; neither is technical expertise. In these days of rapidly increasing knowledge, an engineer of thirty may be out-of-date, may be an old-fashioned toolbox with old-fashioned tools.

There are some odd and horrible losses in this temporary world. We both grow "old" too quickly and stay "young" too long. We can't really *be* young and adventuresome. Got to get going—moving and dealing and making it, right out of college. The cream of the crop has the new techniques, the stamina to survive, and is unformed enough to continually adapt.

So there is the constant fear of being old. Being out of technological date. Being too slow to move and too much of a person to adapt to every silly change.

The temporary world robs both the rush of being young and the true pleasure of aging.

There is an amazing curse put on the young—a curse that goes with our age. It's called potential, and young people almost always have it. One could easily call it a social disease. I'm pleased not to be in college, or even in my twenties. I'm just beginning to glimpse the horrors we put on the young. The weight of the word *potential.*

There is a denial of personal power, a taking away (a not-granting) of a sense of self. Sure you're whole, but empty. Young and hollow. *What does it mean?*

At least two things.

First, all ages seem to have been corrupted. Everyone wants to be young, and young people are denied the essences of life. Second, in our temporary world, emotions get *democratized* and *discounted.*

Let's go back to encounter-type groups and look at them a little differently. The real trap in our pop-psychological instant-intimacy groups is something like this: To be "healthy," one must "express one's own per-

---

5  One particularly vivid and depressing forecast of the future is that it will be like Fort Lauderdale when students are there over spring break. See Alvin Toffler, *Future Shock* (New York: Bantam, 1970); also, of course, see Christopher Lasch, *The Culture of Narcissism* (New York: Warner, 1979).

sonal feelings." To apply a good social science concept to that, a lot of it is just bullshit.

There are many things that are really unimportant ... even some of your very own emotions. To make all emotions equal means you will never be able to see what's important and what's unimportant. When another person or an event really is an intrusion into your life—really does affect the who-you-are in the world—what do you do if you've just been to an encounter group and have let it "all hang out"? Been "up front"? Been "honest" and are "emotionally spent"? What do you do for something important? Just chill, as the expression goes.

We've made love/hate/anger/joy all silly and meaningless by elevating petty moods into important events of our personal lives. We seem all too willing to throw away empathy and care and probably a great deal of our politics and humanity for a cheap version of self-indulgent, childish whimpering.

*We democrats go to encounter groups and vote on emotions.*

What a place we've gotten to.

The temporary society makes no allowance for the very young, for the old, for those not involved in technology. Part of the glue it uses—groups—seems systematically to take us away from our emotional self by flooding us with "emotion." What does it mean? To quote Kurt Vonnegut:

> The problem is this: How to love people who have no use?
>
> In time, almost all men and women will become worthless as producers of goods, food, services and more machines, as sources of practical ideas in the areas of economics, engineering and probably medicine, too. So—if we cannot find reasons and methods for treasuring human beings because they are human beings, then we might as well, as has so often been suggested, rub them out.[6]

Rub them out? Is *that* the ultimate solution of the temporary society? Probably not, but it is an idea.

6  Kurt Vonnegut, Jr., *God Bless You, Mr. Rosewater* (New York: Dell, 1965), p. 183. It should be noted that "doing away" with people is not Vonnegut's message.

Eternal moving affects us in less obvious but equally real ways. When you were a child and you went away for a vacation, did you ever say "goodbye" to your house? (Do you still?) That simple, seemingly childish thing to do is an emotion that is tied to our constantly moving. Our house, our block, our neighbors form a good deal of our everyday reality; it is exactly that reality that we need to better understand.

Our world, at one level, is made up of millions of sense impressions. We take those impressions, sort out the important ones, and give attention and meaning to them. If we stay in the same place for a period of time, the things in that place take on a collection of meanings. Also, if we stay in the same place long enough, there is a certain kind of stability that we simply take for granted.

From the very beginning of white people settling in America, this kind of stability has been forsaken for moving West. The discussion of moving was one of the central points in the chapter on freedom. I understand that to say there is a certain kind of stability in living in the same place sounds very un-American; but because our moving has changed once again, we must look at it once again. After all, a hundred years ago there was land to move to, an environment in which people could create what they wanted, an openness of opportunity.

Change today is from city to city, from set environment to set environment, from bureaucratic role to bureaucratic role. Moving disorients us in some ways, and stabilizes us in others. The worker, the person who is getting transferred, is best off. He or she still has job stability. Although everything else has changed (except for family members), the job is essentially the same. Same product, same basic set of rules, same basic characters with whom to deal. While the building is different, the basic phenomenon of an eight-hour work day remains the same.

The worker's family, however, has lost all stability (except immediate family members). New everything: home, room, friends, schools, stores, social pressures, interests, neighbors. There is a tremendous effort to take everything in, sort out what is important, and give it meaning. After enough of these moves, loyalty to a place, loyalty to neighbors and community, is not much of a possibility.

We become familiar *not* with everyday physical things in our lives, but with constantly changing social pressures reported by the ever-vigilant popular press, magazines, and electronic media.

Do not think that I am ignoring the remarkable bigotry and ignorance that can develop in places where people never move. Our history is rich in examples of the intolerance of wrong-headed communities. Our history is also full of stories about how individuals moved and changed for the better. But to constantly give up a familiar environment in order to escape the possible narrow-mindedness of some communities is foolishness.

To give up the familiar is to give up, in a strange way, meanings you have given the world. Until those meanings are replaced, it is difficult to be as active and vital as you once were.

When we were kids and we said goodbye to our house, we were saying that we were leaving a source of our strength, but that we would be back. We were leaving the easiness of familiar surroundings. Now think about that everyday dynamic/emotion in organizational and political terms. As a leader, wouldn't it make you more secure if your workers or citizens were made to periodically say "goodbye" to a source of their strength, never to see it again?

While it may sound silly to think that merely living in the same place may well be a source of power for the citizen, the possibility should be considered. One of the points of the book is that there are too many everyday things we are willing to ignore (or, to put it less kindly, unwilling to look at). Maybe it would help if what I've been saying is presented in a more formal manner.

How about this for a dynamic to be discussed: As individuals move, power tends to centralize. That holds for organizations and government … at least in the United States.

## Coercion

Enough about the setting of groups. What about the workings of the group itself, the interactions among those people who compose the group?

For several reasons—not the least of which is that they are manageable—many empirical studies have been done on the behavior of small groups. The conclusions of the studies are not surprising. In a small-group setting, the pressure to conform to group norms is great. In a simple, now classic, study, S. E. Asch demonstrated how powerful group pressure could be.[7]

The experiment involved eight people seated in a room. They were shown lines of various lengths and were asked obvious questions about the lines. The whole "test" was very easy and monotonous. As the "test" progressed, one individual began to find him- or herself being contradicted by the rest of the group. His or her "right" answer did not correspond with the answers given by the other seven. What had happened, of course, was that seven members of the group had been coached to give incorrect answers.

In this very simple exercise involving the judging of lengths of lines, the results were "clear and unambiguous. There was marked movement toward the majority. One third of all the estimates in the critical group were errors identical with or in the direction of the distorted estimates of the majority."[8] The reasons why a person would contradict what he or she had visually perceived are instructive. When each subject was asked why he had responded to the "test" the way he or she had done, the most common explanation was that the group had answered that way. The majority of the group seemed to be acting without hesitation, indeed, with confidence, so the outsider assumed they were right.

Being in a minority seemed to make things hard on the individual. Asch writes that the "principal impression" of the subject was "so caught up by immediate difficulties that he lost clear reasons for his actions, and could make no reasonable decisions."[9]

All of that is a little abstract. There are, regrettably, less abstract examples. Let me offer an example that, if it had not happened, would have been very difficult to imagine. The example is Jonestown. It is an example of many things, only one of which is group.

Do you recall Jim Jones? He was a cult leader who, in the late 1970s, led his group of followers to commit suicide. His is an interesting/sick story because, in some ways, he was an authentic do-gooder. He encompassed

---

7   S. E. Asch, "Effects of Group Pressure upon the Modification and Distortion of Judgements," in Bernard Hinton and H. Joseph Reitz, eds., *Groups and Organizations* (Belmont, Calif.: Wadsworth, 1971), pp. 215–23.

8   Ibid., p. 216.

9   Ibid., p. 217.

some of America's best ideals. He really seemed to believe in equality, in justice, in the races living in harmony. He worked hard, he had a certain gift of persuasion, and he was charismatic. In a move that seemed insightful and full of good sense, he and his followers moved to a place where they could be left alone to establish their community.

There was one real shortcoming, one real shame: Jim Jones had some serious psychological problems along with his high ideals. The problems got increasingly worse. We know how the story turned out. Jones's charismatic paranoia, along with the enormous amount of group pressure that was multiplied in the jungle, turned out to be a deadly combination. Kool-Aid will never be the same. The children died first. Jones died yelling the word *mother* over and over.

While it is a fact that not all groups end this way, it is wrong to ignore or dismiss the power of group pressure.

We have, in a sense, extremes in which we are literally given our choice of poisons: To be isolated is to be totally without power. It is to be lonely, alienated, desperate. Giving yourself entirely to a group may well be giving yourself entirely. Jonestown shows us that is not always a good idea.

If the Asch experiment and the Jonestown example are any indication, it is not difficult to conclude that small groups are potentially very coercive. But it would be wrong to stop at that obvious insight. It would be equally wrong to suggest that all groups are evil or that all groups are bad for their members. In order to begin to understand groups as something other than coercive, we must try to envision changes in our attitudes.

## Leadership and Power: An Introduction

To get at the problem of living in groups—the problem of participation—is a complicated task. It involves leading and following and membership. Also involved are ideas about democracy and authority and all those themes political scientists should be concerned with. But a discussion that considered all these ideas would be misplaced here. We are, after all, trying to make sense of groups. We are trying to figure out how we can make groups—an everyday fact of life—a more meaningful everyday fact of life. We are trying to understand how to free ourselves from current group practice by becoming conscious of the benefits groups have to offer.

It is important to realize that people being together—in groups, or politically, or whatever—must come to some kind of understanding of how they will behave. I am not talking about a strict code of rules, or law and order, or even order; I am just suggesting that we make an effort to shape the group toward common interests and goals. We should be aware that power and leadership exist whether we acknowledge them or not.

If that is so, if leadership and power do exist in groups, then their forms should be understood and agreed upon by the members of that group, if they are not to be tyrannized by them. An example may be useful. It is the example of the group living of the people in the Haight-Ashbury during 1966 and 1967. It was an interesting time, a good one to learn from for a couple of reasons. First, there was a great deal of energy for change. Second, even with that energy there was failure. Given history, it is only appropriate that we learn from failure. The hippies accepted a different lifestyle during this period, and by example tried to change society. Their dealings with groups point up questions with which we must deal. John Howard explains:[10]

> Stated simply, the argument is as follows. The hippies assumed that voluntarism (every man doing his own thing) was compatible with satisfying essential group and individual needs and with the maintenance of a social system in which there was an absence of power differentials and invidious distinctions based on, for example, wealth, sex, or race. That assumption is open to question. Voluntarism can work only where the participants in the social system have a sufficient understanding of the needs of the system to be willing to do things, which they do not want to do in order for the system to persist ...

Howard asked one of the Diggers why they were no longer distributing food in the park and received this answer:

---

10 John Robert Howard, "The Flowering of the Hippie Movement," in Terrence Cook and Patrick Morgan, eds., *Participatory Democracy* (San Francisco: Canfield, 1971), p. 209. Reprinted from *The Annals of the American Academy of Political and Social Science*, vol. 382 (March 1969), p. 47.

"Well, man, it took a lot of organization to get that done. We had to scuffle to get the food. Then the chicks or somebody had to prepare it. Then we got to serve it. A lot of people got to do a lot of things at the right time or it doesn't come off. Well, it got so that people weren't doing it. I mean a cat wouldn't let us have a truck when we needed it or some chick was grooving somewhere and can't help out. Now you hate to get into the power bag and start telling people what to do ... but without that, man, well ..."

The point that is important to make is that the "power trip" is not, by definition, a bad thing. What is essential is that power be understood and then used when and how the group wants it used. Back to the hippies:

We had all kinds of people there at first and anybody could stay if there was room. Anybody could crash out there. Some of the motorcycle types began to congregate in the kitchen. That became their room, and if you wanted something to eat or a beer you had to step over them. Pretty soon, in a way, people were cut off from the food. I don't mean that they wouldn't give it to you, but you had to go on their "turf" to get it. It was like they had begun, in some very quiet and subtle way, to run things.[11]

In sum, for a group to fulfill the intentions of each individual, elements of the relationships among the members—like power and leadership—must be understood and agreed upon. If that is the case, the chances of the group's becoming a good or even an extraordinary experience are greatly increased.

## Oh My God ...

*They are playing a game. They are playing not playing a game. If I show them I see they are, I shall break the rules and they will punish me. I must play their game, of not seeing I see the game.*

—*R. D. Laing*

11 Ibid., p. 207.

Because we have no public place to be political, no space in which we may be citizens, we are forced to make each of our actions a political statement of one sort or another. From our diet to our dress we make ideological choices. There are lots of serious folks who really do live their politics.

To be fair (not a terribly noble aim, but adequate enough in this case), at least something should be said about religion. In an important way, believers are taking their actions almost ponderously heavily, their day is a reflection of His Day or Her Day, and theirs is a "politics" of True Belief.

I don't want to push this "fair" thing too far. There is much more about religion that I will not discuss than I will. If your God is real and not mentioned and vengeful, you don't have to worry. I'll get what's coming to me for the oversight.

We are, when we get down to it, Americans. That rates pretty high on a Simple-Minded Scale, but it is a fact that is helpful to remember. Some of us, and I mean a very, very few, are able to un-Americanize ourselves. The rest of us are Americans and it gets into and influences just about everything we do. From hamburgers to God, we are red, white, and blue.

That's not at all a bad thing; in fact, there's something good and noble about it. The problems don't appear while you're being yourself; the real trouble starts when you start being one or another kind of an unself.

But this is about religion. We know, in our very beings, about lip-service religion. A Sunday morning in church if you happen to be with your parents, or two days a year in temple, or catching up on a busy week of sinning in a confessional. Check in as if there was a god for an after-life insurance policy. Motives that are not all that pure, but it's good just to be sure: A comfortable eternity is worth a few boring sermons.

For some years now, there have been people who were willing not only to say that that approach to religion is silly, but also to actually do something about it. There are chanters and freaks and preemies and an amazing variety of orthodox Christians and Jews and believers in the Buddha and different kinds of Zen, and a variety of Islamic beliefs.

Many of these people are making serious and impressive efforts at making sense of a world they didn't ask to be born into; they are trying to live a good life. A life that takes into account the problems of our society and compels them to do something different. I'm not really concerned if they are right- or wrongheaded; I am much more concerned with the statement they make and what we have to learn from them.

There is some sense in starting with what we (mostly) are, and ending up with what we are not. A few years back, the biggest turn-on, the fastest growing and most popular new nonreligion religion was TM. The Transcendental Meditationists. TM'ers. Ommmm. Hummmm.

If we—a committee of us—were to invent a business (group-life) for our fellow Americans, there are some obvious sorts of things we would want. In order to make lots of money, we could offer a product easy to make and use, promise it would do all sorts of things (reduce crime in the streets, improve sexual performance, make dull work happier, help you get better grades, help you make more money, and bring about world peace), make it religious/nonreligious pop-culture exotic, and let people still smoke, drink, and be junk-food junkies, and sell it with something close to a scientific guarantee.

Why, if we did it right we'd be rich.

We could start a university, sell to 30,000 new people a month, and have $12 million in yearly revenue coming in. Fat City.

We could also be sued by the World Plan Executive Council–US (the TM central office) because they did all of these things. (We can learn a whole lot about ourselves by learning about Transcendental Meditation in America. It may turn out that we are what we hum.)

One might want to argue, probably rightly, that what I wrote is not true. It is wrong in particular, but not in spirit. What seems most wrong is the fact that no committee could invent such a wonderful business. I apologize.

The TM'ers sold an impressive list of "up your" promises.[12] For example: Up Your Recall, or Up Your Productivity, or Up Your IQ,[13] and there are lots more. The point—if it's possible to oversimplify—is that the world is always going at an out-of-control pace and we poor people can't cope. Who can argue with that? In order to make sense and keep up, TM offered a solution—what we need to do is relax (to be precise, it only takes forty minutes a day) and get in touch (in direct contact) with the source of thought. We need only tap into the pure energy in the mind.

---

12  The source of much of the following is Denise Denniston and Peter McWilliams, *The TM Book: How to Enjoy the Rest of Your Life* (New York: Warner Books, 1975).

13  Ibid., pp. 79, 93, 74.

Step right up. Buy into your own mind.

Anyone can do it. It is effortless to do, and it actually takes only hours to learn.[14] The magic mantra gives you a rest deeper than sleep (there is scientific proof), and can make you more creative and even give you a faster reaction time (there is scientific proof). With the stress off your nervous system, you can avoid those nagging heart attacks, and your mind can use its full mental potential. You could lick the tense twenty-first century and reach enlightenment.

Let me interrupt this commercial with some clarification. Upon investigation, we find that enlightenment is a fairly heavy-duty concept, which comes from many of the Eastern religions. For TM it means having 100 percent of one's potential available for use. More curious still, it is claimed that enlightenment is everyone's birthright. Should we now say "Life, Liberty, and Enlightenment"?

Back to our commercial.

The TM technique is "a great scientific discovery." It "makes suffering in life a thing of the past." Not only that, there is nothing to believe in (even an atheist can do it), no special clothes to wear (not even sandals), no change of lifestyle; you don't even have to concentrate. But there will be changes: "Some will find calculus a breeze. Others will have no difficulty writing epic poems before breakfast."[15]

All that, and you can still eat McDonald's hamburgers.

And, as a footnote, if just 1 percent of you in your community do this, the whole community will "suddenly … increase its efficiency, orderliness, and productivity."[16]

All this for less than $200.

## Groups Reconsidered: Passive and Active

This may sound like a paradox, but I do not think that it is: For groups to be less coercive, we must become more involved in them. Let me try to explain briefly.

Small groups are potentially very important to the way we act and the things we do. We know that. Further, we know that we are constantly in-

14 Most of these words come from *The TM Book*. These, for example, come from p. 51.

15 Ibid., p. 116.

16 Ibid., p. 336.

volved, to a greater or lesser degree, in groups. Whether it is a sorority or fraternity, a bridge club or basketball team, or just some snobby little social group, we are involved. The problem is that we are not *consciously* involved. Too often we passively accept membership while never actively taking part in the direction of the group. We accept coercion without accepting participation; we are acted upon without acting.

To put it a little differently, to be a part of a group is to be subject to its rules. This is true whether we accept the fact or not; it is true whether we are actively engaged in the group's decision-making, or whether we feel we are different from the group or really not a part of it at all. In part, our identities stem from these small groups. What is necessary to understand is that the group is part of you no matter how you feel about it. To belong to a group and not take it seriously is to limit the power you have over who you are.

What I am arguing is that groups are important to one's self and, as such, should be treated importantly.

## Particular Groups

Right now, there are between fifteen and twenty million people who belong to some kind of support group or self-help group. Some of these groups are familiar, like AA, and some are not. Sloppy people have a group (Messies Anonymous), older women in relationships with younger men have a group, as do fat people (the National Association to Aid Fat Americans) and people who like to consume (Compulsive Shoppers). The list is astonishing. It is very clear that a lot of people have a lot of issues to work on. The question is, just what is going on every night in all of those meetings? What, if anything, can we make of it?

The first thing of note is that most of these groups are similar in that they exclude professional helpers. These people do not want the kind of structure that an "expert" will bring to the meeting. During a time, and in a nation, where experts often get top billing (and even more often, bill top money), it is more than a little interesting that all of these people are consciously rejecting them. The change that the people in these groups are after, or at least one of the changes, seems to be away from analyses and toward getting better.

It is important to take a minute and think about experts. Traditionally, we have had mixed feelings about them. As the world becomes increasingly complicated and complex it is only natural to take advice from experts. There are experts in everything, so it's not surprising that our government hires high-powered specialists. And it's not surprising that when something goes wrong in our personal lives, we literally read the Yellow Pages in order to find the right person to help.

The highly individual, equality-demanding part of us really dislikes and even distrusts experts. They tend to be—gasp—intellectuals who seem to set themselves up as holier-than-thou. Each of us would like to think that our common sense is equal to, or better than, the all-too-often daffy advice of experts. After all, it seems that money can buy expert advice on any side of any question. Check out most congressional hearings; the opposing experts are all very certain of their position. You know that at least half of them have to be wrong.

The point that started this discussion was that these new self-help groups had made a decision not to include experts. It might be helpful to offer a little evidence about expert helpers. In 1979, Daniel Hogan published a book titled *The Regulation of Psychotherapists*. It was four volumes long. One of his findings was that there was a huge difference between what a person had to do to be qualified to *get* the job, and what was needed in order to *do* the job well.

In order to get a license to practice, the psychotherapist had to do well at hard, scientific training. What Hogan found was that "the effectiveness of the therapist was more determined by the presence or absence of certain personality characteristics and interpersonal skills than technical abilities and theoretical knowledge." Those traits, by the way, were a warm, empathic personality, reliable, unpretentious, and so on. Hogan says that the "necessary qualities are very similar to those one looks for in a good friend." There are studies, for example, that show that laypersons with only limited training are more effective than highly trained experts.

In another study, people faked their way into mental hospitals. Once they were admitted, they stopped faking symptoms and acted in a totally normal way. What happened was amazing. "During the pseudopatients' entire hospital stay, none of the psychiatrists, nurses or other professionals suspected that these people might be normal. Interestingly, the ward patients were quite suspicious …"

There is no real reason to only pick on the helping professions. The fact is that many of them do wonderful work. But we are dealing with groups of people who need help, and who have consciously decided not to turn to experts. They have always helped me.

In these days of media madness one can encounter self-help groups at home. If you are too busy to attend a group there is always the TV. The VCR records it and you can watch it at a time convenient for you. From shows like Jerry Springer, where chairs are often thrown (along with punches), to Montel Williams, who tries to be a bit more understanding and sympathetic (and who talks about his own personal battle with MS), you are likely to find someone with the same, similar, or even more problems than yourself.

There are ways in which these new, problem-specific groups are very American. It is a kind of frontier approach to your very own problems. In the old days (the myth goes) the community gathered around and helped with various things. Need a barn? There was a barn raising. Neighbors got together and did community work.

But not many of us have barns to build anymore. We engage in nothing so straightforward. What we now seem to have in common is a great desire to improve ourselves. To get rid of those awful, depressing personal faults/traits/habits/addictions/illnesses, and be free from the compulsions, crummy families, bad marriages, seems to have evolved into a kind of group effort.

In our pragmatic way, we isolate our troubles and find the right group to work on them. Since close communities seem to no longer exist, families have long since broken up, and there is a healthy mistrust of a therapy that can go on for years, we have invented ways to re-create the more positive parts of each of them.

The groups have rediscovered talking and listening in public. They have relearned the old lesson that finding you are not alone in the world—with whatever bad habit or bad luck has brought — is somehow comforting. They have remembered that others' experiences may, indeed, prove helpful. But while these groups are wonderfully American, they are also too typically American. While the meetings are public, the issues are personal and private. There is no politics here, just an emphasis on peer-help and self-help.

As we have seen, groups have a long past in our politics. The factions of Madison and the voluntary associations of Tocqueville help us see the extremes of how groups operate. It could well be that these self-help groups may make very important discoveries—but I think they will be medical, not political.

## Another Vision

> *If I don't know I don't know*
> *I think I know*
> *If I don't know I know*
> *I think I don't know.*
> — *R. D. Laing*

> *Crowned with garlands, the three-year-old child plays the drum;*
> *The eighty-year-old man plays with a balloon.*
> — *Thich Nhat Hanh*

As a treat to myself, I was reading a skinny book—*Zen and the Art of Archery*—before trying to sleep every night. It was written by a German who went to Japan and tried to learn Zen through a Master who taught archery. I would read a few pages, do some thinking about it, and was enjoying it.

I even flattered myself into thinking I understood some of it.

Somewhere around the middle of the book—somewhere around the second or third year of archery/Zen—the Master introduced the concept of the target and how the arrow and the target should meet at a certain point.

To tell you the truth, I had been aiming at the target since page one. Oh, American me.

The Zen life is one that we seem to be trained and taught not to understand. To grow up in America is to grow up with a set of instincts that close us off from the essences and meanings of Zen. If that is true, and I have to admit I believe it is, it would be silly for me to write in an authoritative way about what Zen really is.

There are a couple of obvious things that might give us the proper distance on those people—and those groups of people—who study Zen. The fact seems to be that one is not "taught" Zen, nor does one actually "study" Zen. Two quotes may be helpful:

> One would not even be able to talk about teaching it since Zen cannot be taught, that is, taught through symbols; it passes directly from master to student, from "mind to mind." The image employed here is a *seal* imprinted on a mind, not a seal of wood, copper, or ivory, but a "mind seal."

and

> But Zen is not the study of Zen; Zen is life. Zen is direct contact with reality ... Zen can only be lived and experienced. As Master Tue Trung Thuong Si said, "This marvelous piece must be played." What is the good of discussing a musical masterpiece? It is its performance that counts.[17]

Let me try another way of getting at not getting at Zen. There are certain Zen monasteries where, upon entering, the novice is given a book called the Little Manual. It is a small book, and a famous one. The instinct of the Western mind would be to think of the book as one of philosophy. After all, it is the first book people trying to learn Zen are supposed to read.

In the Little Manual there is no Zen philosophy. The book, basically, is about how to control your mind and concentration, the discipline and behavior required for life in the monastery, and an essay encouraging Zen disciples to "take to heart the fact that their time and life are precious and should not be vainly dissipated." The book is used by all monks no matter what their age or the amount of time they have studied Zen.

The essence of Zen is found in the Little Manual in part because it suggests an individual focus on each thing he or she does; this action leads to the "Awareness of Being." As I understand it, one would be ill advised (unless he or she wants to prove stupidity) to write much more. It takes a

---

17 Thich Nhat Hanh, *Zen Keys* (Garden City, N.Y.: Anchor, 1974), pp. 31, 131. Emphasis in original.

full lifetime of considered acts by serious and good people with a different mind-set to truly understand the Awareness of Being.

There are few if any actions taken that are not subject to self-awareness and meaning. From the closing of a door to the washing of one's hands, a student of Zen must be conscious and understanding. There are "acts of majestic behavior" and "subtle gestures."

"It is said that in Buddhism there are ninety thousand 'subtle gestures' the novice must practice."[18] That's a fairly serious project, a lifetime's worth. It's certainly not the only kind of serious project; in fact, it seems remarkably out of our grasp. But it serves as a fine example of how taking the quality of your life seriously can easily be a full-time job. There is something almost magical about those people, but there are equally magical—if not totally different—examples of a more recognizable kind. Before looking at them, it seems right to end with a story about enlightenment.

> Little Toyo was only twelve years old. But since he was a pupil at the Kennin Temple, he wanted to be given a koan to ponder, just like the more advanced students. So one evening, at the proper time, he went to the room of Makurai, the master, struck the gong softly to announce his presence, bowed, and sat before the master in respectful silence.
>
> Finally the master said: "Toyo, show me the sound of two hands clapping."
>
> Toyo clapped his hands.
>
> "Good," said the master. "Now show me the sound of one hand clapping."
>
> Toyo was silent. Finally he bowed and left to consider this problem.
>
> The next night he returned, and struck the gong with one palm. "That is not right," said the master. The next night Toyo returned and played geisha music with one hand. "That is not right," said the master. The next night Toyo returned, and imitated the dripping of water. "That is not right," said the master. The next night Toyo returned, and imitated the cricket

18 Ibid., p. 25.

scraping his leg. "That is still not right," said the master.

For ten nights Toyo tried new sounds. At last he stopped coming to the master. For a year he thought of every sound, and discarded them all, until he finally reached enlightenment.

He returned respectfully to the master. Without striking the gong, he sat down and bowed. "I have heard sound without sound," he said.[19]

## Power and Magical Groups

The truth of the matter is that there is very little "hard," empirical objective information—not much social science data—on magical groups. I know that. But *magical* is the word I want to use.

Part of the argument of this book is that human beings are capable of doing wonderful, never-before-imagined things. Further, one of the results of politics can be remarkable events. When we human beings go beyond the normal and the expected, it seems almost like magic. Not all groups, it seems to me, need to be normal.

Up to now, we have been involved with what we know, with ordinary groups doing those things to individuals that ordinary groups generally do. But it seems to me that there is another kind of group, one in which the members are somehow transformed, somehow special, somehow engaged in an enterprise different from the rest of us. The examples of this come from fiction, and close to it: Hermann Hesse's *The Journey to the East* and Tom Wolfe's *The Electric Kool-Aid Acid Test*.[20]

The point of the books and the point I shall try to make is this: Far from the common uses of groups we are generally taught, far from the "normal politics" view of American groups, some groups may actually point the way to different kinds of relationships and to a different kind of politics.

To begin at a common beginning point of political scientists, let us start with power. There are some bad feelings about power, some honest mis-

19 Excerpt from *Zen Buddhism: An Introduction to Zen with Stories, Parables and Koan Riddles of the Zen Masters* (Mount Vernon, N.Y.: Peter Pauper Press, 1959), pp. 24–25. Reprinted with permission of Peter Pauper Press.

20 Hermann Hesse, *The Journey to the East* (New York: Farrar, Straus & Giroux, 1970); Tom Wolfe, *The Electric Kool-Aid Acid Test* (New York: Bantam Books, 1969).

givings about "getting into the power bag." If understood in the conventional way, these misgivings are very understandable. Power is dominance over; it is—to use the common definition—the ability of A to make B do something B would not otherwise have done.

In that sense, power is in part negative. The definition may be both limiting and harmful; it may influence us to act in certain ways. First, as students or as citizens, we can well understand what B feels like. We can understand what it means to be made to do something we otherwise would not have done.

Second, although A has power, he or she is also caged by the relationship. The person holding power is limited to his or her own imagination. There is little chance that A can become different, can qualitatively change, can get beyond his or her own thoughts. Seen from that point of view, from the point of view that has A making B do something he or she would not otherwise do, we can understand why power seems abusive and limited.

The conventional definition of power prescribes "reasonable" ways to behave. Given that definition as a guide to action, we could be expected to "hoard" power, and to "spend" it only when necessary. There would be no sharing or spreading of that kind of power, only spending and losing it. But power need not be like that; there can be a different view of power, a different definition of it, that might alter the way we act. There might be a view of power that would make it creative rather than limiting.

In order to redefine power so that it would apply to a "magical group," we need change only one word: power is the ability of A to make B do something he or she *could* not have done before. Power then becomes a source of creative energy: ability or skill that will help induce someone to take an action, to strike out anew, to do something that in the past was impossible. Just as significantly, power becomes a shared commodity, something that *increases* when used, not decreases.

The most obvious place for power to become a shared commodity is in a small group, but it must be a group that is stable, not temporary, one that understands power, not one that ignores it; finally, it must be a group that is working for something in common, not one in which there is little coincidence of interests.

The idea of leadership must also change. In a bureaucratic world, leadership is pictured as involving a supervisor/subordinate relationship. The leader is at the top, the rest of us at the bottom. That seems natural enough, and it is certainly an adequate description of everyday life. To envision being a leader is to envision being at the top of something and possessing a good deal of power. It is, in a sense, to assume responsibility for all those underneath you. A plantation owner "took care" of his or her slaves, a school principal "takes care" of his or her students.

That view of leadership depends on a repressive view of power. It may be important to understand leadership as being not on an up-and-down scale with followership but rather as on a continuum with it. Leadership and followership are two ends of the same line. One is not "over" the other. One person may have some qualities or traits or skills that makes that advice or those directions more acceptable than those of others. In those areas, that person leads.

What is important to understand is that a leader is also a follower. That it is a relationship in which sometimes one leads, sometimes another. If one has the ability to lead a group of people to do things collectively that they could not do individually, and if the members of a group want that to happen, then one person should "lead." But this important fact remains: The relationship between leader and follower is an essentially equal one. From that relationship, the creative powers of the people individually—and of the group as a whole—are increased.

That has the makings of a magical group.

The essence of this discussion—at least the point I am most interested in making—is that we are foolish to take groups and group theories at their face value. Involved in what we think ordinary and obvious are a whole set of assumptions that need to be examined. Such terms as *power* and *leadership* really do mean something, and the way we define them may have an influence on the way we act. It would be at the far reaches of silliness to suggest that by changing the way we define words, the whole world would automatically change. I am not suggesting that. I am trying to make the point that we are tied to concepts and activities we rarely try to understand, to ones we seldom challenge.

There do seem to be other ways to see the world—and maybe that other vision is a better one.

*They had all voluntarily embarked upon a trip and a state of consciousness that was "crazy" by ordinary standards. The trip, in fact the whole deal, was a risk-all balls-out plunge into the unknown ... Stark Naked had done her thing. She roared off into the void and was picked up by the cops by and by and the doors closed in the county psychiatric ward, and that was that, for the pranksters were long gone.*

*— Tom Wolfe*

# Friendship: Just Friends

*Friendship, friendship: just the perfect blendship*
*When other friendships have been forgot*
*Ours will still be hot*

— *Cole Porter*

This is not really a whole chapter. It is a part of one, a piece of a whole. The ideas that follow are most closely tied to the preceding discussion of groups. The chapter on groups is incomplete. There is something basic to, as well as prior to, small groups. Friendship is an ingredient of groups, and it is a topic that deserves some attention.

It is important that at least two things be said before we begin to work through the idea of friendship. First, it is a fantastically complicated topic, one that is possibly impossible to fully understand. In order to make our effort more reasonable, more manageable, we will limit the discussion to friendship in America.

Second, the effort is worth making because it might give us insights into our social and political environment. If we are the system, if we carry a miniature version of the system in our heads—and act as the system would have us act—then we need to think about how we act.

## Things Change?

Back in 1990, our son Ben and his buddy (almost teenagers at the time) were talking about world politics one evening. The buddy says that he can't understand why everybody liked John Kennedy so much. I saw a speech Kennedy gave, says the buddy, and I didn't like his politics. He seemed like a hawk, a real macho guy.

Didn't like his politics, indeed.

But Kennedy's voice, I wanted to say. But he was young and Eisenhower was so old, I wanted to say. I kept my mouth shut.

The kid was right. To hear JFK's speeches today is to remember what a Cold Warrior he was. What I liked was what I heard from Ben and his buddy.

Maybe we'll see a little political action again pretty soon. Who knows? For example, civil rights thinking has changed. Sure, the traditional stuff is still around: the calls for equality, dignity, and the like. The old focus of civil rights politics was legislation, because people believed that laws would change how minorities and women were treated. In a sense, they were right, and things did change. But we were not, for a while, in touch with that kind of thing, as illustrated by the smart scholarship winner—the woman going places and doing things in *Say Anything*. It seems that young people had come to assume that discrimination was foolishness and just shouldn't exist.

Shortly after that conversation with Ben and his buddy, Barbara and I were having lunch with good friends. Not surprisingly, we talked about how our kids were doing. The friends had recently asked their daughter, Becca, what one thing she would change in her life. "One thing?" she said. "One thing," they said. "My skin," Becca answered. "I'd be black." No great legislative dreams for her, no new laws about who has the right to do what. No, Becca wanted black skin.

In truth, Becca's answer came as no surprise to us; Ben had wanted to be black for years. Ever the casual empiricist, I began checking around. Guess what? A lot of white people wanted to be black in 1990. This is more than a little shift in the civil rights movement. It certainly seems important enough to speculate about.

It could well be that, culturally, the most interesting people in the public eye were black. Rap music, and rappers, seemed to have more life and honesty than most of the pasty white boys you see on MTV. Spike Lee is laced with tension, and Michael Jordan flies. Yo.

For some reason, blacks seem more real than whites. Who cares whether that is true or not. Not all blacks have rhythm, and not all whites are pasty nerds. But that isn't the point. The point seems to be that there has been something compelling about what blacks see, how they look, and what they are doing. Color envy. Culture envy.

I guess if the presidents during your lifetime have consisted of an old, out-of-it, white B-movie actor and an aging preppy, then wanting to be black makes a lot of sense.

On the other hand, when Bill Clinton moved into the White House, the world of the young looked like the 1950s with birth-control pills. God had made a big comeback. Most hair was neat and short and people dressed for success in their power clothes.

Billionaires came and went in the 1990s, and a "born-again" Bush was made president by a majority of the Supreme Court. The small-government Republicans want to fight wars, spy on everything we do, and begin *every* meeting with a prayer.

We need only remember the words of Chris Rock: You know things are out of control when the world's best golfer is black and the world's best rapper is white.

## Friendships: American Myths

These myths, which had been so alive when we were growing up in the 1950s, seemed so near extinction when the last edition of the *Preface* was published that the chapter on friendship was left out. They may no longer exert their power in the same way, but power and groups and friendship still count. So, let's revisit the past—the young *Preface*—and see how things have changed.

Our first myth is somehow true, and somehow not. The kind that we do not want to believe, but for some reason act as if we do. The myth involves women. The first old myth we may still share is this: Men make better friends than women.

The myth is/was amazingly degrading. It contends that two women are rarely true friends, rarely friends who honestly share and honestly give, friends who are able to stay close for years and years.

But why? Lurking in us is the thought that the essence of women's failure to be friends with other women lies in their jealousy. In a male chauvinist pig sort of way, men seem to believe that each woman is too insecure to be the friend of another woman. The idea is that what women need are strong males, someone to whom they can talk, someone on whom they can lean.

Do Americans seem to believe that women together are either hens or bitches, but never friends?

Women were succeeding in their fight for equality and Ronald Reagan was president—a very strange combination. It was the 1980s and one of my favorite social science "laws" clearly fit the situation: For every wrongheaded action there is an equal and opposite wrongheaded action.

The cross-currents are strong. While there is an image of the woman who tries to be more masculine than males in the business world, there is also the realization that women can be wonderful friends. From Thelma and Louise on, it has become clear that the old "women can't be friends" idea is merely part of our past.

What about men and women? Can they truly be friends? Again, our vision is clouded with doubt. We know that men and women can like each other; but is that friendship?

The stereotypical thought is obvious to all. They can be lovers, or they can be "just like sister and brother," but the idea of being friends with someone of the opposite sex? We are in a strange time: a time when we realize men and women are not the same, yet are the same. It is a time when we must not assume that women doing "men's jobs" is a sign of liberation, or men doing "women's jobs" is a sign of weakness. In the flux of our identity crises, friendship is tough to find.

For men, women are okay to sleep with, but is it still foolish to try to be too friendly with one? The tension of sex is sometimes too much to overcome. Friendships between men—so goes the myth—are also limited. The first obvious limitation—obvious indignation—concerns black men and white men. The myth is that for a white, the black man is everything but a friend. For two hundred years, whites were taught to believe that the black was a "boy." A grinning, happy boy. It's tough to be best friends with a boy. Then there was the myth that black men were sexually superior. It's tough to be best friends with a rival—a rival who was better. Finally, in enlightened, liberal circles, the black man became a status symbol. Whitey had to have one at every party. But the black was not there as a friend; he was there to be on display.

So blacks hated whites and whites hated blacks; and friendship was limited in yet another way. Certainly things are much better than they were thirty years ago, but it would be foolish to believe we have overcome issues of race. As I write, we are still fighting over affirmative action. It is a retro-issue, brought to you by a retro-administration.

The results of all this are limiting. White men end up being friends with white men. If one is not too much richer than the other, two white men seem to be able to be friends in America. They can drink together, tell dirty jokes, and sometimes even talk about important things. The only limitation is that they cannot love each other. For males to be friends, they have to prove to society that they are more attracted to women than to men. They can neither cry nor comfortably kiss in public.

Friendship as it used to be understood in America made little sense, and did little good. We failed to take seriously the sometimes special world of women or of men and we couldn't grant the trait of humanness to most of those who are black or red or yellow or brown.

In doing so, we were forced to define the world as violent—as unemotional and masculine, as unsentimental and white.

Have we changed our wrongheaded ways? Did *My Big Fat Greek Wedding* remind us that there might be special bonds in each ethnicity? While we waited to exhale, did we see that women really can be friends? As a culture, have all of us made progress?

What is interesting, and ironic, is that white males are the group that seems to have made the least progress. The stereotypical white male remains too guarded and unemotional to have friends. The time of the "sensitive" male has passed (he was so sensitive he couldn't make a commitment), and the stereotype is back to the familiar beer-drinking, TV-watching "guy."

But we know that just isn't true for every young man.

We also know that it's almost impossible to figure out what is really going on.

## Toward the Last Chapter

*He swallowed a whole lot of wisdom, but it seemed as if all of it had gone down the wrong way.*

*James Thurber wrote that a moth never burned its wings by flying toward the stars.*

There is little reason for one to bother reading this "Toward," since it does not rightly belong to the preceding chapter, or to the one that follows. It has to do with some of what goes into—but rarely comes out of—writing.

Like many endeavors, writing consists of a series of traumas; with a book, these traumas are numbered in chapters. I suppose an eleven-and-one-half-chapter book is not so traumatic. It is hard to imagine a twenty-three-chapter book. But that is not the whole point. The point is that The Last Chapter is somehow different from the others. It is (or, maybe, should be) different for a number of reasons.

The Last Chapter is the final chance to make whatever point one has been trying to make throughout the book. It is the last, best, and only chance one has left. It is the obvious place in which to sum up, to make clear, and to explain precisely. That should be pressure enough, but there is more. The Last Chapter is the place to right all the wrong things that have been implied, to apologize for the tricks employed, or the shoddy arguments, or whatever. Some of that is easy enough to do, if one is so inclined.

It seems to me, though, that there is a great urge to come up with The Final Answer in The Last Chapter. To write is often to make up both the answer and the question (the order is not terribly important) and to create an illusion that things are thereby better, or that they soon will be. This book is probably in that tradition. The only problem is that I am still not quite sure about either the answer or the question.

Certainly there have been "answers" in almost every chapter. Just by dealing with this particular set of problems, I have assumed much. But it seems unlikely that this textbook should end with a neat series of solutions, a Last Chapter that contains "strategies" for completely renewing society. It is not that I believe that all is well; indeed, complete renewal may be the minimum we need. The problem is: I do not know of a neat plan to solve our problems.

The real problem is this: I do not believe in neat plans.

The last chapter does a little of all those things I have mentioned. There is a summing up, a final point making, and some apologizing. For certain, it does not reflect the wishes I had for it, which is my last apology.

> *Today is gone. Today was fun.*
> *Tomorrow is another one.*
> *Everyday,*
> *From there to here*
> *From here to there*
> *Funny things are everywhere*
> *From there to here*
> *From here to there,*
> *Funny things are everywhere.*[1]

---

1    From Dr. Seuss, *One Fish Two Fish Red Fish Blue Fish* (New York: Random House, 1957). Reprinted by permission.

# chapter 12

# The Last Chapter

*There was once a company of six dancers who were part of a circus in the local village. Five of the dancers could leap about three feet. The villagers followed these five closely, knowing just how high each could jump. They would applaud enthusiastically at the dancer who would leap just a few inches higher than the others.*
*The sixth dancer could leap almost six feet. The villagers ignored him, wishing to reward the others in his company. When asked why he continued to leap so much higher than the others, while being unappreciated, he replied simply: "Because the other dancers understand."*

— *Søren Kierkegaard*

*Happiness is a warm gun: Bang, bang, shoot, shoot.*

— *The Beatles*

## Happiness

It seems fairly obvious that if we had our choice, we would choose to be happy rather than unhappy. We want to be happy; we aim at it and plan for it and sometimes even strive toward it. But it seems to me that we have more of a passion for happiness than we have knowledge of it. As with so many seemingly important things, the greatness of our wants is equaled only by the greatness of our ignorance.

Happiness seems a reasonable topic to discuss when one considers the preceding topics. Maybe all those other things really do have some relationship to the ways we act and to how we feel. Maybe those things can make us happy, or unhappy, without our even knowing it. Maybe not. But happiness is a subject that should be explored.

Happiness is not the goal of humanity, or even of politics, and I do not want to argue that it is. I would simply like to suggest that to begin to think about how we think about happiness might help us to understand not only what we have but also, possibly, what we don't have. By exploring happiness, we may be able to see more clearly how to get what we want, and also to ask ourselves if what we want is worth getting. To begin with, we should try to understand a little of what happiness consists of in ourselves and in our relationship with society. Then we will explore different ways of dealing with society.

There is no obvious beginning point to a discussion of happiness, no point that is so natural a place to begin that it cannot be ignored. Dictionaries may help; so too may Aristotle or Augustine or Jesus. But a discussion that thorough may serve to confuse as much as to clarify.

For a laugh, we could start at an unlikely place—with the Puritans. They serve as models for many things, but I doubt that they have ever been a model for happiness. H. L. Mencken once wrote that Puritanism was the gnawing feeling that someone somewhere might be happy.

So much for the Puritans.

At the very beginning we had already established in the Declaration of Independence that happiness—at least the pursuit of it—was something "originally" guaranteed. The apocryphal story goes that when Thomas Jefferson was working out the wording, he wrote about the right to life, liberty, and property. That is the true (Lockean) phrasing of the thought, but it was not much artistically. So Jefferson rewrote it. Instead of pursuing property, we were to pursue happiness. The point is an obvious one: In many American minds, there is no difference. Any subtle distinctions are unclear. They are the same: Property is happiness and happiness is property.

But what does that mean now? What does it mean to us? One could easily imagine that it means something like this. Before, to have property was enough. An individual was thought to be more or less happy if he or she owned things. But times have changed. We have changed. We have become sophisticated in our tastes and modified our styles; today, we consume. Maybe happiness is no longer just the pursuit of property.

Maybe happiness in America is to buy things we won't use, use things we don't need, and waste things we don't want. To consume is to destroy; yet our happiness is in the consumption. Our credit revolves, our purchasing power increases, and this dynamic is supposed to bring smiles to our faces and happiness to our hearts.

Of course, as middle-class, cared-for, mostly pampered college people, we think the consumption formulation vulgar and offensive. "No," you think, "that is for the others. They have to buy to be happy. Not me. Not us. No sir. For us to be happy, we just have to have fun."

So that is what you do: run after fun. Have a drink, smoke some dope. Now that is fun. Or you might ski. Or you might play bridge. Or you might go out and kill animals. Now that is really fun. What more could we want? Aren't we all happy now?

But is happiness just fun? Fun is cheap. Fun may be little more than a way to fill empty hours, or it may be a way to achieve status and social approval. In the final analysis, fun may have about as much to do with happiness as buying things does. Buying and having fun may simply be methods of display, motion, and instant reward.

We somehow squander our right to pursue happiness for the security of mindless, inoffensive fun. We confuse internal pursuits—beauty, nobility, and excellence—with the pursuit of happiness understood as the fulfillment of desire. We are too well trained in our own evilness and too used to our own self-interest to accept the task of trying to be happy while living with other people or while seeking values that do not have an obvious, tangible reality.

Maybe there is no such thing as happiness in our society. The harder we look, the more hopeless we become. We grow further apart and pretend somehow that loneliness is happiness. We consume, and we kill, and we read and watch things that only limit our perceptions, dull our imaginations.

To begin to think hard about happiness is to begin to feel cheated. It is to feel that there is an empty space where fullness should be. The more we pursue happiness in a society based on the presumption of our own evilness, the less well off we are as human beings.

But to end our discussion of "happiness" in great despair does not make much sense, at least not much good sense. If I really agreed with Archbishop Whately that happiness was no laughing matter, I should be forced to believe that happiness was probably not worth the trouble of figuring out.

No, I want to argue that I have seen people happy, and have even felt it, and certainly enjoyed it. Not only that: Happiness might be important. It was Hawthorne who suggested the likeness of happiness to a butterfly, which flits away when chased, but which may come and light on your hand if you will only sit quietly, occupied with something else.

It is wholly possible that we have been searching in the wrong place, pursuing the wrong question. If we take Hawthorne seriously, it may be best to occupy ourselves with that "something else."

## Beyond Butterflies

I have no desire to set out a reasoned and reasonable argument about what one should do, about what that "something else" would look like if we wanted to have the butterfly light on our hand. Indeed, the implication of my remarks up to now is that happiness may simply be a nice by-product. It may not be worth pursuing in its own right.

Nor do I wish to agree fully with Hawthorne. While his insight into the chase seems a good one, his analogy is not quite accurate. Just sitting may be good for butterfly landings, but I am not certain that it is the best condition for happiness. Indeed, happiness may be, in some part, the connections between one's self and others and society. It may have to do with how one thinks and sees and acts, not with how well one sits still.

If what has been said so far is right—if a portion of happiness is both personal and societal, and if our society is more limiting than fulfilling—then we must consider some general notions of what might be done. No plans (specifically); no Final Answer; nothing that hasn't already been suggested. Certainly each chapter has contained ideas about how we might begin to politicize our politics and possibly take our public selves and actions more seriously. No need to repeat that.

It is important to understand a little more about how to deal with what is going on now. If the preceding chapters have been at all successful in defining the present—and how we got here and where we are logically heading—then something should be said about the ways in which this "reality" might be confronted. It seems clear that almost everyone can get along, that most can cope, and that many can even "succeed" according to the present rules. But if what has been said is correct, that seems a foolish option to take.

College seems to be a good place to begin to confront conventional definitions. It is centered on the future, but held in the present by the questions we all seem forced to ask, and live by: What should I study? What will I be? Who will I love? Where will I live? What? What? Who? Who?

What makes real college so hard is that no one has the answers. Who knows what you should do or what you will be? Who knows whether what you believe is rightfitting? Certainly not us, or the person teaching this—or any other—course. But the truth of the answers lies at the heart of much of education.

It seems a good idea to start the conversation somewhere, so what follow are ways to do life. Each has a certain appeal; each has the potential to be an aesthetically pleasing way to live. None may work for you. Read and see.

## Way One: Do Not Do It

There may be a point, for some people, when it seems impossible or unlikely that what has been going on can keep going on. A point at which all seems hopeless or insane or inane, wicked or vile or cruel. A point when they just cannot continue doing whatever it is they have been doing. There are those who believe that nothing they do is getting them anywhere, yet who cannot quite figure out the next move.

One next move might be this: Stop doing those things that are not helping. Begin to understand—and don't do—the things "they" do.

What follows is an elaborate story that helps illustrate the point. It is suggested as an obvious move if what you are doing doesn't seem worth much. It is just a suggested move, not a stance toward life or an ultimate political action. It is simply a story of breaking away. The story is about Ken Kesey and a speech he once gave to protest the war in Vietnam.

Before beginning, a word about Kesey. As we saw in the introduction, he is a fine (I would vote for "great") American author. *One Flew Over the Cuckoo's Nest* and *Sometimes a Great Notion* are beautifully written, powerful books. Kesey lived in California and was heavily involved with LSD in the 1960s. He returned to Oregon to live out his life writing, farming, teaching, and doing politics. To understand his acid life-style of the mid-1960s, read Tom Wolfe's *The Electric Kool-Aid Acid Test.* But that, mostly, is beside the point. One can learn from Kesey without using heavy drugs. He can conceptualize important things fantastically well. Enough background.

In 1965, Ken Kesey was invited to a teach-in held by the Vietnam Day Committee at Berkeley. According to Wolfe, no one was sure just why he was invited, but he was and he accepted the invitation. So Kesey and his friends dressed up in funny war costumes, painted themselves and their big old school bus in bright Day-Glo colors, took horns and electric guitars, and went to Berkeley.

When they arrived, a whole series of speakers were talking about "genocidal atrocities" and the need for great marches in the streets. Pretty soon it was Kesey's turn and this is what he had to say:

> You know, you're not gonna stop this war with this rally, by marching ... that's what *they* do ... they hold rallies and they march ... They've been having wars for ten thousand years and you're not gonna stop it this way ... ten thousand years, and this is the game they play to do it ... holding rallies and having marches ... and that's the same game you're playing ... their game.

Kesey stopped talking. According to Wolfe, he reached "into his great glowing Day-Glo coat and produced a harmonica and start[ed] playing it right into the microphone, *"Home, home on the range, hawonking away on the goddamn thing—Home ... home ... on the ra-a-a-a-ange hawonk-awonk ...""*

And his friends behind him began to play their guitars, and dance, and blow their horns. But the crowd—the Berkeley serious people—could not quite understand. This was a serious thing: the teach-in before the march. Home, home on the range? "We know about that *home!* We know about that *range!* That rotten U.S. home and that rotten U.S. range—" Maybe that is what the audience was thinking; but they just misunderstood. Kesey stopped playing and began to speak:

> I was just looking at the speaker who was up here before me ... and I couldn't hear what he was saying ... but I could hear the sound of it ... and I could hear *your* sound coming back at him ... and I could see the gestures and I could see his jaw sticking out ... and you know who I saw ... and who I heard?... Mussolini ... I saw and I heard Mussolini here just a few minutes ago ... Yep, you're playing their game ...

Most of the crowd simply was not with Kesey or his friends. Some booed; most were just confused. That changed nothing on the stage. There was more music and more talk, more guitars and more "Home on the Range." The message was always the same: You're playing their game. And then another message:

> There's only one thing to do ... there's only one thing's gonna do any good at all ... and that's everybody just look at it, look at the war, and turn your backs and say ... Fuck it ... "-*hawonkawonkawonkawanka-*"

Then the music got louder and madder and the Day-Glo crazies were really into playing and dancing and strutting to variations of the old classic "Home on the Range." And the Berkeley people weren't ready, and were a little shocked, and maybe a little drained of their desire to march, of their desire to "be like them." And Kesey repeated his message—and our first way out:

> Just look at it and turn away and say ... Fuck it
> — *hawonkawonkawonka* blam
> —fuck it—
> *Hawonka* fuckit ... friends ...

## Way Two: Do It

It is not at all difficult to imagine some people's unhappiness with the above advice. For a whole group of individuals, both the style and the substance are potentially as distasteful as they are disagreeable. The style is a matter of taste, which is important—but not necessarily to this discussion. To walk away takes a good deal of understanding and nerve; but it is not necessarily the way for everybody. Some people want to know where they are going, just what they are getting into. They ask the naturally conservative (but reasonable) question: Will it be better than what we have now?

To cling to that question is to limit what will be to what one is sure of, to what one knows. While Kesey's advice is precise, it is limited. He has no thoroughgoing view to offer us. It seems to take a certain kind of person to leave what is without really knowing what will happen. In part, it takes an individual who knows that what is, is not enough, is lacking something, is wrong; and who, because of that, is willing to try to create something else. Leaving—or not doing—something that seems wrong is not necessarily a negative act.

But it is clear that most of us, most of the time, need more than the advice to leave. We need some kind of direction. Moreover, we want that direction to be built on a rather explicit view of the world. Given that, Kesey is not our man. Possibly, Georges Sorel is.

In order to get any meaning out of Sorel, in order to understand his politics and his influence, it is necessary to talk about some of his ideas of society. Basically, Sorel believed that societies ebbed and flowed; they were founded and destroyed, they decayed and were renewed. There was no permanent answer, no state of peace. There were just continual cycles of change.

Europe, at the turn of the twentieth century, was in what Sorel believed to be a state of decline. Indeed, he thought the people bland, compromising, and corrupt. The institutions were as bad: both Church and State seemed to him decadent. We are familiar enough with more contemporary versions of this kind of analysis to see why Sorel may be of some use, why he may illuminate some points.

The problem for Sorel—to oversimplify—was this: How can things be reformed and renewed? How can the decadence and the old ways of acting be cut out, be changed? His goal was a new style of being, a new way of acting. He wanted people to involve themselves in creating new societal forms, and he wanted this done in a new atmosphere of liberty. These were no modest aims.

What Sorel tried to do was involve the majority of the people—in his term, the proletariat—in the change. To his way of thinking, there was a slave morality and a master morality. It was only the master morality that was noble enough to cause heroic action. It was the master morality that the people had to acquire. Moreover, this morality had to be shared, had to be public, had to be political. If society was to be renewed, there had to be a collective force stronger than society. There had to be political action by a great mass of people.

Sorel proposed that people be reeducated—but with a difference. People were to be taught through a concept of their own hope. They were to be given a new myth, a new ideal of what might be, a new vision to do battle for. It should be made clear that this myth cannot be characterized as a single idea, or as a series of small changes, or as a blueprint. It isn't logical or rational or open to critical analysis. The new myth is a complex of pictures and images of what we believe. It contains what we hate and what we want and what we will fight for.

We have a myth of America. It may or may not be worn out. If it is old, out of date, decadent, then, according to Sorel, we must create a new myth. The new one will be built on our hopes, on our own best thoughts.

The idea of the myth is important in understanding Sorel and in understanding what we must do. For at the heart of his myth is a commitment to violence, a commitment to starting afresh. Through this commitment, people begin to take action, to reeducate others by their example, and to develop a sense of the master morality. In the creation of the myth and through commitment to it, an individual will turn more and more to the interests of the community and to the fate of his fellows.

In the end, the state is destroyed and a new one created. But according to Sorel the individual is not only creating a state, he or she is also creating virtue. To take it to the next step, the individual is achieving a remarkable aim: By creating virtue the individual is also helping to create himself or herself.

The themes of Sorel are instructive; he is able to help us understand that the state and politics are beyond the rational, the routine, and the bureaucratic. The whole idea of remaking—indeed, of creating—through political action enables us to glimpse an important vision we now lack. It is, in part, to begin to know that change is connected with the creation of, and then the substitution of, one way of looking at the world for another, of one myth for another myth. Finally, Sorel teaches us that there is a close tie between the development of the political and the individual, and that ultimately the virtue of the one is tied to the virtue of the other.

For those who do not want to walk away but who believe that the state of the state is beyond repair, Georges Sorel might point the way. Certainly his arguments are too powerful to simply ignore, his aims too grand to put aside. Sadly, he may have been wrong about us: It is possible that we are all corrupt, all bland and compromising. Maybe we are slaves to a morality that effectively blocks us from the new myth —from the Myth of the General Strike.

But that is off the point.

## Way Three: Returning

As the 1960s and 1970s burned themselves out, as acid eroded brains and revolts got torched, and as the 1980s fried us with greed, Ways One and Two began to seem not quite right for these times. This was a quiet, try-to-be-happy regrouping time.

There is not vast literature about such times. Yet there is one book—one story—that is just about right. It has to do with American virtues, happiness, know-how, and family. If there is any one drawback in the book, it is the size of the family it describes, since we live in a militantly zero-population time. You see, the size of this family is impressive: There is a father, a mother, and a dozen children.

The name of the book is *Cheaper by the Dozen,* and it was written by two of the children. It was published in 1949 and records events from 1910 to 1924 or so. Way Three is fun; or at least it sounds fun.

There really were a dozen children:

> "How many would you say we should have, just an estimate?" Mother asked.

"… an even dozen," said Dad. "No less. What do you say to that?"

"… a dozen would be just right. No less … Boys or girls?"

"Well boys would be fine," Dad whispered. "A dozen boys would be just right. But … girls would be all right too. Sure. I guess."

"I'd like to have half boys and half girls. Do you think it would be all right to have half girls?"

"If that's what you want," Dad said, "we'll plan it that way." He took his memorandum book and solemnly wrote: "Don't forget to have six boys and six girls."

So they did—they being Lillian and Frank Gilbreth. In seventeen years they had six girls and six boys. And there was something uniquely American about the plan and the planners. Lillian and Frank, interestingly enough, had the same vocation: They were industrial engineers. They were early advocates of efficiency, followers of Frederick Winslow Taylor. The Gilbreths were true believers: "… Mother the psychologist and Dad the motion study man … believed that what would work in the factory would work in the home."

The house, according to the book, was fun to live in … and very well organized. There was a chart in the bathroom where each child old enough to write had to sign in after he or she had taken a bath, brushed his or her hair and teeth, and made the bed. Also, each child had to plot a graph showing his or her weight, progress in homework, and the like. Everything was done regularly—and routinely—and was done in the most efficient way. Frank Gilbreth buttoned his vest from the bottom up instead of the top down because it saved him four seconds.

The children were organized so that each older child was responsible for one of the younger ones. Lillian took care of the baby, and Frank took care of himself.

There was, not surprisingly a division of labor in the house. The boys would cut the grass; the girls would sweep and dust. Tall girls would dust tabletops; short girls would dust table legs. And it was all like that. When there was an extra job, the children would submit bids for it, and the lowest bid won.

Clearly, the parents were extraordinary. The book documents the amazing interest Frank had in efficiency—how he saw so much of the world as inefficient. For example, there was the time when several of the children needed to have their tonsils taken out. Frank understood surgeons to be simply skilled mechanics, and decided to improve on their efficiency. He talked the doctor into doing the operation in the Gilbreth home and into having each operation filmed.

The plan was easy enough to understand. By comparing six operations of the same kind, Frank believed he could find the least wasted motion in every phase of the procedure and in the end make everything more efficient. There were some problems, though; one healthy child had her tonsils removed by mistake, and some funny things happened, but all the while the cameraman was in the operating room with his camera going.

Can you imagine living in a house where one of the adults wanted to reform the world by making it faster? Can you envision the mass removal of tonsils as a wonderful way to collect data to save time? Isn't it *American* to think that way? Don't we want efficiency in our lives, and in government, and even when we buy tickets to a movie?

It is fair to tell you how this particular venture in efficiency turned out: The cameraman forgot to remove his lens cap from the camera, so naturally there were no pictures.

The cameraman quit before Frank could fire him.

The world—or at least the part of the world in which people deal with physical objects—was understood in terms of Therbligs. (The term *Therblig* is Gilbreth spelled backward, almost.) A Therblig is a unit of motion or thought. Time and motion studies in a factory or in a home were concerned with trying to reduce those dreaded Therbligs. Frank and Lillian were really good at it.

In the last chapter of the book we are told that Frank had a weak heart and knew he would die young. In spite of that, in spite of the fact that he would leave a widow with twelve children, he wanted those dozen kids. His children seemed to think that "one of the principal reasons" why "he had organized the house on an efficiency basis" was so that things would be easier for Lillian when he died.

Maybe that is so. I'm not convinced, but it is a nice thought.

What Frank could not have counted on was Lillian's reaction after his death. After being "taken care of" all of her life, first by her parents and then by Frank, she simply came into her own. She sat in Frank's chair, was no longer a weepy, frightened woman, and assumed a great deal of authority.

She was, to use today's word, liberated.

She became, in an odd way, just like Frank.

Way Three, then, is an American way. It is the mix of fun-family and efficient-factory. It is warm, without wasted motion. It's home ... the Way we want to return to.

## Way Four

There is a Way Four, but it's not obvious enough to sum up in a catchy phrase. In a sense, this fourth way counsels us to do the best we can, no matter what. Although it might seem pessimistic (it counsels that, no matter what, we all die and rot), I do not believe that it is. While not as obviously political as Sorel or as direct as Kesey, this way does provide a basis for action. While it comes from the Bible, from Ecclesiastes to be precise, it certainly is not religious. Indeed, it pretty much ignores the God-problem. It involves what we should do, if anything, and why. It involves the same questions raised in the discussion on happiness and by Kesey and Sorel.

*Vanity of vanities, all is vanity.*

The son of David, the king of Jerusalem, wrote Ecclesiastes. The best guess is that King Solomon wrote Ecclesiastes, a person reputed to be wise, just, wealthy, and virtuous. An impressive combination. It is from this vantage point that he writes his advice, that he tries to explain their merits in accordance with what he understands to be the human condition.

First, Solomon explains that we cannot count on being different than we are; we cannot count on having something new. All has happened, all will happen again. We will continue unsatisfied, unfulfilled, if we continually expect something new. "I have seen all the works that are done under the sun; and, behold, all is vanity and a striving after wind."

But there are goals other than trying to be different. There is wealth:

I made me great works; I builded me houses; I planted me vineyards ... I acquired me manservants and maidservants, and had servants born in my house ... I gathered me also silver and gold and treasure ... So I was great ... and whatsoever mine eyes desired I kept not from them; I withheld not my heart from any joy, for my heart had joy of all my labour; and this was my portion from all my labour.

Then I looked on all the works that my hands had wrought, and on the labour that I had laboured to do; and, behold, all was vanity and a striving after the wind ...

Other verses recall the effort to achieve wisdom and virtue, and the conclusion is always the same: All is vanity, a striving after the wind. That is a part of our condition we cannot ignore. It is a part of our condition, in part because we all must die.

"There is one event to the righteous and to the wicked; to the good and to the clean and to the unclean; to him that sacrificeth and to him that sacrificeth not; as is the good, so is the sinner ... there is one event unto all ... the heart of the sons of men is full of evil, and madness is in their heart while they live, and after that they go to the dead."

And when we "go to the dead," that is it.

"For to him that is joined to all the living there is hope; for a living dog is better than a dead lion ... the dead know not anything, neither have they any more a reward; for the memory of them is forgotten. As well as their love, as their hatred and their envy, is long ago perished; neither have they any more a portion for ever in anything that is done under the sun."

No heaven, no hell: just vanity and chasing the wind. Then no more a portion forever in anything. But this forth way—this advice of Solomon—is not depressing. These are not grounds for despair. The advice is twofold: First, enjoy life. "Eat thy bread with joy, and drink thy wine with a merry heart ... let thy garments be always white; and let thy head lack no oil ... Enjoy life with a wife when thou lovest ... whatsoever thy hand attaineth to do by thy strength, that do; for there is no work, nor device, nor knowledge, nor wisdom, in the grave, whither thou goest."

Second, be with people. "Two are better than one ... if two lie together, then they have warmth; but how can one be warm alone? And if a man prevail against him that is alone, two shall withstand him; and a threefold cord is not quickly broken."

Enough Bible. Maybe too much. But the points are sufficiently important to be made explicitly. For some, Kesey's advice was obvious and good; for others Sorel or the Gilbreths were as good. Yet there are many who cannot quite make blind leaps, who are not ready for an ideological stand, who just have to think things through as far as possible. That is the point here: To understand vanity and death is not to be immobilized, is not to despair, is not to avoid action. It is to do all these things—to act, and to move, and to accept happiness. It can easily be the basis of politics, for it is all we have; and if Solomon is right, we only have one chance at it.

So the last way is the most vague of all, but maybe the most urgent.

## Where to Begin: What to Talk About

*Freedom is fire, overcoming this world by reducing it to a fluctuating chaos, as in schizophrenia; the chaos, which is the eternal ground of creation. There is no uni-verse, no one way.*

*We are always in error*
*Lost in the wood*
*Standing in chaos*
*The original mess*
*Creating*
*A brand-new world*

*Thank God the world cannot be made safe, for democracy or anything else.*
*— Norman O. Brown*

Before ending this chapter, it is necessary to explore one more problem. Where do we begin to talk about politics? By where, I simply mean to ask what the logical entry point for a discussion of politics is.

It is clear that, for some, the "real" concerns of politics have not even been mentioned, or that they have been mentioned only in passing. Many would think that any discussion of politics should inevitably center on "real-life" issues: schools, health care, income distribution, and the like.

Those are the problem areas; those are the concerns of politics and political science. To concentrate on alienation, aloneness, or privatization is, for many political scientists, to concentrate on all the wrong things.

In a sense, it is difficult to disagree. It would be hard to say that better health or better schools or more food were not really the point. Of course, they are the point. They represent, in great measure, the concerns of society and are the issues any community must deal with. Yet we should know by now that to deal exclusively with such problems is to doom the search to only one dimension and to almost certain failure.

Think of it like this. If we concentrate entirely on issues like housing, food, health, and the like, part of what we are assuming is that government is like a huge household. We automatically limit our public activities—the press calls it politics—to the issues of running a house. We are like a very big impersonal family. Somehow, we all want the best bedroom, our own phone, and a television. One of the lessons of this book is that politics is more than family affairs.

We must understand the reasons for the problems, in what way we are involved, and how these two things are connected. We must ask how the problems are going to be solved and whether the proposed solutions involve change or just more of what we have. We must be constantly aware that there are "solutions" that are even worse than the original problems.

Put another way: There are a number of fundamental questions we must come to terms with before we can answer the "better health" problems of everyday, obvious politics.

In order to get to a more fundamental level of discussion, we must first ask what we can expect from the political system and from politics. It seems to me obvious that we have been taught to make unnecessary distinctions. That there is any tension between the "cultural" problem of aloneness and the "political" problems of food and money may, in part, stem from the very narrow view of politics we have been brought up on. A view that is limiting in subject matter as well as scope, one that is set off from rather than inclusive of the idea that political action can be the resolution of the creative tension between individual and societal virtue.

Before discussing the "real" problems, it is necessary to understand the context of the discussion. It is necessary to realize that until the context contains a definition of politics that includes the qualitative values of those involved, the solutions to the problems will only be "tricks," only variations on the themes that helped bring about the problems in the first place.

I am suggesting that the study of politics is twice the work some think it is. First, we must define politics in such a way that it helps us to define who we are. We must understand politics as a creative process—both for our society and ourselves. Second, with that definition, we must try to solve the critical problems around us. But the order, in this instance, is critical. We can't do the second until we have done the first.

It is necessary to understand that to talk about politics is to talk about both the process and the problem, about both the individual and the outcome.

One of the results of this approach is to take us into the area of political theory. Norman Jacobson writes, "The genius of all great political thinkers is to make public that which is of private concern, and to translate into public language the more special, idiosyncratic vocabulary of the inner man in hopes of arriving at public solutions which might be internalized in each of us.

This book in large part has tried to get at our "normal" context of politics, and to suggest that there are many ways in which it is inadequate. We have tried to make explicit the implicit ideology into which we were born and which dominates our thinking. With that in mind, we can finish the book.

## On Trying to Understand the Whole Book

This is meant to be an introduction to politics, some ideas that may lead one to begin to understand a few important problems.

What was done seems reasonable enough to do at a beginning level. An effort was made to try to understand the elements of politics. Pretty obviously, the book has been concerned with much more than how a bill becomes a law or how to be elected mayor or president. Simply and reasonably and logically, we have found that politics is prior to and more important than our governmental apparatus.

In many ways, politics is a function of how we think of each other and of how we relate to the whole. It is we and they, and we and I, and I and thou, in all combinations. To understand that, we began at the beginning.

The beginning was a simple search into how we related to each other, into how society wanted us to understand ourselves, and—somewhat closer to the root of the matter—into how much we counted. So we read *Federalist* No. 10 and tried to figure out what it means and how we acted according to it. The conclusion was unhappy, but fairly accurate: Madison's account of society—of us—was true. We Americans built a society on the evilness of us all. Somehow we chose to emphasize those things least desirable in ourselves. We discovered that we believed each other to be evil, and that our belief had become a self-fulfilling prophecy.

Larry Spence has named this whole way of thinking. He calls it *the principle of the fewest sons of bitches.* ■ gSince it is the nature of man to steal, kill, cheat (that is, increase chaos) at every opportunity, the chances for survival are enhanced if a few men are designated a government with certain rules as to where, when and how the cheating, stealing and killing are to be done. The supposition is that getting robbed and beaten by a few men at designated times and places is better than getting it from all sides at all times and at any place."

There was the whole question of how we know things, of what things are real. The conclusion was rather an odd one: We found that we believed knowledge was something that could be touched, or felt, or seen. We believe that we know things by rationalizing them, by objectifying them. So there is little opportunity to think about "unreal" things, about knowledge that is neither wholly objective nor rational.

A world in which all things were rational and objective would be a world without humans; it would be mute testimony to our own stupidity.

So we hunted hard for our own humanity. We began to realize that the political state was more than laws and elections, that politics had something to do with who we were. So we tried to be free but saw that we were made to be alone; we tried to understand justice but could only talk about being judged.

There were depressing times doing some of this work. To work through the problems and to think about the answers was often no fun. But it seemed to make sense to begin the study of politics by talking about what politics is doing to you. And, just as importantly, about what you are allowing to happen to you, simply out of ignorance.

Everything means something; nothing is entirely obvious. So we tried to understand what was happening and how it happened. There were discussions about how groups could pressure you, freedom isolate you, voting degrade you, and happiness sadden you. It was no mistake that we reached the conclusions we did.

What was discussed, much of what was decided, are real, hard, true facts. They are, to some degree, the facts with which we have lived up to now. They seem imprecise simply because they are difficult to measure; but, in the long run, they are much more important than most things easily quantifiable.

The study of political science—of politics—can be the study of these facts. I think it can, at its best, be an attempt to understand how to relate to our society in a public, open, and political manner. My bias is obvious: It seems important to understand what is happening, which things must be kept, and which things should be changed. We are free to study any aspect in any manner; but it seems a great loss when we fail to relate what goes on to our human condition. To discuss politics without people seems as silly as discussing economics without goods, or history without the past.

There is a possibility that some of you find this a little depressing. Vanity? Violence? A dozen children? Who needs another set of seemingly silly or disappointing choices? It's just too much like presidential elections. It is like trying to pick the least bad candidate.

The book was not written to depress you. I promise: a little outrage, anger, insight—whatever—but certainly not depression.

Earlier there was a discussion about a plan and an answer, a discussion in which both seemed wrong. I was serious about that. What I am not against is doing things: I am for action. It is clear that politics is much too important to be left to the politicians, to the bureaucrats, to the technicians. We are better than that.

Now here's the rub.

The difficulty is figuring out the best thing to do, finding people to do it with, and then doing it. What do you believe? What do you do? Until you begin to think about the world and act in it, "they" have you. Just knowing the critique of society is not enough; constant looking in the mirror does not count as a political act.

Odd as it may seem, it doesn't matter—on one level—if you choose any of the suggested "ways" in this chapter, or if you choose something else. What matters is that you choose and that you do. What I want to argue is that there is something that is necessary and important for the human spirit. Equally important, belief and action are needed to resist the quiet, deadening tyranny of our times.

When you do something—when you act—you affect the world; you add to the sum of stories about trying to make the world better. Maybe it is having a huge family; maybe it is getting involved with Day-Glo. The choice has to do with what you know, and believe, and enjoy. It is a matter of knowledge and taste. Maybe what is best is just turning your back at just the right time, and doing it in public.

The thing that matters most is that each of us has the capacity to act.

So, there you have it—it is not depressing at all.

*Once there was a flock of geese. They were kept in a wire cage, by a farmer. One day, one of the geese looked up and saw that there was no top to the cage. Excitedly, he told the other geese:*

*"Look, look: There is no top. We may leave here. We may become free."*

*Few listened, and none would turn his head to the sky.*

*So, one day, he simply spread his wings and flew away—alone.*

*— Søren Kierkegaard*

Printed in the United States
20379LVS00001B/41-266

9 780883 165720